CLINICAL HEALTH PSYCHOLOGY
IN MEDICAL SETTINGS

CLINICAL HEALTH PSYCHOLOGY IN MEDICAL SETTINGS

A PRACTITIONER'S GUIDEBOOK

Revised Edition

Cynthia D. Belar & William W. Deardorff

American Psychological Association
Washington, DC

First edition published 1987 as *The Practice of Clinical Health Psychology* by Pergamon Press. Revised edition published 1995 by the American Psychological Association.

Fourth Printing June 1999

Copies may be ordered from
APA Order Department
P.O. Box 92984
Washington, DC 20090-2984

In the UK, Europe, Africa, and the Middle East, copies may be ordered from
American Psychological Association
3 Henrietta Street
Covent Garden, London
WC2E 8LU England

Typeset in Minion by GGS Information Services, York, PA

Printer: Data Reproductions Corp., Auburn Hills, MI
Cover and Jacket Designer: Supon Design Group, Washington, DC
Jacket Illustrator: Elizabeth Wolf
Technical/Production Manager: Kathryn Mary Lynch

Library of Congress Cataloging-in-Publication Data
Belar, Cynthia D.
    Clinical health psychology in medical settings : practitioner's
guidebook / Cynthia D. Belar, William W. Deardorff.
        p.   cm.
    Includes bibliographical references and index.
    ISBN 1-55798-277-5—ISBN 1-55798-287-2 (pbk.) (acid-free
paper)
    1. Clinical health psychology.   I. Deardorff, William W,
II. Title
    [DNLM: 1. Psychology, Clinical.   WM 105 B425c 1995]
R726.7.B445   1995
616.89—dc20
DNLM/DLC
for Library of Congress   94-41375
                                                       CIP

British Library Cataloguing-in-Publication Data
A CIP record is available from the British Library

Printed in the United States of America

To my parents,
Herbert and Glennie Belar,
the wisest people I have ever known.
To my husband,
Jean-Louis Monfraix,
for his loving patience.
C. D. B.

To my wife,
Janine,
for her enduring love,
patience, and support.
To my sons,
James and Paul.
W. W. D.

Contents

Preface

Since the writing of our book *The Practice of Clinical Health Psychology* nearly 10 years ago (Belar, Deardorff, & Kelly, 1987), the scientific knowledge base of professional practice has continued to expand. In addition, board certification is now available for clinical health psychologists through the American Board of Professional Psychology (ABPP), and health psychology has the potential to be a major player in the health care system of the future. Given these developments, we believe it is timely to update our prior reference, taking into account new knowledge, current issues in practice, and trends for the future.

This guidebook stems from more than two decades of experience in clinical health psychology practice, education, training, and research. The issues dealt with (e.g., core content, professional roles, assessment, intervention, ethics, and malpractice) represent those areas we have found to be of special importance in clinical practice in medical settings. Each case example is one with which one of us has had personal experience, although identifying data have been changed. Throughout the book, we note common pitfalls in practice and attempt to provide ideas for their effective management. Reference materials for further study are provided for each major topic.

This guidebook is not designed for the novice clinician but is intended for the clinical student or practicing professional psychologist who wishes to develop special expertise in clinical health psychology. It might also be useful to other mental health professionals who want to retool for practice with medical–surgical populations and environments. It is best viewed as an overview, and it is written with an underlying assumption of already developed competence in basic clinical skills on the part of the reader.

Acknowledgments

Special acknowledgment is given to Karen E. Kelly, who was a coauthor in the earlier version of this book.

Acknowledgments are also given to Joe Matarazzo for his sustaining influence on the field and on my own thinking; to Nathan Perry and Philip Shulman for supporting my development of education, training, research, and practice programs in clinical health psychology; and to all of my students, whose intellectual curiosity, need for guidance, and enthusiasm for learning have enhanced my learning and commitment to the field.

C. D. B.

Acknowledgments are given to my mentors, Wilbert Fordyce, Judy Turner, Joan Romano, Saul Spiro, Harold Dengerink, Herbert Cross, and Cynthia Belar, for introducing me to the complex and challenging field of clinical health psychology.

W. W. D.

Introduction to Clinical Health Psychology

DEFINITIONS

Millon (1982b) was the first to offer a concise definition of *clinical health psychology* that captured the elements of the science and its applications:

> the application of knowledge and methods from all substantive fields of psychology to the promotion and maintenance of mental and physical health of the individual and to the prevention, assessment, and treatment of all forms of mental and physical disorder in which psychological influences either contribute to or can be used to relieve an individual's distress or dysfunction. (Millon, 1982b, p. 9)

This definition represents a merging of clinical psychology, with its focus on the assessment and treatment of individuals in distress, and the content field of *health psychology*, which is defined as follows:

> the aggregate of the specific educational, scientific, and professional contributions of the discipline of psychology to the promotion and

maintenance of health, the prevention and treatment of illness, and the identification of etiologic and diagnostic correlates of health, illness, and related dysfunctions. (Matarazzo, 1980, p. 815)

Although professional activity in *clinical health psychology* has long preceded the usage of this term, we believe this designation best describes this area of practice for psychologists. As Millon (1982b) stated, "the label chosen to represent the field is of no minor import; it will certainly shape its focus as a research realm and its viability and character as a service profession" (p. 9). Related labels are either inappropriate, confusing, or too narrow for the practice of psychology. Examples of these include *behavioral medicine, medical psychology,* and *psychosomatic medicine.*

Behavioral medicine is an interdisciplinary field. A psychologist cannot "practice" behavioral medicine; psychologists can only practice psychology. This is evident from the most commonly accepted definition of behavioral medicine:

> the interdisciplinary field concerned with the development and integration of behavioral and biomedical science, knowledge and technique relevant to health and illness and the application of this knowledge and these techniques to prevention, diagnosis, treatment and rehabilitation. (G. E. Schwartz & Weiss, 1978, p. 250)

Stemming from a landmark conference at Yale University in February 1977, and further refined at a meeting of the National Academy of Sciences in April 1978, this definition was specifically intended to *not* represent either a single theoretical orientation (behavioral) or a single discipline (medicine). However, it is often misinterpreted and even asserted as such by the more chauvinistic. All health psychologists and all clinical health psychologists are contributors to the field of behavioral medicine, as are social workers, nurses, epidemiologists, physicians, nutritionists, and members of other disciplines who choose to practice, to teach, to develop policy, or to conduct research related to the integration of behavioral and biomedical sciences relevant to health and illness.

Another term, *medical psychology,* can be confusing in that it has at least three well-accepted definitions and it conveys a narrowness of focus (e.g., it excludes psychologists practicing primarily with dental populations). These definitions include the following: (a) the practice of psychology in the medical school establishment (Gentry & Matarazzo, 1981, p. 12); (b) the study of psychological factors related to any and all aspects of physical health, illness, and its treatment at the individual, groups, and systems levels (Asken, 1979, p. 67); and (c) traditional psychiatry in Great Britain.

The term *psychosomatic medicine* has historically been the most prominent. Originally intended to refer to the unity of mind–body relationships, it usually conveys the notion of psychological causation of physiological disorders to most health professionals and to the public. As such, it carries with it some pejorative overtones. Again, the use of the term *medicine* would be inappropriate for the practitioner of the discipline of psychology. Other labels found in the field, such as *pediatric psychology*, *rehabilitation psychology*, and *neuropsychology* are pertinent to more narrow content and practice areas.

In summary, we believe that the term *clinical health psychology* best conveys the breadth of the field (health) while designating a focus on applied practice (clinical). The practice is discipline specific (psychology); however, the recognition that many other disciplines practice in the field of health makes much of the following information relevant to those practitioners as well.

HISTORICAL PERSPECTIVES IN CLINICAL HEALTH PSYCHOLOGY

In Western culture, the roots of clinical health psychology date back to the fifth century B.C. and the Hippocratic school of medicine. Health was viewed as a natural balance of both physical and emotional aspects, mediated by a harmonious mixture of the humors (phlegm, choler, blood, and melancholy). Centuries later in 1747, Gaub, a professor of medicine, wrote "the reason why a sound body becomes ill, or an ailing body recovers, very often lies in the mind" (cited in Lipowski, 1977, p. 234). However, it was during the years between 1920 and 1950 that the more formalized field of psychosomatic medicine emerged. Two major frameworks dominated: psychodynamic and psychophysiologic. One of the best representatives of the psychodynamic viewpoint was Franz Alexander (1950) who, inspired by psychoanalytic theory, developed a specificity theory of illness. Specific unresolved unconscious conflicts were thought to produce specific somatic disorders in this *nuclear conflict theory* (e.g., frustrated oral and dependency needs result in duodenal ulcer).

In the area of psychophysiology, Harold G. Wolff (1953) used highly innovative experimental designs to study the effects of psychological stimuli on physiological processes. By means of these methods, Dr. Wolff developed a theory of psychological stress, which he applied to a wide range of somatic diseases. For example, he noted that during subjects' discussion of relationship problems (stress), resentment was associated with increased blood pressure, whereas despair and depression were associated with lowered blood pressure (Wolff & Wolf, 1951). These results were particularly true of hypertensives. In general, the first half of this century was marked by the passage of mind–body processes from the province of philosophy and religion to the domain of respectable scientific inquiry. Shorter (1992) provided an interesting historical account of cultural and scientific influences on theories of mind–body interactions.

The past three decades have been marked by a decrease in the influence of psychodynamic theories and an increased focus on psychophysiological processes in attempts to explain mind–body processes. There has also been the addition of social and ecological dimensions to these models and the development of psychological interventions to prevent or ameliorate disease and improve the health care system. Psychology as a discipline has made significant contributions in this endeavor.

From the experimental psychology laboratory has come information about learning and bodily processes, with subsequent successful efforts at physiological self-regulation through biofeedback. Studies of cognitive processes have revealed the importance of meaning, belief systems, and information processing and have underscored the need for attention to issues such as compliance, help seeking, and pain tolerance in health care. Research in psychoendocrinology has helped us to understand relationships between physiological processes and emotions, and behavior-change technology has been applied in attempts to reduce behavioral health risks. Some of the most exciting developments are occurring in the field of psychoneuroimmunology, which holds promise for delineating the mediating mechanisms between psychological processes and health (Ader & Cohen, 1993; Hall, Minnes, & Olness, 1993). Psychology, as the science of behavior, will continue to be an integral part of the now widely accepted biopsychosocial model of health.

THE GROWTH OF HEALTH PSYCHOLOGY

As a specialty within the discipline, health psychology has mushroomed since the mid-1970s. Gentry (1984) summarized some of the possible reasons: (a) failure of the biomedical model to adequately explain health and illness; (b) increased concern with quality of life and prevention of illness; (c) shift of focus from infectious disease to chronic disease as the major challenge in medicine, with concomitant recognition of the influence of life-style factors; (d) increased maturity of research in the behavioral sciences, including the application of learning theories to disease etiology and illness behavior; and (e) increased cost of health care and the search for alternatives to the traditional health care system.

Those of us who were involved in this rapid growth remember the fervor with which we worked to establish new professional groups. The year 1978 was a high point in this developmental process. The Academy of Behavioral Medicine was established in April, with Neal E. Miller as its first president. On November 16, 1978, we held the charter meeting of the Society of Behavioral Medicine in Chicago. This group is an interdisciplinary organization with over 3,000 members. And at the 86th Annual Convention of the American Psychological Association in 1978, we celebrated the recognition of the new Division of Health Psychology, which now has over 3,500 members and is one of the largest divisions of the American Psychological Association. Also that year, the *Journal of Behavioral Medicine* began under the editorship of W. Doyle Gentry. Four years later, the journal *Health Psychology* began publication. And in 1994, the *Interna-*

tional Journal of Behavioral Medicine began publication, reflecting the international developments in the field.

As health psychology developed, our concern for quality led to the Arden House National Working Conference on Education and Training in Health Psychology. This conference developed recommendations for education and training at the predoctoral, apprenticeship, and postdoctoral levels for research and professional career paths in psychology. These guidelines remain the standards for the field (a full report can be found in G. C. Stone, 1983).

In the mid-1980s, the American Board of Health Psychology (ABHP) was established to promote excellence in the professional practice of health psychology. Board certification is now provided to individual practitioners who demonstrate advanced competence in the science and practice of psychology related to health, including the prevention, treatment, and rehabilitation of illness. In 1993, this board gained full affiliation status with the American Board of Professional Psychology (ABPP), the oldest national credentialing body for professional psychologists. Thus, clinical health psychology has now received formal recognition by the profession as a psychological specialty practice area. As such, practitioners wishing board certification have access to well-established and respected mechanisms. In fact, in recognizing the breadth of the specialty, the ABHP Board of Directors decided in 1992 to begin the process of developing certificates of special expertise in subareas of practice such as pain management, rehabilitation, and psychosocial oncology. The first area to be developed is pain management.

The 1970s and 1980s were a time in which many of us felt that we had a mission to accomplish in "spreading the word" about health psychology and the potential for practice in this area. Yet we knew that we were certainly not the first to recognize the importance of psychological factors in health and health care.

PSYCHOLOGY'S ROLE IN HEALTH CARE

The role of the psychologist in the health care system began early this century as a teacher of medical students (see G. C. Stone, 1979). The area most frequently represented was physiological psychology, as related research flourished. However, there was little application of psychology to the problems of the health care system itself. As the field of clinical psychology developed after World War II, the focus was primarily on mental disorders. There were some studies on overutilizers of the health care system, some pathology-oriented treatment reports on classic psychosomatic disorders, and an important body of work by Janis (1958) on psychological preparation for surgery. However, Schofield's (1969) report on the role of psychology in the delivery of health services marked the beginning of an explosion of this area in the psychological literature.

Until more recently, the role of clinical psychology continued to be somewhat limited. As Millon (1982b) pointed out, with but few notable exceptions (e.g., Schofield, 1969), clinical psychology "was misguided in its evolution when it followed a dualistic mind–body model and thereby limited itself to ministering to the 'mentally' disordered" (Millon, 1982b, p. 9). In a clever reworking of Engel's (1977) well-known critique of the medical model (p. 129), Millon (1982b) suggested that clinical psychology's crisis stemmed from its logical inference that because behavior disorder is defined in terms of psychosocial parameters, psychologists need not be concerned with somatic issues, which lie outside psychology's responsibility and authority. This attitude divides the patient illogically and spuriously segments health care in the same manner for which medicine has been criticized in the past.

Indeed, the senior author remembers well the times in the early 1970s when she was required, while attempting to establish herself in academic clinical psychology, to justify to skeptical senior professors her clinical interest in medical–surgical patients and the treatment of chronic pain problems. The usual challenge ("Is this real clinical psychology?") reflected the mind–body dualism extant in the field. Actually, that process proved helpful, in that it facilitated critical thinking about the field. It also increased sensitivity to many professional and political issues involved in extending the boundaries of professional practice.

Subsequent experiences have confirmed that mind–body dualism is as alive and well in psychology, psychiatry, and psychiatric social work as it is in general medicine. Remarkable numbers of mental health practitioners feel no need to review a patient's medical chart before undertaking psychotherapy. Many such clinicians actually dislike dealing with medical–surgical patients because these patients have "real" (meaning insoluble?) problems. When consultations are conducted by these practitioners, findings are often expressed in *either–or* and *functional versus organic* terminology.

Mind–body dualism continues to be deeply ingrained in health policies (including the Clinton administration's Health Security Act of 1993, despite its recognition of the importance of behavior in prevention and health promotion). Throughout the insurance industry and health care reform efforts, there is a division and disparity in coverage between mental health and medical–surgical insurance benefits, with mental health coverage being less extensive. Conceptually, this poses difficult problems when attempting to determine which coverage is responsible for such things as psychological management of a hypertensive medication compliance problem, biofeedback treatment of surgically induced fecal incontinence, or cognitive–behavioral management of headache.

Typically, psychological services are covered only under mental health benefits, a health policy that tends to perpetuate rigid mind–body dualism. For example, within the Southern California Kaiser Permanente system, a region of the nation's largest health maintenance organization (HMO) and nongovernmental health care system, all psychological counseling is covered under the mental health benefit, suggesting that such treatments are only appropriate for mental health problems. Indeed some indemnity insurance policies dictate that psychologists can only treat "mental illness," and insurers will reject the claim if psychological approaches are being used to address physical problems.

Dualism is also found in administrative structures, as evidenced by geographically separate clinics. Many mental health clinics are actually located at some distance from the medical center, the mainstream of health care. Clearly, the attitudinal set of mind–body dualism and related administrative issues have significant implications for the professional functioning and practice of clinical health psychologists. Indeed the reader is advised to be alert to the instances in which mind–body dualism seeps into our own writing—a product of our language system, our cultural heritage, and our own struggle to integrate psychological and physiological concepts.

In summary, our model of clinical health psychology actually incorporates mental health psychology as a complete subset in the domain of clinical health psychology. However, for the purposes of this book, we have chosen to deal primarily with practice in medical–surgical settings. In general, we shall assume existing expertise in more traditional areas of professional clinical or counseling psychology.

ROLES AND FUNCTIONS OF CLINICAL HEALTH PSYCHOLOGISTS

Clinical health psychologists have a diversity of roles and functions. Although there are no survey data specifically on clinical health psychologists, we do have information about activities of health psychologists from Division of Health Psychology surveys (Houston, 1988; Morrow & Clayman, 1982). In general, more than half of the division members obtained their original training in a health service provider field (primarily clinical or counseling psychology). According to the 1988 survey, primary employment settings were educational (55%), service delivery (42%), and industry–government (9%). The top three professional activities were practice (65%), research (55%), and teaching–supervision (50%).

With respect to health care activities, the heterogeneity of activity in assessment, intervention, and consultation is enormous. Exhibit 1.1 contains samples of these activities.

Clinical health psychology practitioners use the range of diagnostic and therapeutic techniques available to professional psychology: diagnostic interviewing; behavioral assessments; psychometric testing; insight-oriented psychotherapies; behavioral therapies; psychophysiological self-regulation and biofeedback; family, marital, and group therapies; psychoeducational counseling groups; and staff-level interventions. Their theoretical orientations include but are not limited to psychodynamic, behavioral, systems,

Exhibit 1.1

Health Care Activities

1. Assessment of candidates for penile prosthesis surgery, back surgery, organ transplantation, in vitro fertilization, or oocyte donation
2. Desensitization of fears of medical and dental treatments—including needles, anesthesia, childbirth, or magnetic resonance imaging (MRI) procedures
3. Treatment to enhance coping with or control over pain, including chronic back pain, headache, or severe burns
4. Interventions to control symptoms such as vomiting with chemotherapy, scratching with neurodermatitis, vasospasms with Raynaud's phenomenon, or diarrhea with irritable bowel syndrome
5. Support groups for chronic illness, cardiac rehabilitation, HIV-positive patients, or families of the terminally ill
6. Training to overcome physical handicaps after trauma, cognitive retraining after stroke, or training to use prosthetic devices effectively
7. Behavior-change programs for behavioral risk factors such as smoking, weight, and stress
8. Consultations and workshops to deal with issues of staff burnout, communication, and role conflict
9. Consultations and program development regarding patient compliance (e.g., special aids for the elderly or inpatient units for insulin-dependent diabetic children)
10. Consultations with industry to develop worksite health-promotion programs and management of occupational stress
11. Development of psychosocial services for oncology patients
12. Neuropsychological assessments for baseline, diagnostic, and treatment-planning purposes

existential, and social learning theory approaches. They deal with the problems of coping with illness, compliance, psychophysiologic disorders, the doctor–patient relationship, health care systems design, differential diagnoses, rehabilitation, occupational health, and prevention of disease. No one clinical health psychologist is an expert in all possible areas of practice. Because of the diversity and volume of information in clinical health psychology, it is not possible, within the context of this book, to provide an educational background in each potential area of practice. Thus, we focus our comments on more generic issues of preparation and clinical practice for the health psychologist, emphasizing process issues and pitfalls.

SUGGESTED READINGS

Engel, G. L. (1977). The need for a new medical model: A challenge for biomedicine. *Science, 196,* 129–136.

Schofield, W. (1969). The role of psychology in the delivery of health services. *American Psychologist, 24,* 565–584.

Stone, G. C., Weiss, S. M., Matarazzo, J. D., Miller, N. E., Rodin, J., Belar, C. D., Follick, M. J., & Singer, J. E. (Eds.). (1987). *Health psychology: A discipline and a profession.* Chicago: University of Chicago Press.

2

Becoming a Clinical Health Psychologist

EDUCATION AND TRAINING

S urveys of education and training in health psychology have attempted to delineate programmatic offerings at the predoctoral, internship, and postdoctoral levels. From a survey of graduate departments of psychology, Belar, Wilson, and Hughes (1982) identified 42 programs that offered predoctoral training in health psychology. Although 6 of these described a specialized program, the predominant model (almost 70%) was that of a specialized track within another area of psychology, usually clinical, counseling, social, or school psychology. Between 80% and 95% of the identified programs offered training in consultation, assessment, intervention, or all three areas. In comparison, the most recent directory from the Division of Health Psychology (1991) listed 46 doctoral programs with a primary focus in health psychology.

Of perhaps greatest interest is the finding of Sayette and Mayne (1990) in their survey of American Psychological Association accredited clinical psychology programs. Health psychology was the most popular area of clinical research, with 75% of programs offering opportunities in the area, and the second most frequent specialty clinic for clinical training. Clearly, health psychology is now part of mainstream clinical psychology.

From a survey of American Psychological Association accredited internship training programs, Gentry, Street, Masur, and Asken (1981) identified 48 programs with formal training in health psychology, although only 19 programs required such training. Assessment and intervention were equally emphasized.

With respect to postdoctoral training, Belar and Siegel (1983) identified 43 programs offering postdoctoral training in health psychology, 90% of which emphasized applied research. The 1991 Division 38 directory listed opportunities for postdoctoral fellowships at 42 sites.

The Association of Psychology Postdoctoral and Internship Centers publishes an annual directory, which facilitates the identification of relevant professional psychology postdoctoral and internship programs. Other major sources of current information on health psychology education and training are the Education and Training Committee of the Division of Health Psychology, the Society of Behavioral Medicine, and the Council of Health Psychology Training Directors (see Appendix C).

Guidelines

As indicated in chapter 1, the Arden House Conference detailed a set of recommendations for the education and training of health psychologists (Stone, 1983). Although a summary of these is beyond the scope of this guidebook, certain recommendations with respect to service provision in the field deserve highlighting.

Perhaps most important, for the professional practice of health psychology (thus for clinical health psychology), the scientist–practitioner model was endorsed at every level of training. As a later national conference affirmed, the scientist–practitioner model is essential for the ever-changing discipline of psychology and "ideal for psychologists who utilize scientific methods in the conduct of professional practice" (Belar & Perry, 1992, p. 72). Arden House Conference delegates also agreed that professional training in health psychology should include a broad set of experiences leading to knowledge and skills in the following core areas: (a) biological bases of health and disease; (b) social bases of health and disease;

(c) psychological bases of health and disease; (d) health assessment, consultation, intervention, and evaluation; (e) health policy and organization; (f) interdisciplinary collaboration; (g) ethical, legal, and professional issues; and (h) statistics and experimental design in health research.

In addition, exposure to health care settings, a multidisciplinary faculty, and experienced professional health psychology mentors were considered crucial. Furthermore, it was decided that programs offering such education and training should meet American Psychological Association accreditation criteria.

Belar (1980) described what is transportable from traditional clinical psychology training and what needs to be added to better train graduate students to function effectively in this growing field. A basic assumption is that the understanding of the fundamentals of human behavior and the critical-thinking, hypothesis-testing approach to research and clinical problems are transportable to any area in which the psychologist chooses to work.

We support the scientist–practitioner model for service providers in health psychology and underscore our belief that competency in research methodology is fundamental to functioning as a clinical health psychologist. This is in keeping with the American Psychological Association Utah Conference on Graduate Education in Psychology Resolution 1.3: "It is essential in the graduate education of applied and professional psychologists to include education and training in the conduct of scientific research as well as the application of products of psychological research" ("Resolutions Approved," 1987, p. 1071).

Research skills are necessary to the critical evaluation of research reports in this burgeoning area, to the conduct of program evaluations so often required as an aspect of accountability, and to the design of research capable of making contributions to the science base of this expanding field. However, in this book, we focus on practitioner activities, and our discussions assume that the reader is either a fully trained professional clinician or a student in an organized professional training program.

Core Content Areas and Courses

With respect to specific content, one can develop one's own course of study through readings or enrollment in basic courses. The basic areas needing attention include anatomy, physiology, pathophysiology, applied pharmacology, social and psychological bases of health and disease, health policy and health care organizations, and health assessment and intervention. One needs to understand not only disease—its treatment, its course, and its emotional and behavioral correlates—but also the context within which the health care system operates. (Changes are so dramatic in this area that references over a year old on health policy and the health care system should be considered outdated!)

Courses basic to other health professions are often useful (e.g., nursing, physical therapy, occupational therapy, respiratory therapy, and health education), thus, the reader is encouraged to investigate local university or community college offerings. For the general clinical health psychologist, we have found that the courses offered in medical schools are frequently too detailed, although some prefer the anatomy and physiology offered there. We are aware that our neuropsychologist colleagues report that the neuroanatomy courses obtained in academic medical centers are fundamental to their areas of practice. However, in general, these courses are probably less accessible to the practicing clinician than to the graduate student.

The reader might also investigate the availability of courses in medical terminology that are frequently found in hospital administration and secretarial programs. Familiarity with the language of the health care system is a must, as is understanding the most commonly used medical abbreviations, if one is to be able to read medical charts. We have witnessed scores of students and fellow professionals struggle with these language and code issues. There is considerable potential for negative outcomes in terms of efficiency, communication, and rapport with medical colleagues, as well as in misunderstandings of the nature of referral questions.

If the clinician is planning to work in a general hospital setting, it would also be wise to obtain cardiopulmonary resuscitation (CPR) training, if not already certified in this skill. Certification and renewals are often required for staff privileges. Courses are available through community service agencies such as the Red Cross.

It is important to remember that the goal of these didactic experiences is not to become a "junior physician." In our experience, such an attitudinal approach meets with disdain on the part of physicians, who frequently criticize their psychiatrist colleagues for not being "real physicians" when it comes to up-to-date medical knowledge and practice. Rather, an analogy might be learning enough of a foreign language to be able to get around in another country, which also means being willing and able to ask for help from the natives. We find physicians much more open to and respectful of this approach.

Reference Materials

The neophyte clinical health psychologist will want to obtain a familiarity with core readings in the field. The Suggested Readings at the end of this chapter can provide a general background. Appendix A consists of a list of relevant scientific journals, which publish research as well as theoretical articles in health psychology, although it is noteworthy that in recent years articles relevant to health psychology can be found in many of the traditional medical and psychological journals as well. In addition, at the end of subsequent chapters, we provided suggested readings, which detail the theoretical frameworks and empirical data related to chapter topics.

Appendix B contains a list of common medical abbreviations. Note, in reviewing this list, that small differences might indicate significant changes in meaning. For example, BS means breath sounds, whereas bs means bowel sounds. Also, Gr indicates gravida, whereas gr is the abbreviation for grain. Although the context of the abbreviation can sometimes prevent errors in interpretation, this might not always be so. Note the small difference between NC (no change) and N/C (no complaints). Because different institutions have different approved medical abbreviations, it is imperative that the clinician obtain the appropriate list for his or her site of practice. For example, at the University of Florida's Shands Teaching Hospital, AS means aortic stenosis; at the Los Angeles Kaiser Foundation Hospital, the same abbreviation means arteriosclerosis!

Worthwhile purchases include a good medical dictionary, such as *Stedman's Medical Dictionary* (1990) and an up-to-date *Physician's Desk Reference* (1994), which provides information about medications (e.g., indications, contraindications, and side effects). *Harrison's Principles of Internal Medicine* (Isselbacher et al., 1994) contains a thorough review of medicine. However, many clinicians find the less expensive *Merck Manual* (Berkov, 1992) to be very useful in that it provides brief descriptions of symptoms, course, laboratory findings, and prognosis of various diseases. Taken together, these references provide a comprehensive resource list for basic study in clinical health psychology.

Additional Resources

One can also obtain information through continuing education workshops and courses. The Society of Behavioral Medicine, the Association for Applied Psychophysiology and Biofeedback, the American Psychosomatic Society, and the American Psychological Association, among other professional groups, organize workshops at their annual meetings. Other specialized groups (e.g., the Arthritis Foundation) have educational programs designed specifically for health professionals, in addition to those targeted to the general public. For example, the Association of Rheumatology Health Professionals (ARHP) regularly offers foundation courses in the rheumatic diseases appropriate for the clinical health psychologist interested in gaining further expertise in this area.

Nearly every major disease has a related organization among whose goals is public and professional education (e.g., American Lung Association, American Cancer Society, American Tinnitus Association). Many of these groups provide substantial information at no cost. A list of names and addresses of relevant scientific societies and special-interest groups can be found in Appendix C.

Finally, hospital libraries are reservoirs of audiovisual aids provided by pharmaceutical houses. These are often used by physicians to obtain continuing education credits and are at a level that psychologists can usually understand.

Supervised Training

Note that didactic experiences, while necessary, are not sufficient for the practice of clinical health psychology. As is true of all professional training, the availability of appropriate role models, supervisors, and mentors is crucial. The implementation committee appointed at the Arden House Conference delineated a number of techniques and skills that should be acquired through supervised training (Sheridan et al., 1988). Exhibit 2.1 lists the techniques and skills at least six of which the clinical health psychologist should develop competence.

Obtaining appropriate training requires a careful assessment of the program faculty, or if one is already in practice, the pursuit of an ongoing formal consultation relationship. Exhibit 2.2 displays areas to assess in a potential supervisor.

The need for clinical supervision cannot be overemphasized. First, psychologists are bound by their ethical code to practice only in areas of competence. Second, the wisdom acquired from clinical practice will never be

---

Exhibit 2.1

Competence Areas for Clinical Health Psychologists

1. Relaxation therapies
2. Short-term individual psychotherapy
3. Group therapy
4. Family therapy
5. Consultation skills
6. Liaison skills
7. Assessment of specific patient population (e.g., pain patients or spinal cord injury patients).
8. Neuropsychological assessment
9. Behavior modification techniques
10. Biofeedback
11. Hypnosis
12. Health promotion and public education skills
13. Major treatment programs (e.g., eating disorders, stroke rehabilitation, or pain programs)
14. Compliance motivation

Exhibit 2.2

Competence Areas for Clinical Health Psychologists

1. Special competencies in clinical health psychology (do they match the desired areas of practice?)
2. Sensitivity to ethical issues in supervision
3. Model of supervision to be used (including goals and methods)
4. Availability to the supervisee
5. Perspective and knowledge of the field of clinical health psychology
6. Knowledge about the health care system
7. Affiliation with appropriate professional groups

---

totally communicable in a purely didactic framework. This would be analogous to expecting that one could learn psychotherapy through a set of readings or to conduct research by reading reports. As all trained clinicians are aware, one of the hallmarks of professional training is a developmental process under the tutelage of "masters." Third, with increasing malpractice litigation, there is increased risk of successful suit without proper training and supervision in this area of practice (ethical and malpractice issues will be fully discussed in chapters 6 and 7).

Fourth, naive or incompetent practitioners do a disservice to the rest of their profession. We have, on numerous occasions, heard stories about health care units being "spoiled" for entry by new psychologists because of previous experiences with traditionally trained (and, in our view, insufficiently trained) clinical psychologists or health psychologists who lack training in applied professional practice. Sometimes these difficulties arise from lack of specific knowledge or technique (e.g., gross misinterpretation of medical abbreviations, what physicians call "stupid questions" and "irrelevant reports," inappropriate charting, or misapplication of psychodiagnostic instruments). However, they often occur because of a failure to comprehend the sociopolitical features of health care, as medical settings have their own cultures, which require understanding if the clinician is to be an effective participant. This culture has significant implications for professional role behavior, because the personal conduct and attitude of the psychologist could determine the difference between the success of a service and its death due to disuse.

PERSONAL AND PROFESSIONAL ISSUES

Knowledge of specific facts and expertise in technical clinical skills are not sufficient for the successful practice of clinical health psychology. The health care system itself, along with its various subcultures, must be understood, for one to achieve credibility and acceptance as a professional health service provider. In addition, we have found that professional behaviors, attitudes, and personal characteristics of the clinician are related to performance as a clinical health psychologist.

Clinical health psychologists frequently practice in one or more of three settings: medical–surgical hospitals, outpatient clinics, or independent private practices. Given the nature of the work, close collaboration with medical–surgical or dental specialties is required wherever the practice occurs. Historically, many psychologists have been unaware of the customs, practices, and sociopolitical issues associated with the practice of medicine or dentistry or with the hospital environment. As discussed previously, in recognition of the need for such understanding, the Arden House Conference (Stone, 1983) declared that professional health psychology training should occur in multidisciplinary health service settings under the tutelage of experienced psychologist–mentors who themselves were bona fide members of those settings.

As an example, one requirement of a graduate level medical psychology course taught by C. B. involved a semester-long observational experience on either an inpatient or outpatient service (e.g., the dialysis unit, women's health clinic, oncology service, coronary care unit, or genetic counseling clinic). The purpose of this assignment was to provide an opportunity for experiential learning about the medical setting, its language, its culture, and the nature of interdisciplinary functioning. It also provided in vivo exposure to what it was like to be a patient and to the stressors the health care staff experienced. Students could then compare notes with respect to such things as differences among settings, types of personnel who tended to work there, and clinical problems likely to surface. On course evaluations, every student has reported that this experience was crucial to his or her learning. It facilitated the integration of published clinical research findings, provided numerous hypotheses for future investigations, and stimulated ideas about potential professional roles on each of these services. Perhaps most important, students became much more sophisticated about the sociopolitical aspects of health care. Such observational experiences are relatively simple for students to obtain, but the practicing clinician might have to seek special arrangements with community-based practices or settings. We believe that such experiences are extremely useful.

Formalized Aspects of Health Care Settings

To facilitate learning about the hospital setting, the American Psychological Association (1985a) published the *Hospital Practice Primer for Psychologists*. This document, which is currently being updated, provides needed information about such issues as staff privileges, organized staff membership, legal and regulatory matters, and hospital organization. Hospitals are typically organized into three systems of authority and responsibility: the board of directors (with ultimate responsibility for the activities of the hospital), the hospital administrator (responsible for the day-to-day operation of the hospital), and the medical director (responsible for all clinical care within the hospital). The hospital administrator and medical director work jointly to carry out the goals of the board. Hospital professional staff report to the medical director. The board also has a number of committees, such as the credentials committee (to review credentials of professional staff), the executive committee (usually consisting of chiefs of service and department heads), the quality assurance committee (to maintain standards of practice), and the medical records committee (to ensure proper documentation).

Hospital bylaws delineate qualifications for practice at the hospital, categories of professional staff, conditions of appointment, issues of quality assurance, and personnel due process procedures. *Hospital rules and regulations* are documents that accompany bylaws and contain specifics regarding practice. Rules and regulations concern documentation, standards of care, admission and discharge procedures, infection-control procedures, and so forth.

Psychologists who wish to develop successful clinical health psychology practices must be aware of these rules and avoid their violation. For example, there are actual dress codes in some hospitals (in other settings, the code is not explicit but is just as important to understand). Identification badges are required, and their absence is taken seriously. (C. B. recalls one instance when, in a hurry to deliver a final consultation report to a ward, she left her white coat with badge behind and received an embarrassing lecture from the chief of nursing.) Both the traditional white coat and identification badge are important means of quick identification of authorized personnel.

Another example of specific rules of the health care setting are the guidelines for making chart entries (e.g., using military time, black ink only, and specific procedures for correcting errors). Infractions are actually monitored by special committees. Bylaws and rules and regulations can vary across hospitals. It is imperative that the clinical health psychologist obtain copies of these documents, to learn what privileges and responsibilities are relevant to a particular institution before undertaking practice there.

There are various categories of membership of the hospital staff, as defined by hospital bylaws. Although these categories vary from institution to institution, they are generally organized as follows (American Psychological Association, 1985a):

Active organized staff. This is the highest level of hospital privilege and responsibility. Members of this group are eligible to vote on hospital policy and may hold office. They have a full range of clinical responsibilities within their area of competence. Sometimes nonmedical personnel are excluded from membership within this category.

Courtesy organized staff. Members of this group are limited in the number of patients they may admit to the hospital and may not vote on hospital policy. Usually, these staff hold active organized staff privileges at another facility.

Consulting organized staff. Consulting staff members act only as consultants in their particular fields of expertise. They have no voting privileges and may not hold office. They may attend staff meetings and can be asked to serve on various committees.

Affiliate or allied health staff. Affiliates tend to be "allied health professionals" and ancillary or paramedical personnel. They are granted privilege to participate in patient care under direct supervision of active or courtesy staff members. They hold no voting privileges and may not serve on committees. Although there is change nationally, psychologists are often relegated to affiliate or consulting categories (without voting or admission privileges). Psychologists have long fought for admission and discharge privileges; however, in the field of clinical health psychology, this professional issue seems relatively less important—if hospitalization is required, it is usually for reasons of physical health, necessitating that the primary provider be a physician. What we find more important is the psychologist's ability to vote on rules and regulations, to participate in setting standards, to serve on staff committees, and to participate in health policy formation for the hospital.

Psychologists must apply for *staff privileges*, to practice in a hospital. These privileges are specifically delineated in the application materials (e.g., patient admission; the writing of orders, consultation reports, and progress notes; personality and neuropsychological assessment; individual, family, and group psychotherapy; hypnosis; biofeedback; crisis intervention–emergency care; pain management; and staff development). The applicant's training, experience, and demonstrated competence in requested practice areas are reviewed by the credentials committee and approved by the executive committee.

The process will generally include the application process, including documentation of training, hospital experience, and appropriate malpractice coverage (usually $1 million/$3 million). On approval of the application, the psychologist will go through a "proctoring period," which is required for any discipline applying for staff privileges. During this period, one might be expected to contact the proctor before doing a consultation or simply send reports for the proctor to review as the consultation and treatment progress. Once the proctoring period is complete, advancement to active staff (or active allied health staff) can be completed. Note that application for privileges in a psychiatric hospital may be quite different than those in an acute-care hospital. Often, in an acute-care hospital, the clinical health psychologist will be under the Department of Medicine, because there may not be a Psychiatry Department.

Professional behavior and practice are also governed by the standards of the Joint Commission on Accreditation of Healthcare Organizations (JCAHO), by state laws that regulate practice, and by federal policy that affects health care, usually through the reimbursement process (e.g., Medicare). For example, JCAHO is a private, nonprofit organization developed to set standards for hospitals to ensure proper health care. Guidelines for JCAHO accreditation affect professional behavior through requirements for charting, quality assurance, staff privileges, and so forth. JCAHO also requires attention to patients' rights, and most hospitals have a formal Patients' Bill of Rights, which specifies rights to privacy, dignity, knowledge about treatment and the treating professionals, interpreter services, and so forth.

State statutes affect practice with respect to limits on confidentiality in cases of child abuse and dangerousness, as well as through licensing requirements. Federal policy is having a profound effect on health care practices through the reimbursement system and proposals for health care reform. For example, the prospective payment system (Public Law No. 98–21; Social Security Amendments of 1983) was designed to stem the tide of increased hospital costs. It calls for Medicare reimbursement to hospitals on the basis of fixed rates for diagnosis-related groups (DRGs) and has had a significant effect on length of hospitalization. In summary, the clinician should review state statutes; JCAHO guidelines; hospital bylaws, rules, and regulations; and relevant health policy before practice in any particular setting.

Informal Aspects of Health Care Settings

In addition to formal structures, there are the informal rules that govern behavior in a medical setting and affect professional roles and effective functioning.

Professional Role Issues

It is important for the clinician to understand both the implicit and the explicit power hierarchy. An important question is, Who has credibility in the system? It is sad but true that some physicians who see themselves as holistic have the least credibility with their colleagues, although in some cases this might be justified. These physicians can be very anxious to collaborate and to affiliate with the beginning clinical health psychologist and can make the newcomer feel most welcomed. However, these alliances could prove disastrous if the reputation of the psychologist suffers as a result.

It is important to observe and learn about the hospital environment and "the players" before solid alliances are established. As an example, we are aware of a clinical health psychologist who was attempting to establish a pain management service within an acute-care hospital. In doing so, he developed close relationships with the hospital administration and a few orthopedic surgeons in the hospital to the exclusion of the Anesthesia Department and other orthopedists who also operated out of the hospital. The establishment of the service, over the objections of the Anesthesia Department, resulted in intense turf wars between orthopedics, anesthesiology, and psychology. The service was ultimately closed, because the disciplines were unwilling to cross-refer or cooperate. Yet, another pain service was opened a short time later within the Department of Anesthesia. This service did not include the expertise of a clinical health psychologist.

Stories abound of professional mistreatment of psychologists by physicians (e.g., as "one-down," "second-class citizen," or "technician"). Although we have a few scars in this regard, in general, we have been viewed with respect as professional experts in our own areas. When dealing with more aversive situations, we have found it helpful to keep task oriented and to look for areas of mutual agreement. This usually means realizing that we all have the same goal: good patient care. Focusing interactions over this mutual goal, and not engaging in unnecessary power struggles, is not only more effective for the patient but can also be a major professional coping strategy.

Being a psychologist, and thus somewhat outside of the normal medical hierarchy, has also been of benefit. As a profession, we have sufficient status to warrant attention from other health care professions but are not so intimidating as to thwart communication at various levels. It is often necessary for us to seek medical information from the referral source, which can make it easier for the physician to learn from us about psychosocial material. We become mutual students in the biopsychosocial understanding of the patient. We never have to prove ourselves as "real physicians," as do our psychiatric colleagues.

Referral Customs

Understanding referral customs in both inpatient and outpatient settings is very important. For instance, a hospital consultant does not provide feedback to a patient about results unless given permission to do so by the attending physician (which is usually easily obtained). This can present special ethical issues regarding psychological testing feedback; these are addressed in chapter 6. In most hospitals, a psychologist should never see a patient unless it is requested by the attending physician, even if nursing staff have requested help. However, good relationships with nursing staff are very important for a number of reasons: (a) these staff members are frequently responsible for initiating consultations, (b) they have valuable information to offer about the patient, and (c) they are often critical to the intervention process.

It can also be important to understand the roles of all the physicians involved in the patient's care. W. D. once experienced a situation in which a chronic-pain consultation was ordered by the physiatrist (a physical medicine and rehabilitation doctor) for a patient on the acute-rehabilitation unit. Per accepted standards, this consultation included a Minnesota Multiphasic Personality Inventory (MMPI) assessment. The physiatrist was very familiar with the instrument and expected it would be used. In addition, the patient was openly willing to complete the test. Even so, when the attending internist came into the room and observed the patient completing this "ludicrous" questionnaire, he became very agitated and took the test away from her, telling her she should not complete it. This was followed by what would be considered an inappropriate note in the chart regarding psychological assessment along with an order canceling any further consultation or psychological treatment.

In this rehabilitation situation, patients are commonly followed by both an internist (who addresses any general medical problems) and a physiatrist (who dictates the rehabilitation treatment). The latter of these is usually much more involved in the treatment of these patients. In addition to suspending patient contact immediately, W. D. discussed the issue with the physiatrist rather than going directly to the internist. The physiatrist was able to educate the internist as to the necessity of the evaluation (including the testing) and elicit his cooperation. The consultation was reordered and completed. W. D. then followed up by presenting the results to the internist (in a nondefensive manner), providing concrete and *usable* information. In addition, the internist was sent an article on the use of psychological evaluation and assessment in treating chronic-pain problems. This feedback further educated him as to the validity and usefulness of such procedures.

In outpatient consultation work, it is important to remember that one should never refer a patient to a medical or dental colleague for consultation without going back to the original referral source to tactfully obtain his or her permission (we've never been denied). This is especially important in clinical health psychology, because the psychologist clinician constantly has to assess whether previous medical workups have been adequate, without having competence in that area. It is best to have established relationships with specialty physicians in whom the clinician has confidence. The clinical health psychologist will often obtain "curbside consultations" from these specialists, as well as refer to them and thus contribute to their practices.

An important aspect to keep in mind is that when physicians request services from psychologists, they might actually feel somewhat threatened about admitting that they do not understand a patient or that they cannot handle a particular situation. In fact, this might be more of an issue when it comes to behavioral and emotional problems than when consultations are required of other specialists in medicine. In our culture, it appears that many people consider themselves to be experts in human relations. Breakdowns in interpersonal relationships are frequently blamed on the "other," but not without significant personal fears concerning one's own failure. So it is with health care providers and their patients, and this can result in defensiveness or increased emotional reactivity on the part of the consultee.

This kind of problem needs to be handled with tact. Any type of arrogance or condescending behavior will only exacerbate the problem. Indeed it is hypothesized that professional arrogance in psychologists is relatively more damaging to collaborative relationships with physicians, in part due to the nature of problems being addressed, than would be arrogance displayed by another medical specialist (e.g., cardiologist to family practitioner). In general, we believe that there are a number of professional behaviors and personal attributes that can facilitate or hinder successful clinical health psychology practice.

Special Issues in Professional Behavior

Another discipline often cannot judge the quality of psychological services, but physicians can judge whether such services are delivered in good professional style. Unfortunately, *quality of care* is often confused with *quality of service*, although the latter is certainly also important. However, style is frequently the only frame of reference from which physicians can judge, and the standards used are those of their own profession. Given this understanding, we suggest that the clinical health psychologist should do the following: (a) avoid overidentification with medicine, (b) fine-tune communication skills, (c) be prompt and follow through, (d) accept his or her limits of understanding, (e) be prepared for patient advocacy, and (f) advocate for quality of services.

Avoid overidentification with medicine. Although there is a need to understand the health care system and to behave in a fashion that can gain credibility for the clinical health psychologist, it is also important to be aware of the potential for inappropriate medical socialization of clinical health psychologists. Elfant (1985) articulated the traditional medical model, with its authoritarian stance and action orientation, and expressed his concerns that health psychology practitioners will overidentify with it. In doing so, they might forgo the psychological treatment model that insists on autonomy and freedom of choice for both patient and therapist.

Elfant (1985) also stated, "The fact that psychological assessment raises a multiplicity of hypotheses, issues and clinical guesses is disturbing news in the hospital environment where quick action is the norm"(p. 61). There are strong pressures in health care to come to bottom-line decisions: "to fix" people. This is especially relevant to psychologists in the area of compliance with medical regimen, where the clinician must carefully evaluate who the actual client is: the health care system or the patient. We agree with Elfant that clinical health psychology must avoid the mistakes of the traditional medical model, which portrays the patient as sick and dependent and the professional as imperialistic and heroic.

Fine-tune communication skills. Suffice it to say that competence in the eyes of physicians will *not* be demonstrated through the use of psychological jargon, be it psychoanalytic or behavioral in orientation. We have witnessed physicians' reactions range from sarcasm to bemusement to terms such as *oral fixation, cognitive restructuring, projective identification,* and *contingency management.*

The rule of thumb is to be *concrete, practical, brief,* and *succinct.* Recommendations should be relevant to the consultee's behavior. It is often said that the longer the report, the less likely it is to be read.

Be prompt and follow up. In hospitals, consultations usually must be initiated within 24 hr or less, with full reports available immediately. Many consultations require more than one contact. A frequent complaint about psychological consultants is that they "drop the ball" by rendering an opinion and then leaving the case to the attending physician to manage without either specific directions or proper follow-up support.

Outpatient services are sometimes accused of being "rabbit holes" for patients, who are thought to disappear after the referral is made. Often this is not the result of inattention to the patient's needs, but a lack of follow-through in communication back to referral sources.

Accept limits of understanding. Every discipline has its limits in understanding. Clinical health psychologists must not overestimate or overstate the boundaries of knowledge. As psychologists attempt to prove themselves in medical settings, this might be tempting, but it is ill-fated. One needs to know and to accept the limits inherent in the state of psychological knowledge and therapeutic efficacies and to be able to ask for help or information when appropriate. The psychologist should not project the image of a general "fixer" of human behavior; rather, she or he should convey a more limited range or expertise. Lipowski (1967) described the physician's view of the psychiatrist as "a scientifically unsophisticated, medically ignorant, and impractical man, given to sweeping statements about other people's motives based on abstruse theories of questionable validity" (p. 158). For over 20 years, he called on psychiatrists to contradict this image, a message never completely heeded by either psychiatrists or psychologists, given some of the consultation reports we have seen.

Be prepared for patient advocacy. A final issue has to do with patient advocacy. Often the clinical health psychologist will find him- or herself in a mediating role between the health care system and the patient, sometimes having to actively advocate for patient needs. For example, a previous psychiatric diagnosis can affect physicians' willingness to pursue medical evaluations. We remember well the case of a 45-year-old former alcoholic who complained of back pain and was considered a "crock." It was ultimately determined that the woman was actually suffering from a recurrence of bowel cancer. Thorough documentation of the nature of the complaints, the lack of evidence for psychological mechanisms to explain the symptoms, and several phone calls to the attending physician persuaded him to do a more extensive workup. As a result, the patient felt more "authenticated" and, throughout her remaining therapy, worked out her anger at caregivers as she became increasingly dependent on them until her death.

Setting-related issues can also be extremely important in patient advocacy. For example, it has been said that in an HMO, in which the patient has less autonomy and control than in fee-for-service health care, health care professionals have special obligations to advocate for the patient and to act as internal critics of unfair HMO policies and colleagues' practices.

Advocate for quality services. If the psychologist witnesses a violation of patient rights or an inappropriate standard of care, appropriate action must be taken. Psychologists must know the local professional mechanisms, chains of authority, and structures available to deal with such problems.

According to Keith-Spiegel and Koocher (1985), psychologists' ethical principles implicitly encourage whistle-blowing if other mechanisms fail to resolve the problem. However, such activity is not without personal and professional self-sacrifice and risk. Keith-Spiegel and Koocher have encouraged the use of questions developed by Nader and his colleagues (Nader, Petkas, & Blackwell, 1972), which could assist the clinical health psychologist with decision making concerning this issue:

1. Is my knowledge of the matter complete and accurate?
2. What are the objectionable practices, and what public interest do they harm?
3. How far should I, and can I, go inside the organization with my concern or objection?
4. Will I be violating any rules by contacting outside parties and, if so, is whistle-blowing nevertheless justified?
5. Will I be violating any laws or ethical duties by *not* contacting external parties?
6. Once I have decided to act, what is the best way to blow the whistle—anonymously, overtly, by resignation prior to speaking out, or in some other way?
7. What will be the likely responses from various sources—inside and outside the organization—to the whistle-blowing action?
8. What is expected to be achieved by whistle-blowing in this particular situation? (Nader, Petkas, & Blackwell, 1972, p. 6)

Many of these questions are also useful in determining for oneself how far one wants to go, either within a setting or within a profession, to resolve problems related to professional practice.

Personal Characteristics

Before undertaking work in clinical health psychology, it is important to review some of the personal issues that we have found to be related to one's ability to adjust to practice in this area. There are some individuals who are just not suited to the work; thus, it is better to examine these issues early in the process of training.

Because clinical health psychology is receiving increased attention, individuals might be drawn to it for inappropriate reasons or with unrealistic expectations. Mismatches between personal characteristics and professional requirements are costly in terms of time spent and emotional well-being. We have seen mismatches result in early burnout and, in the worst cases, pervasive anger, resentment, and nihilistic thinking. These attitudes not only are damaging to the individual practitioner but also can reflect negatively on the field as a whole. Personal characteristics thought to be related to successful practice include the following:

Understanding one's own stimulus value. It is important for the clinician to assess whether he or she has any striking peculiarities that could interfere with early establishment of rapport, because rapport must often be accomplished very quickly in this field. Given the bad press mental health professionals have had in the past, the more "shrinklike" person might be at quite a disadvantage. When we think of the most successful clinical health psychologists we have known, the descriptors *active, engaging, open, direct, assertive* and *energetic* come to mind. In a survey of Veterans Administration physicians, Schenkenberg, Peterson, Wood, and DaBell (1981) found the following adjectives used to describe important qualities for a psychological consultant: *pleasant, personable, friendly, compassionate, empathic, sensitive, interested, available, able to communicate effectively, cooperative, intelligent, open, perceptive* and *displaying common sense.*

Possession of a high frustration tolerance. The clinical health psychologist must be a persevering, patient person who, given the frustrations in the field, can manage on a very thin schedule of reinforcement. We believe this to be very basic to work in the area. One must be able to tolerate the fluctuation of interest by the medical community in behavioral and emotional components of health. Despite all the current focus on comprehensive health care, it can still be lip service. Some physicians care little about the values psychologists hold most dear. Physicians can be ambivalent, hostile (covert or overt), or indifferent. An attitude of "benevolent skepticism" is welcomed. Physicians sometimes fail to carry out recommendations (about 30% of the time, according to Billowitz & Friedson, 1978–1979), discharge patients before evaluation or treatment is completed, refer patients without adequate preparation, or fail to acknowledge the expertise of the psychologist (everyone is a "psychologist").

Of special note is the need for clinicians to respond nondefensively to what could be perceived to be an MD versus PhD prejudice. As Shows (1976) pointed out, psychologists' prejudices against the medical model (which they equate with medicine) can lead to a readiness to project conflict into almost any situation. When a defensive or aggressive stance is taken, it can make collaborative efforts difficult. As one becomes more sophisticated in the health care system, it becomes evident that some conflict is a natural, ongoing part of the system and that it occurs among medical specialties as well.

In our experience, psychologists with strong needs for external validation and recognition are not likely to do well on a long-term basis; they soon become angry and resentful. Rather, we believe the work is more suitable if one is primarily motivated by internal belief systems and achievement needs. This is because the system often yields too little external reinforcement.

Avoidance of professional fanaticism. Although we indicated the importance of being motivated by internal beliefs, and earlier mentioned the somewhat missionary zeal with which a number of us embraced the field, we believe it important not to be fanatical in our beliefs about the importance of the biopsychosocial model. Nor should we be wedded to any single treatment technique. We have witnessed the suspension of critical

34

thinking by a number of colleagues who threw themselves into the wellness movement or the use of biofeedback, only to suffer a loss of credibility when they could not deliver the results they anticipated.

Tolerance for a demanding work schedule. This is especially true if inpatient work is involved. Much consultation work in the hospital setting is unpredictable, and the psychologist must be available on short notice. Follow-through is essential, and must be completed despite whatever else has already been scheduled. The work is not leisurely. Pressures can mount, especially when there are demands for immediate solutions to very complex problems, as is often the case. Of course, settings do vary, and there are some systems in which clinical health psychologists maintain a 9-to-5 schedule, with few deviations even in hospital work. Scheduling in outpatient practices is much more under the control of the clinician.

Ability to deal with hostile–reluctant patients. Specific suggestions for handling hostile patients are given in chapter 5, but it is noted here that clinical health psychologists frequently see patients who are upset about the referral. They often display indifference, if not outright antagonism, when meeting the clinician. This is sometimes due to poor preparation by the physician but is most often due to the mind–body dualism that is alive and well in patients as well as physicians. If the clinician has strong needs to see patients who are actively seeking psychological help, this is not the most suitable area of practice.

Ability to cope with diverse sets of data. The clinical health psychologist needs to be comfortable with diverse sets of data (biological, social, and psychological) and to attempt to integrate these while recognizing that no single theory of behavior provides an adequate conceptualization. The clinician must remain flexible in operating within a variety of conceptual models, depending on the case. The clinical health psychologist must guard against being too easily intimidated by biological models (which are often presented as being more precise than they actually are) while being overly self-critical of the behavioral sciences.

Ability to work with the physically ill. Patients seen by the clinical health psychologist are sometimes gravely ill, deformed, mutilated, disabled, or dying. A period of acclimation is needed as one struggles within oneself with such potential stressors as the sight of blood, the burn unit, the fears of chronic pain, and the acceptance of terminal illness. The clinician's reactions to the patient in these areas are critical. The colostomy or mastectomy patient who is concerned with body image and fears of unacceptability must not be treated with squeamishness. Yet it is easy to be distracted from addressing patient feelings and attitudes in the presence of massive physical changes (such as those found on a head and neck surgery service; Petrucci & Harwick, 1984).

Clinicians need to design their own programs to facilitate dealing with these issues. Medical libraries are full of pictures and videos that can provide stimuli for desensitization purposes. Colleagues, supervisors, personal therapists, and families are important resources in dealing with personal issues regarding death, dying, and threats to body integrity.

Empathy for the health care providers' perspectives. It is important to be able to communicate respect for the consultee and his or her problem (e.g., a demanding or noncompliant patient). Collaboration with medicine requires empathy not just in the evaluation of the patient but also in dealing with the referral sources. The clinician needs to understand consultees' thinking styles and perspectives on patient care. This requires an in-depth understanding of the roles, functions, and stressors in various hospital units and outpatient clinics. This is perhaps best obtained through naturalistic observation.

Acceptance of dependence on another profession. Psychology is an independent profession, but the practice of clinical health psychology has aspects of a forced dependency on the expertise and performance of another profession, usually medicine or dentistry. Some psychologists we have known have had special difficulty with this forced dependency, especially when it involved a profession of greater social status.

Appropriateness as a health model. Weiss (1982), in his 1980 Presidential Address to the Division of Health Psychology, highlighted the importance of health psychologists' assessing their personal suitability as role models. The clinical health psychologist should be aware of personal habits such as smoking, overeating, alcohol usage, and physical fitness. Modeling of appropriate personal health behavior is related not only to therapeutic effectiveness, if one adopts a social learning theory model, but also to ethical principles, as discussed in chapter 6.

In summary, beyond acquiring the core body of clinical health psychology knowledge and skills, preparation to become an effective clinical health psychologist requires significant attention to professional and personal issues.

SUGGESTED READINGS AND DESK REFERENCES

Ader, R., Weiner, H., & Baum, A. (1988). *Experimental foundations of behavioral medicine: Conditioning approaches.* Hillsdale, NJ: Erlbaum.

Berkov, R. (Ed.). (1992). *Merck manual of diagnosis and treatment* (16th ed.). Rahway, NJ: Merck Research Laboratories.

Bernard, L. C., & Krupat, E. (1994). *Health psychology: Biopsychosocial factors in health and illness.* Orlando, FL: Holt, Rinehart & Winston.

Gatchel, R. J., & Blanchards. (Eds.). (1993). *Psychophysiological disorders: Research and clinical applications.* Washington, DC: American Psychological Association.

Gylys, B. A., & Wedding, M. E. (1988). *Medical terminology: A systems approach* (2nd ed.). Philadelphia: Davis.

Isselbacher, K. J., Braunwald, E., Wilson, J. D., Martin, J. B., Fauci, A. S., & Kasper, D. L. (Eds.). (1994). *Harrison's principles of internal medicine* (13th ed.). New York: McGraw-Hill.

Kaplan, R. M., Sallis, J. F., & Patteson, T. L. (1993). *Health and human behavior.* New York: McGraw-Hill.

Maxmen, J. S. (1991). *Psychotropic drugs fast facts.* New York: Norton.

Physician's Desk Reference. (1994). (48th ed.). Montvale, NJ: Medical Economics Data Production.

Spence, A. P. (1982) *Basic human anatomy.* Menlo Park, CA: Benjamin/Cummings.

Stedman's Medical Dictionary. (1990). (25th ed.). Baltimore: Williams & Wilkins.

Sweet, J. J., Rozensky, R. H., & Tovian, S. M. (1991). *Handbook of clinical psychology in medical settings.* New York: Plenum.

3

Clinical Health Psychology Assessment

As has been previously documented, psychodiagnostic assessment is a frequent activity of clinical health psychologists (Morrow & Clayman, 1982; Stabler & Mesibov, 1984). It is also probably one of psychology's most unique contributions to patient care. Although assessment is often used by psychologists as the first step in developing a treatment program for their own patients, in clinical health psychology it is frequently used to answer questions and thus solve problems regarding patient care for other health professionals. As Sir William Osler, the esteemed physician, so aptly stated, "it is more important to know what kind of man has a disease than to know what kind of disease a man has" (Osler, 1971, p. 14). For clinical health psychologists, the assessment activity is, then, inextricably intertwined with the consultation activity.

The kinds of consultation requests made of clinical health psychologists depend on the type of practice that one has delineated. Clearly, the referral bases developed (e.g., pediatric, oncology, or neurology) influence the types of assessment questions posed. Lipowski (1967) described the diagnostic issues that the consultant in a multidisciplinary consultation–liaison team is likely to encounter: (a) psychological presentations of organic disease (e.g., pancreatic cancer presenting as depression), (b) psychological complications of organic disease (e.g., post cardiotomy delirium), (c) psychological reactions to organic disease (e.g., depression subsequent to amputation), (d) somatic effects of psychological distress (e.g., angina) and (e) somatic presentations of psychiatric disorder (e.g., masked depression).

A report by Shevitz, Silberfarb, and Lipowski (1976) on 1,000 referrals for psychiatric consultation in a general hospital found that approximately 57% of the patients were referred for differential diagnosis, 56% were referred for management problems (disturbing behavior on the ward, psychiatric disorders that complicated a known organic disease, and somatic problems with no known organic pathology), and 28% were referred for disposition, especially after a suicide attempt that mandated a psychiatric referral.

From C. B.'s experience in developing a medical psychology service in an academic health science center, a wide variety of medical–surgical patients are likely to be referred specifically to clinical health psychologists. The psychiatric services at the same center tended to receive the consultations concerning suicidal and combative behavior, psychotropic medication, and mental status changes. In contrast, the psychologists received relatively more consultation requests concerning such issues as coping with illness, compliance, preparation for surgery, presurgical screenings, diagnostic and treatment issues associated with chronic pain, and, of course, neuropsychological evaluations.

We have more recent data from our experience in developing a behavioral medicine outpatient team in an HMO setting. Nearly 600 referrals were received per year. Over half of those involved requests from neurology, internal medicine, and family practice units to provide services in the areas of headache management and neuropsychological assessment. A significant number of other clinical problems were also seen for consultation or treatment purposes and these included such varied disorders as angina, asthma, arthritis, back pain, blepharospasm, bruxism, cancer/cancer phobia, cardiac disease, chronic obstructive pulmonary disease, compliance issues, deafness, diabetes, fibrositis, hyperhidrosis, hypertension, interstitial cystitis, irritable bowel syndrome, multiple sclerosis, neurodermatitis, penile prosthesis surgery, Raynaud's phenomenon, temporomandibular joint pain, tinnitus, and vomiting.

We believe that the growth of knowledge provided by applied research in health psychology has resulted in an increased need for clinical services. This is especially true in areas not always addressed by traditional consultation and liaison psychiatry or clinical psychology models. In general, these include (a) consultations and treatments involving psychophysiologic self-regulation or the application of learning theory, either as the treatment of choice for a medical problem or as an adjunct to standard medical care, (b) consultations involving predictions of response to medical–surgical treatments, (c) reduction of health-risk behaviors.

Given the possible range of consultation and assessment activities in clinical health psychology, it will not be possible to detail problems associated with specific diseases or to address the utility of specific assessment measures, which are well described elsewhere (see Suggested Readings). Instead, we focus on a *model* for assessment in clinical health psychology and briefly describe the most common procedures used. Chapter 5 focuses on more process-oriented issues, which are common among various settings, roles, and types of illnesses.

A MODEL FOR ASSESSMENT IN CLINICAL HEALTH PSYCHOLOGY

Following the medical model, psychological assessment has traditionally had two primary purposes: identification and treatment of psychological disorders. As such, psychological assessment measures have been developed to focus on a single dimension of the patient—namely, the state of the patient's mind—without complementary consideration of the patient's body. Conversely, medicine has traditionally focused on the treatment of disease to the exclusion of personality or emotional factors. Each approach has some value, but the field of clinical health psychology requires an integration of these divergent attitudes, often in the absence of adequate conceptual models. Adequate assessment does not exclude one for the other.

The clinical health psychologist's tasks are to assess the interactions among the person, the disease, and the person's environment and to formulate a diagnosis or treatment strategy on the basis of that understanding. Given the necessity of incorporating physiological, psychological, and sociological information, the clinical health psychologist typically works from a biopsychosocial perspective of health and illness (Engel, 1977).

On the basis of Engel's (1977) work and that of Leigh and Reiser (1980), we have elaborated a model for assessment that we find useful in approaching clinical situations because it facilitates organization of information and subsequent decision making about assessment strategies. Unfortunately, this model reduces various aspects of the biopsychosocial perspective in a manner that could enhance thinking in a compartmentalized, reductionistic fashion about complex, interrelated processes. Note that this is not reflective of our overall orientation toward assessment issues but rather is an artifact of inadequacies in current schemata representing the biopsychosocial model.

TARGETS OF ASSESSMENT

Table 3.1 describes the *targets of assessment* by *domain of information* (biologic or physical, affective, cognitive, or behavioral) and *unit of assessment* (patient, family, health care system, or sociocultural context). Within each block are listed examples of the kinds of information that need to be gathered in conducting the assessment or of which the clinician should be aware when attempting to understand the patient from a biopsychosocial perspective.

Each block also has an associated developmental or historical perspective that could be critical to a full understanding of the present condition. In each area, the clinician should attempt to understand the patient's (a) *current status*, (b) *changes since onset of the illness*, and (c) *past history*. The focus of the assessment should be not solely on identification of problems but also on delineation of assets, resources, and strengths of the patient and his or her environment.

Patient Targets

Biological Targets

The most obvious biological targets are the patient's age, race, sex, and physical appearance. In addition, the clinician needs to gain a thorough understanding of the patient's current physiological symptoms and how they are similar or different from past symptoms. Recent physical changes could be particularly salient to the assessment, because they are often the precipitating events that elicit the referral (e.g., recent hair loss due to radiation treatment, incontinence, or gross pedal edema after noncompliance with dietary regimen). The clinician will want to obtain information on the specifics of the particular disease: nature, location, and frequency of symptoms; current treatment regimen; and health status within the disease process (e.g., Stages I through IV in cancer).

Other sources of biological information include the physical exam, current and past vital signs, the results from relevant laboratory tests (e.g., creatinine levels, blood alcohol levels, and HIV status), medications, and use of illicit drugs. Furthermore, a history of the patient's constitution and general health—including previous illnesses, relevant genetic information, injuries, and surgeries—should be obtained.

Depending on the problem, biological targets might also include variables associated with the autonomic nervous system or musculoskeletal activity (e.g., electromyographic [EMG] recordings or peripheral temperature readings) obtained in both resting and stress-related conditions. For example, a psychophysiological profile involving frontal EMG activity under relaxed and stressed conditions could be obtained on a patient suffering from tension headache.

Affective Targets

The assessment of affective targets involves understanding the patient's current mood and affect, including their contextual elements and historical features. In addition, an assessment would be incomplete without having obtained information about the patient's *feelings* about his or her illness, treatment, health care providers, future, social support network, and, of course, self.

Table 3.1

Targets of Assessment

Domain of information	Patient	Family	Environment	
			Health care system	Sociocultural context
Biological or physical	Age, sex, race	Characteristics of the	Characteristics of the	Social services
	Physical appearance	home setting	treatment setting	Financial resources
	Symptoms, health status	Economic resources	Characteristics of	Social networks
	Physical examination	Size of the family	medical procedures	Occupational setting
	Vital signs, lab data	Familial patterning	and treatment regimens	Physical job requirements
	Medications, drugs	(e.g., headache history)	Availability of prosthetic	Health hazards
	Psychophysiological data	Other illness in family	aids	
	Constitutional factors			
	Genetics			
	History of injury, disease,			
	and surgery			

	Patient	Members	Providers	Culture
Affective	Mood Affect Feelings about illness, treatment, health care, providers, self, family, job, and social network History of affective disturbance	Members' feelings about patient, illness, and treatment	Providers' feelings about patient, illness, and treatment	Sentiment of culture regarding patient, illness, and treatment
Cognitive	Cognitive style Thought content Intelligence Education Knowledge about disease Health beliefs Attitudes and expectations regarding illness, treatment, health care, and providers Perceived meaning of the illness Philosophy of life Religious beliefs	Knowledge about illness and treatment Attitudes and expectations about patient, illness, and treatment Intellectual resources	Providers' knowledge Providers' attitudes toward patient, illness, and treatment	Current state of knowledge Cultural attitudes toward patient and illness

(*continues*)

Table 3.1

(*Continued*)

Domain of information	Patient	Environment		
		Family	Health care system	Sociocultural context
Behavioral	Activity level	Participation in patient care	Providers' skills in education and training patients	Employment policies
	Interactions with family friends, providers, and coworkers	Reinforcement contingencies for health and illness	Reinforcement contingencies for health and illness	Laws regulating health care practice, disability, provision of care, health habits
	Health habits			Handicapped access
	Health care utilization (previous medications and psychological treatment)			Customs in symptom reporting and help seeking
	Compliance			
	Ability to control physical symptoms			

Again, it is helpful to obtain data that allow for comparison between current affective states and those of the past, in that it is often the contrast that has prompted the referral. For example, a request we once received stated the following: "Patient recently diagnosed with colon cancer. Had been adjusting well to pending surgery, now crying frequently. Please evaluate." It was the *change* in affective state that led to this referral, a change that turned out to be related to a family problem rather than maladaptive coping with illness. Previous history of an affective disorder must also be obtained.

Cognitive Targets

Assessment of the patient's cognitive functioning involves gathering information about the patient's knowledge, perceptions, and attitudes, as well as the content and pattern of thinking. It is imperative that the clinical health psychologist be aware of cognitive abilities and limitations of the patient, from both current and developmental perspectives. Cognitive targets include the following: general intelligence; educational level; specific knowledge concerning illness and treatment; attitudes toward health, illness, and health care providers; perceived threat of illness; perceived control over psychological and physical symptoms; perception of costs and benefits of possible treatment regimens; and expectations about future outcome.

Another important target is the perceived *meaning* of the illness to the patient. More generally, the clinician should be aware of the patient's general cognitive style and philosophy of life, including religious beliefs.

Behavioral Targets

Behavioral targets include what the patient is doing (the action) and the manner in which he or she does it (the style). Action primarily involves assessment of motoric behaviors, such as facial expressions, foot tapping, bruxism, bracing, body posture, and eye contact. Styles are varied but include flamboyant, hesitant, age appropriate, hostile, restless, and passive. The clinical health psychologist will want to understand the patient's overall level, pattern, and style of activity in areas of self-care and interpersonal, occupational, and recreational functioning, as well as specific behavioral targets related to the reason for referral.

Of special interest is the patterning and nature of the physician–patient relationship, as well as whether the patient can voluntarily control any of his or her physical symptoms. Once again, a historical perspective is important, because past behavior is often the best predictor of future behavior.

Extremely important in clinical health psychology is the assessment of current and previous health habits (e.g., smoking, exercise, eating patterns, and alcohol usage) and health care utilization. The clinician should be able to answer the following questions about the patient: (a) What are the nature, frequency, and pattern of past contacts with health-service providers, and (b) what have been the antecedent stimuli and consequences of these contacts (i.e., history of previous help-seeking and treatments)?

Finally, an assessment would be incomplete without information concerning the patient's current and past history of compliance or adherence to treatment regimens, with specific reasons noted for noncompliance whenever it has occurred. Areas of assessment here include medication usage as prescribed, history of keeping appointments, and follow-through on previous recommendations.

Environmental Targets

The clinical health psychologist also needs to assess aspects of the various environments within which the patient interacts. These include the following: (a) the family unit, (b) the health care system with its various settings and providers, and (c) the sociocultural environment, including social network, occupational setting, and aspects related to ethnicity and cultural background. As with assessment of the individual patient, environmental targets of assessment include physical, affective, cognitive, and behavioral domains, with a focus on relevant demands, limitations, and supports.

Family Environment

In assessing the physical domain of the family environment, it is important to know about available economic resources and perhaps even physical characteristics of the home setting, depending on the problem being assessed (e.g., quadriplegia or blindness). The family's developmental history, size, and experience of recent changes are all important aspects to consider. The clinician should also be aware of other illnesses in family members (e.g., history of hypertension or diabetes) and familial models for various symptoms (e.g., headaches).

In the affective domain, it is important to understand family members' feelings about the patient, the patient's illness, and the treatments rendered. Assessment of past or present affective disorders in the family is essential.

In the cognitive domain, the clinician must assess the family's attitudes, perceptions, and expectations about the patient, the patient's illness and treatment, and the future. Family members' intellectual resources, as well as knowledge that they possess about health and illness, should be understood.

In the behavioral domain, the clinician will want to know whether there have been any changes within the family since the onset of the illness. An example might include a shift in roles and responsibilities of family members. It is also important to find out to what degree family members participate in the patient's care.

Assessment of behaviors of family members that could influence the patient's illness or adaptation is crucial. For example, families might model chronic illness, punish patient attempts at self-help, or be secretive in a manner that increases patient anxiety.

Health Care System

The health care system should also be assessed across physical, affective, cognitive, and behavioral domains. For example, in the first domain the clinician needs to know the physical characteristics of the setting in which the patient is being assessed or treated (e.g., coronary care unit, ward, or outpatient clinic). Special considerations include degree of sensory stimulation, privacy, and availability of prosthetic aids. In addition, the clinical health psychologist must understand the physical characteristics of the diagnostic procedures and the treatment regimen to which the patient has been, is being, or will be exposed (e.g., pelvic exenteration, colostomy, hemodialysis, or chemotherapy).

In the affective domain, one must be aware of how health care providers *feel* about the patient and about the patient's illness (e.g., requests for sterilization or HIV-positive status). Special problems can occur, for example, in burn units, where both perpetrators and victims of severely injurious events can be housed within the same unit. Staff and visitors often feel split in their feelings and loyalties to these patients. Also, the attitudes of providers themselves toward the health care system within which they work can enhance or detract from overall health care.

In the cognitive domain, the clinician needs to have some understanding of how knowledgeable health care providers are about the patient's problems, illness, and treatment. One also needs to assess their attitudes and expectations about these issues as well as about the patient's future. Furthermore, it is helpful to be aware of the community standard of care for the problem.

When assessing the "behavior" of the overall health care system, the clinician needs to be aware of policies, rules, and regulations that will affect the patient and his or her treatment (e.g., staffing patterns, single vs. rotating physicians, appointment schedules, and infection control policies). It is also important to understand which specific behaviors health care providers might be displaying that could influence patient behavior. Such behaviors might include transmitting knowledge about disease, providing skill training in self-care, reinforcing verbal complaints, or avoiding affective expression by the patient.

Sociocultural Environment

Physical aspects of the patient's sociocultural environment include both (a) the physical requirements and flexibilities of the patient's occupation and work setting and (b) the social and financial resources–services available to the patient. In addition, the clinician should be aware of the nature of the patient's social network (including size, density, and proximity) and the frequency of the patient's contact with it. Assessment of the natural environment in terms of ecological health hazards (e.g., pollutants and noise levels) is also sometimes necessary.

In the affective and cognitive domains, the clinician should understand cultural sentiments, attitudes, and expectations regarding the patient's race, gender, ethnicity, lifestyle, religion, illness, and treatment (e.g., sentiments about AIDS, homosexuality, and femininity of women who have undergone hysterectomy). What are the cultural attitudes towards prevention? What is the health belief model of the culture itself? Are there prevalent religious beliefs that could impact the patient's willingness to obtain treatment?

In terms of the behavior of large sociocultural systems, the clinician might need to know specific employment policies related to the problem being assessed (e.g., regulations regarding return to work for patients with back problems and hiring guidelines for AIDS patients). In addition, legislation regulating health care provision and health habits is relevant (e.g., disability and smoking in public places). Finally, the clinician should be aware of ethnic customs that could be related to symptom reporting (or underreporting) and health care use.

INTEGRATING ASSESSMENT INFORMATION

It becomes clear from a review of the targets for assessment that these "blocks" are interrelated and that the nature or relative importance of information obtained in one block is often affected by information found in another. For example, type and location of physical symptoms can affect perceived meaning of the illness because of the special psychological significance of certain body parts (e.g., genitalia or heart). Thus, affective reactions might be more pronounced in a patient with cervical carcinoma in situ than those found in a person with an objectively worse health status (e.g., insulin-dependent diabetes). Affective reactions might also be influenced by age. For instance, related to the previous example, the loss of ability to bear children could be significantly less traumatic for a 55-year-old woman than for a 17-year-old teenager. Ethnicity might impact this relationship even further if cultural values equated femininity with childbearing potential. For example, in one rural area, we had a number of women who were past child rearing age express concerns about hysterectomy for such reasons. These women did not want their male partner to know the exact nature of the proposed surgery.

Cultural background affects more than just emotional reactions. For example, we have been aware of some instances of more cavalier attitudes about conducting hysterectomies when the potential recipients were unwed females, of low socioeconomic status, with multiple children. These attitudes could affect not only clinical decision making, but characteristics of the health care environment and the doctor–patient relationship as well. A growing body of research is exploring the role of ethnicity in treatment seeking, symptom perception, and health care provision (Becker et al., 1992).

In conducting an assessment, it is important to understand that the data obtained could be influenced by the type of setting in which the assessment occurs. For example, low-back-pain patients often walk with greater or lesser flexibility depending on who is watching them and in what setting they are being observed. We are reminded of the following example:

> A low-back-pain patient in an inpatient, chronic-pain program was repeatedly observed ambulating with a walker by program personnel. However, on one occasion, when the patient was unaware that he was being observed, he was seen casually carrying his walker over his shoulder while ambulating with appropriate body posture and gait.

Expectations about the purpose of the assessment clearly impact data obtained. As example, the demand characteristics for patients seeking heart transplant surgery as their only hope of survival versus those seeking disability payments for a cardiac condition are tremendously different and must be considered in the interpretation of data. The presence of other people, their roles, and their behavior can also affect responses during assessment. We have more than once witnessed the emotional breakdown of a patient only a few moments after the patient assured the oncologist that he or she was doing well. The breakdown was not observed until the oncologist left the room, in part due to the need to be a "good patient" for the physician, who is perceived as having so much power over life and death. We have also experienced the reluctance of patients to reveal even significant physical symptoms because of the perception of their physician as being too rushed.

Settings also have different base rates of certain phenomena. For example, orthopedic wards tend to have more accident victims, including more risk takers (e.g., motorcyclists), and patients in teaching hospitals report more anxiety than patients in community hospitals (Lucente & Fleck, 1972).

We also know that there are physiological effects of various social environments. An example of this is the well-known "white coat hypertension" phenomenon of elevated blood pressure in the presence of health professionals. Another example is the work by Ulrich (1984), who found faster recovery rates and less pain medication usage in surgical patients who had a view of a wooded park versus those with a view of a brick wall.

Interrelationships among the targets of assessment are obviously complex. We are reminded of the case of the 75-year-old man who, in a late stage of chronic obstructive pulmonary disease, manifested his anxiety by "grumbling at staff." Staff consequently avoided him, thus reinforcing his fear of dying alone and his complaints of poor care. Exhibit 3.1 displays relationships that influence the interpretation of information obtained during assessment.

These represent only a sample of known relationships. In addition, clinical health psychologists must be aware of medical problems that present with psychological symptoms. Appendix D lists the most common of these. To be able to competently interpret the data obtained, the clinician must have a firm grounding in the theoretical and empirical bases of clinical health psychology. In developing a conceptualization of the case, the clinician differentially weights information obtained on the basis of mediating relationships as demonstrated through research and as learned through his or her experience in working with patients. There is no substitute for good clinical judgment.

Exhibit 3.1

**Relationships That Influence the Interpretation
of Information Obtained During Assessment**

1. Medication effects on psychophysiological recordings (e.g., diazepam on EMG level)
2. Fund of knowledge of the physician on accuracy of medical diagnosis (often specialists need to be consulted to evaluate medical record data, as the referral may come from a general practitioner who had not completely evaluated the presenting problem)
3. Family understanding, emotional support, and involvement in treatment on compliance with medical regimen
4. Family members' behavior on self-care activities (e.g., overprotectiveness often impedes patient self-management and, consequently, hinders the development of a sense of mastery)
5. Legislation on sick-role behavior (e.g., disability payments could reinforce chronic-illness behavior)
6. Religious beliefs on the perceived meaning of symptoms and acceptance of medical regimens (e.g., pain as guilt for past sins or refusal of therapeutic abortion for a life-threatening pregnancy)

METHODS OF ASSESSMENT

In performing the clinical health psychology assessment, there are numerous methods that could be used. Many of these give information about one or more targets in our assessment model. The choice of method depends on the target being assessed, the purpose of the assessment, and the skill of the clinician.

We are not wedded to any one particular technique, as each has its strengths and weaknesses. However, we do rely heavily on a good clinical interview as the core clinical method. We also endorse a multiple-measurement model and a convergent/divergent, hypothesis-testing approach to clinical assessment. Detailed descriptions of specific methods will not be provided, but we list the core techniques used in clinical health psy-

---

Exhibit 3.1 (*cont.*)

7. Providers' attitudes about disease on patient affective responses (e.g., nurses' refusal to minister to AIDS patients)
8. Family attitudes toward disease on patients' affective and behavioral responses (e.g., wife's negative attitude about colostomy contributing to patient's impotence)
9. Prosthetic characteristics of environment on patient activity level (e.g., a barrier-free environment facilitates activity level for the spinal cord patient)
10. Occupational requirements on self-esteem (e.g., loss of breadwinning capacity by artist who loses functioning in dominant hand)
11. Providers' attitudes toward treatments on patient suffering, (e.g., negative attitudes about use of narcotics resulting in undermedication of cancer pain)
12. Cognitive factors on course of illness (e.g., maintenance of hope and future orientation facilitating recovery from surgery; unrealistically positive expectations about sexual functioning associated with poor outcome in penile prosthesis surgery)
13. Cognitive factors on physical symptoms (e.g., perceived control of pain results in increased tolerance for pain)

---

chology. The Suggested Readings at the end of the chapter provide excellent references for further study in this area. The methods of assessment discussed are interview, questionnaires, diaries, psychometrics, observation, psychophysiological measures, and archival data.

Interview

The clinical interview is perhaps the most common method of gathering information. It has the capacity to elicit current and historical data across all domains (i.e., physical, affective, cognitive, and behavioral information regarding the patient and his or her family, health care, and sociocultural environments). The interview is also a means of developing a supportive working relationship with the patient. It permits the acquisition of self-report and observational data from the patient, family members, significant others, employers, and health care providers. Understanding one's own stimulus value is crucial to the interpretation of interview data.

Content and style of individual interviews vary depending on the assessment question. The formality of the interview process (unstructured, semistructured, or structured) often depends on the personal preference of the clinician as well as the setting and time constraints. Specific intervention programs (e.g., presurgical penile prosthesis screenings or headache treatment programs) commonly use structured interviews, but we prefer a combination of structured and unstructured approaches. This helps to avoid interviewer bias and to remain open to exploring areas not immediately recognized as important.

One structured interview that has received a good deal of attention in the health psychology literature is the Type A Structured Interview (Rosenman, 1978). Although its development could serve as a model for other such assessment techniques, it tends to be used more for research than for clinical purposes. (A review of the Type A area can be found in Thoreson & Powell, 1992.)

Also of interest is the Psychosocial Adjustment to Illness Scale (PAIS) described by Derogatis (1986). This scale has both structured interviews and self-report (PAIS–SR) formats, designed to assess domains of health care orientation, vocational environment, sexual relationships, extended family relationships, social environment, and psychological distress.

In many situations, it is most useful to develop one's own structured/semistructured interview for a specific patient population. For instance, we have done this for such areas as chronic-pain problems, presurgical screenings, organ transplantation, and craniomandibular disorders. A semistructured interview format allows for flexibility and development of rapport while assuring that vital information is not neglected.

We believe that every clinical interview should include some elements of the Mental Status Examination (MSE). How extensive an MSE is completed will depend on the presenting symptoms and preliminary findings. Elements of the MSE include the following sections: (1) Appearance, Attitude, and Activity; (2) Mood and Affect; (3) Speech and Language; (4) Thought Process, Thought Content, and Perception; (5) Cognition; (6) Insight and Judgment. We commonly find that the MSE yields information that has not been previously assessed by another health care professional. Many of the areas of assessment (e.g., sexual functioning, drug- and medication-use history, and suicidality) are uncomfortable areas for other providers to explore, but they are of great concern to the patient. For instance, in asking about the impact of a pain problem on sexual functioning, we have often had the response, "I am glad someone finally asked me about that! I've been very concerned. . . ."

An excellent mental-status-exam resource is *The Psychiatric Mental Status Examination* (Trzepacz & Baker, 1993; see Suggested Readings).

In some instances, patient interviews are impossible. Occasionally the patient is too agitated or not sufficiently alert to meet the demands of the interview. There are also times in which the patient is uncooperative, in which case the clinician needs to use alternative forms of assessment, delay the consultation, or discontinue the process in the absence of adequate consent.

Questionnaires

Clinician-developed, problem-focused, information-gathering questionnaires are very useful in the assessment process. In the outpatient setting, these can be mailed to patients before the first visit and reviewed at the time of interview. We have found this method to be a considerable time-saver in the evaluation of such diverse areas as chronic-pain patients, potential oocyte donors, and patients seeking penile prosthesis surgery. The interviewer may review questionnaire data with the patient but can focus more time on areas needing further clarification and on more general psychological issues.

Reviewing some questionnaire information with the patient is important, in demonstrating the value of the data to the clinician and in establishing rapport, which could affect future patient compliance. Questionnaires are also a mechanism for the systematic recording of data that can facilitate clinical research and subsequent program evaluation.

Our intake questionnaire for use with chronic-pain patients consists of some 80 questions related to the presenting problem, previous treatments, and effects on daily functioning. In the thousands of patients who have been asked to complete various versions of this questionnaire, refusal has been almost nonexistent. However, given the initial defensiveness of many patients to seeing a psychologist, we have found it important to limit questionnaire items to variables related to sociodemographic features and the chief complaint, leaving broader psychological exploration to the interview.

Questionnaires can also be developed for significant others and health care providers. The form and content of the questionnaire will depend, of course, on the theoretical orientation of the clinician. Questions can be forced choice, open ended, simple ratings, checklists, or pictorial in nature (e.g., pain maps). Clarity and ease of response are important features. However, the clinician must take care not to use questionnaire techniques in a fashion that would substitute for the development of a quality professional relationship with either the patient or the referral source.

Diaries

Patient diaries are commonly used to record behaviors, both overt (e.g., vomiting, tics, activity level, frequency of urination, and medication usage) and covert (e.g., thoughts, feelings, images, blood pressure, body temperature, and pain intensity). They are used as baseline measures and as an intervention to foster learning about antecedents, consequences, and the relationships among internal and external behaviors (i.e., to promote psychological and physiological insights). Diaries are also used to measure the effectiveness of treatment programs. Although there are controversies about the reliability and validity of diary data, these methods continue to be clinically useful.

Diaries should be easy to use, brief, and nonintrusive. Training the recorder in their use is important. The use of mail-in forms and cues as reminders to record information can increase compliance. Note also that not all diaries are maintained by the patient. Medical charting and psychological-process notes are two examples of diaries that are maintained by staff.

Psychometrics

In general, two kinds of psychometric techniques are used in clinical health psychology: broadband and narrow-focus measures. Piotrowski and Lubin (1990) surveyed American Psychological Association Division of Health Psychology clinicians and identified the most frequently used instruments used in health assessment. These and others with which we believe the clinician should be familiar are listed next. Those marked with an asterisk were in the top 10 list of Piotrowski and Lubin. However, one should be cautious in the application of any of these measures to clinical health psychology and should carefully evaluate their suitability for medical–surgical or dental-patient populations and for the specific problems being addressed. Broadband measures include the following:

1. Minnesota Multiphasic Personality Inventory (MMPI; Hathaway & McKinley, 1967). The most commonly used measure in clinical health psychology, the MMPI was originally designed as a measure of psychopathology. Appropriate norms must be used when interpreting results for medical–surgical populations.
2. Minnesota Multiphasic Personality Inventory—2 (MMPI–2; Butcher, Dahlstrom, Graham, Tellegen, & Kaemmer, 1989). The MMPI was revised in 1989 to provide current norms for the inventory, to develop a nationally representative normative sample, and to update item content. In the revision process, an attempt was made to make previous MMPI study results generalizable to the MMPI–2. Even so, some researchers recommend caution in this area (Greene, 1991).
3. Sixteen Personality Factor Inventory (l6PF; Cattell, Eber, & Tatsouka, 1970). Developed as a measure of personality, this test might be more appropriate to medical–surgical populations than the MMPI when the focus is not the assessment of psychopathology.

4. Millon Clinical Multiaxial Inventory. (MCMI; Millon, 1982a). A measure of eight basic personality styles and symptoms designed for psychodiagnosis in clinical populations.

5. Millon Behavioral Health Inventory (MBHI; Millon, Green, & Meagher, 1982) This test was designed specifically with medical–behavioral decision making in mind. It attempts to assess not only basic coping styles but also the feelings and perceptions of the person that are thought to aggravate the course of current disease or increase susceptibility to disease.

6. Symptom Check List—90–Revised (SCL–90–R; Derogatis, 1983). A checklist of psychiatric symptomatology, often used as a screening device.

There are also a number of more narrowly focused instruments used in the practice of clinical health psychology, which measure general psychological constructs, experiences, or symptoms:

1. Beck Depression Inventory (BDI; Beck, 1972). A measure of severity of depression. See Beck, Steer, and Garbin (1988) for a review of 25 years of research. This measure has also been modified for use with pain patients, omitting somatic items that tend to overlap with chronic pain (Wesley et al., 1991).

2. Center for Epidemiologic Studies Depression Scale (CES–D; Radloff, 1977). A self-report measure of depression designed for research in the general population.

3. State–Trait Anxiety Inventory (STAI; Spielberger, Gorsuch, & Lushene, 1970). A self-report measure of anxiety.

4. State–Trait Anger Expression Inventory (STAXI; Spielberger, 1988). A self-report measure of both the experience and the expression of anger.

5. Index of Activities of Daily Living (ADL; Katz, Downs, Cash, & Grotz, 1970). A measure of independent functioning most useful for geriatric and institutionalized populations.

6. Measures of life events such as the Schedule of Recent Experience

(SRE; Holmes & Rahe, 1967) and the Life Experiences Survey (LES; Sarason, Johnson, & Siegel, 1978). The latter includes an assessment of the perceived significance of the event.

7. Cognitive Capacity Screening Exam (CCSE; Jacobs, Bernhard, Delgado, & Strain, 1977). A brief, scorable mental status questionnaire that is easily administered as a screening device.

8. Mini-Mental-State Exam (MMS; Folstein, Folstein, & McHugh, 1975). A method of grading the cognitive status of patients.

9. Family Environment Scale (FES; Moos & Moos, 1981). An assessment of three domains of family environment: (a) quality of interpersonal relationships, (b) personal-growth goals, and (c) system-maintenance factors.

10. Ward Atmosphere Scale (WAS; Moos, 1974). A measure of perceived program orientation and organization and of ward interpersonal relationships.

11. Work Environment Scale (WES; Moos, 1981). A measure of workplace interpersonal relationships, orientation, and work stress.

12. Hassles and Uplifts Scale (Kanner, Coyne, Schaefer, & Lazarus, 1981). A life events scale that focuses on minor hassles and positive events.

Also, a number of health-specific measures have been developed that could prove useful, depending on the targets of assessment chosen:

1. Jenkins Activity Survey (JAS; Jenkins, Zyzanski, & Rosenman, 1979). A self-report measure of the type A behavior pattern.

2. Sickness Impact Profile (SIP; Bergner, Bobbitt, Carter, & Gilson, 1981). A self-report measure of functional status and impact of sickness applicable to any disease or disability group.

3. Arthritis Impact Measurement Scale (AIMS; Meenan, Gertman, & Mason, 1982). A measure of the effects of arthritis on functioning and the quality of life.

4. McGill Pain Questionnaire (MPQ; Melzack, 1975). A measure of perceived pain intensity and sensory, affective, and cognitive components of pain.

5. Cornell Medical Index (CMI; Brodman, Erdman, & Wolff, 1949). A self-report measure of health status.
6. Dental Anxiety Scale (Corah, 1969). A measure of anxiety concerning dental care.
7. Multidimensional Health Locus of Control (MHLC; Wallston, Wallston, & DeVellis, 1978). A measure of the extent to which patients see their health as attributable to fate, powerful others (such as physicians), or their own behavior.
8. Psychosocial Adjustment to Illness Scale—Self-Report (PAIS–SR; Derogatis & Lopez, 1983). A self-report measure of adjustment to illness.
9. Eating Disorder Inventory (EDI; Garner & Olmsted, 1984). A measure of the severity of cognitive and behavioral characteristics associated with eating disorders.
10. Cancer Inventory of Problem Situations (CIPS; Schag, Heinrich, Aadland, & Ganz, 1990). An inventory of problems commonly experienced by cancer patients.
11. Multidimensional Pain Inventory (MPI; Kerns, Turk, & Rudy, 1985). A self-report measure reflecting pain severity; interference with family, occupational, and recreational activities; appraisals of response from significant others; perceived life control; and affective distress.

Obviously this listing is not exhaustive. We cannot over emphasize the need for the clinical health psychologist to be aware of the reliability and validity issues specific to each measure *for each usage*. Failure to recognize limits of interpretation of test results is contrary not only to good clinical practice but also to ethical standards.

Observation

Observation of the patient is one of the most fundamental methods of assessment and can provide the clinician with information applicable to many of the target areas described in our model. Observation can be unstructured or highly structured. For example, it can occur as part of a general clinical interview or in a more naturalistic setting (e.g., a treatment setting involving interactions with nursing staff or response to medical procedures, such as burn debridement). Structured observations can include tasks such as role-playing interactions with family, employer, or physician and in vivo experiences such as observing cold stress challenges for Raynaud's disease patients and self-administration of insulin by the diabetic.

Observations can be made directly by the clinician, by family members, or by health care providers. Furthermore, these observations can be audiotape or videotape recorded. Because this is an obviously reactive measure, the influence of the measurement process on data obtained must be considered in the interpretation.

Observations can be quantified through rating methods (e.g., Hamilton Anxiety Scale; Hamilton, 1959), content analyses (e.g., somatic focus), or frequency scores (e.g., pill counts to determine compliance), among other methods. The clinician can also collect impressions in an effort to generate hypotheses for more precise testing. It is especially useful to compare direct observation of behavior to others' perceptions of the behavior or to the patient's own perception of his or her behavior (e.g., the "demanding patient"). Reasons for the lack of correlation could be clinically very meaningful and thus help target areas for intervention.

Psychophysiological Measures

Psychophysiology refers to the "scientific study by nonsurgical means of the interrelationships between psychological processes and physiological systems in humans" (Cacioppo, Petty, & Marshall-Goodell, 1985, p. 264). Psychophysiological measures are designed to provide information about biologic events (e.g., heart rate) or the consequences of biologic events (e.g., skin temperature). They can also be used to provide feedback to the person and thus serve as psychological interventions (e.g., biofeedback).

Generally, the biologic events of most interest to the clinical health psychologist include muscle tension, skin temperature, blood pressure, heart rate, and respiratory activity. Parameters of interest include average resting levels, within-subject variability, and response of the measure to differing conditions (e.g., stress, relaxation, resting, imagery, and specified activities). Although psychophysiological stress profiles have been used as assessment methods in chronic-pain problems, research has not validated their use in evaluating individual patients for diagnostic or predictive purposes (Flor & Turk, 1989). For example, the lack of correlation between level of muscle tension and the diagnosis of "muscle contraction headache" has been found repeatedly (Philips, 1978; Sutton & Belar, 1982). Although we no longer use profiling in the initial stages of a diagnostic workup, once the decision is made to undertake treatment, psychophysiological profiling can become a very important part of the treatment process.

To undertake psychophysiological measurements, the clinician needs to have expertise in, among other things, bioelectric and physiological processes, instrumentation and recording techniques, signal-processing methods, and potential artifacts and confounds. We believe that advances in telemetric and ambulatory monitoring will increase the ecological validity of these kinds of measures, with a subsequent increase in clinical usage in the future.

Archival Data

Literature reviews of diseases including cause, symptoms, course, prevention, treatment, and psychological components can provide archival data that is useful in the assessment process. Reviews of previous medical and psychiatric charts are valuable sources of information for the clinical health psychologist. Although these records are not always easily obtained, the clinician will find the information contained within them most useful in providing a historical perspective of the patient, his or her problem, and aspects of help-seeking behavior.

It might also be necessary to consult archival data when assessing the potential impact of various environmental variables on the problem, such as the health care system and the sociocultural environment. Hospital policies, insurance coverages, legislation relating to disability, laws regulating the practice of health care provision, and employers' policies need to be understood, to develop an adequate conceptualization for intervention.

Other Methods

There are a number of other methods of assessment available to the clinical health psychologist that could prove useful under specified conditions. For example, pedometers might provide fruitful information about activity level and thus be especially useful in problems such as chronic-low-back pain. Spirometric measures of pulmonary functioning can be used as dependent measures in work with asthmatics. Smoking behavior may be measured by thiocyanate levels in blood serum, urine, and saliva. Skinfold thickness, as an indirect measure of body fat, might be useful in dealing with problems of obesity. Sleep electroencephalograms are useful in assessing sleep disorders. Body weight can be a useful measure of compliance to dietary restrictions in hemodialysis patients. The uniqueness of the problem and the creativity of the professional will aid in identifying other methods of assessment that might be useful.

ACHIEVING THE GOALS OF ASSESSMENT: UNDERSTANDING THE PATIENT

At the end of the assessment process, the clinician will have an understanding of (a) the patient in his or her physical and social environment, (b) the patient's relevant strengths and weaknesses, (c) the evidence for psychopathology, (d) the nature of the disease and treatment regimen, and (e) the coping skills being used.

After integrating relevant information, the clinician should be able to answer the seven questions listed below. These questions were derived from Moos (1977), who delineated these areas as the major adaptive tasks for any patient with a medical illness. The relative importance of answers to each question in determining the overall status of the patient will vary, dependent on the understandings developed through assessment of the previously mentioned targets.

1. How is the patient dealing with pain, incapacitation, and other symptoms?
2. How is the patient dealing with the hospital environment and the special treatment procedures?

3. Is the patient developing and maintaining adequate relationships with health care staff?
4. Is the patient preserving a reasonable emotional balance?
5. Is the patient preserving a satisfactory self-image and maintaining a sense of competence and mastery?
6. Is the patient preserving relationships with family and friends?
7. How is the patient preparing for an uncertain future?

In conclusion, the purpose of the clinical health psychology assessment is to understand the patient and his or her problem, so as to arrive at a treatment strategy or a management decision. One need not be wedded to a particular theory or assessment strategy; indeed, flexibility in this regard is, in our opinion, an asset. However, we do attempt to adhere to the biopsychosocial conceptual framework.

SUGGESTED READINGS

Beck, A. T., Steer, R. A., & Garbin, M. G. (1988). Psychometric properties of the Beck Depression Inventory: Twenty-five years of evaluation. *Clinical Psychology Review, 8,* 77–100.

Brantley, P. J., & Bruce, B. K. (1986). Assessment in behavioral medicine. In A. R. Ciminero, K. S. Calhoun, & H. E. Adams (Eds.), *Handbook of behavioral assessment* (2nd ed., pp. 673–710). New York: Wiley

Dana, R. H. (1984). Assessment for health psychology. *Clinical Psychology Review, 4,* 459–476.

Dana R. H., & Hoffman, T. A. (1987). Health assessment domains: Credibility and legitimization. *Clinical Psychology Review, 7,* 539–555.

Doleys, D. M., Meredith, R. L., & Ciminero, A. R. (1982). *Behavioral medicine: Assessment and treatment strategies.* New York: Plenum.

Greene, R.L. (1991). *The MMPI–2/MMPI: An interpretive manual.* Boston: Allyn & Bacon.

Karoly, P. (1985). *Measurement strategies in health psychology.* New York: Wiley.

Karoly, P. (Ed.). (1988). *Handbook of child health assessment: Biopsychosocial perspectives.* New York: Wiley.

Keefe, F. J., & Blumenthal, J. A. (1982). *Assessment strategies in behavioral medicine.* New York: Gruen & Stratton.

Sturgis, E. T., & Gramling, S. (1988). Psychophysiological assessment. In A. S. Bellack & M. Hersen (Eds.), *Behavioral assessment* (3rd ed., pp. 213–251) Elmsford, NY: Pergamon Press.

Sweet, J. J. (1991). Psychological evaluation and testing services in medical settings. In J. J. Sweet, R. H. Rozensky, & S. M. Tovian (Eds.), *Handbook of clinical psychology in medical settings* (pp. 291–313). New York: Plenum.

Trzepacz, P. T., & Baker, R. W. (1993). *The psychiatric mental status examination.* New York: Oxford University Press.

Widiger, T. A., & Frances, A. (1987). Interviews and inventories for the measurement of personality disorders. *Clinical Psychology Review, 7,* 49–75.

4

Intervention Strategies in Clinical Health Psychology

In chapter 3, we presented our framework for applying the biopsychosocial model to the assessment process in clinical health psychology. At the end of that process, the clinician should be aware of patient problem areas, related environmental contributors, and the variety of resources available. The next step, then, is to translate these findings into some plan of intervention. Clinical health psychology intervention can also be conceptualized by means of our framework, although the focus changes from a historical and developmental one to a focus on the present and future.

Many of the targets of assessment described in Table 3.1 can also become targets for intervention. And as before, intervention for any one target can affect functioning and interventions in others. This issue will be discussed further, after a general outline of each domain of intervention is presented.

PATIENT TARGETS

At the unit of the individual patient, the clinician can attempt intervention in biological, affective, cognitive, or behavioral domains.

Biological Domain

Treatment strategies in this domain are designed to directly change actual physiological responses involved in the disorder. Examples include biofeedback for fecal incontinence and relaxation for hypertension. One can also intervene in an attempt to control specific symptoms associated with the disease or its treatment (e.g., hypnosis for pain control or desensitization for anticipatory nausea associated with chemotherapy).

Of course, medical interventions have a primary focus in this domain, and their interactive effects with simultaneous psychophysiological treatment must be addressed or monitored (e.g., shifting insulin needs during relaxation training or usage of muscle relaxants during biofeedback training).

Affective Domain

In the affective domain, one might focus on such emotional states as anxiety, depression, or hostility. For instance, the clinician could provide such interventions as stress inoculation to decrease anxiety about an upcoming medical procedure, cognitive–behavioral treatment for depression, and anger management for Type A behavior pattern.

Cognitive Domain

Interventions in this domain involve providing information in a psychoeducational approach or changing the manner in which a patient conceptualizes a problem. As examples, one might maximize placebo effects of medical or psychological treatments, provide sensory and procedural information about upcoming diagnostic procedures, challenge unrealistic expectations about sexual activity after penile prosthesis surgery, and use existential psychotherapy to facilitate the development of a philosophy of life in keeping with adaptive coping.

Behavioral Domain

Treatment in this area includes changing the patient's overt behaviors and involves using principles of operant and social learning theory. Thus, the clinician might design a self-monitoring program to enhance compliance with hypertension medication, to teach assertion skills to facilitate communication with the patient's physician, to develop a behavior-change program to modify behavioral health-risk factors (such as smoking or weight), or to consult in the training of the patient in such self-management skills as insulin injections and stoma care.

ENVIRONMENTAL TARGETS

Targets need not be patient focused, however, because the clinician could decide that an environmental intervention is either necessary for change or easier to accomplish. Once again, the environmental units include (a) the family, (b) the health care system, and (c) the sociocultural context. Intervention within each of these units might target physical, affective, cognitive, or behavioral domains as defined above.

Family

Interventions aimed at the physical aspects of the family environment include redesign of living space in accordance with patient limitations (e.g., specified order of spices in the cabinet for the blind housekeeper) and referrals to social agencies for financial resources. In the affective realm, the clinician could use supportive therapy to help family members deal with anxiety about the patient's illness. In the cognitive arena, the clinician could facilitate more realistic expectations through the provision of accurate information or use family therapy to work through potential misattributions of the cause of the patient's illness.

In terms of family members' behavior, it might be necessary to train individuals to give appropriate emotional support or to develop a contingency-management program, so that the family behavior does not unwittingly reinforce unnecessary sick-role behavior.

Health Care System

The health care system is a frequent target of intervention. One of the most important aspects is the physical domain within which services are provided. Interventions can be as simple as suggestions to increase orientation of intensive-care-unit patients through the use of time prompts and of chronically ill patients through the posting of calendars.

Privacy is very important to patients but is often neglected in the health care system. We are aware of a radiation-therapy waiting room situated in a busy hallway, where patients with disfigured appearances often sit uncomfortably, subjected to the stares or grimaces of hospital visitors. Environmental design that is sensitive to and respectful of patient needs can produce a more relaxing, less anxiety-provoking atmosphere; thus, music, ceiling art, and bubbling fish tanks are increasingly used in many waiting and treatment rooms.

The clinical health psychologist working within an institutional context often needs to adopt an advocacy role to bring about these kinds of health care system interventions. Many of the physical environment manipulations are not costly or difficult to implement.

In the affective domain of the health care system, the clinician might also need to work with medical and nursing staffs concerning their feelings about a specific patient, to facilitate a therapeutic relationship between caregivers and patient. An example of this is reframing demanding patient behavior as an attempt to exert control in the face of enforced, threatening dependency. In our experience, it is not uncommon for staff to express angry feelings toward a patient in a passive–aggressive manner that tends to foster retaliatory acting out in the patient. This, of course, sets up a cyclical behavior pattern, which can become exceedingly severe if it is not interrupted.

In the cognitive domain, clinical health psychologists continually find themselves in the role of teacher, because in most interactions they attempt to increase the knowledge of other health care providers about the psychological aspects of health, illness, and patient care. This education also involves dispelling myths and providing correct information about various psychological disorders that present as part of, or simultaneously with, a medical problem.

We suggest that the majority of communications back to referral sources include explicit recommendations about how the health care provider's own behavior could facilitate the treatment of the patient. Sample interventions aimed at the behavior of health care providers include instructions to (a) increase attention for well behavior, (b) provide medication on a fixed interval rather than on an as-needed basis for chronic-pain patients, (c) unify source of communications to the patient regarding prognosis and care, (d) check for patient understanding of treatment instructions, and (e) train the patient in self-care when possible, even when hospitalized, to maximize a sense of mastery and self-control. Advocacy for progressive health care policies is often warranted (e.g., development of interdisciplinary teams).

Sociocultural Context

Often, only certain aspects of the sociocultural context are available for immediate intervention, as other features require interventions outside the control of any individual clinician. It is possible to intervene in the patient's social network and thus use its resources to the benefit of the patient. We have counseled friends of patients on ways to facilitate coping in patients and have given them information about the grieving process, which enhanced their understanding and ability to support the patient. We have also worked with employers in designing a gradual return to work and resumption of activity for the patient recovering from a serious illness or learning to live with a chronic-pain problem. (Interestingly, we are aware of one major health care system that does not permit its own employees to return to work gradually. Instead the employee must be released to return to "100% functioning" if the worker is to be reinstated, a frequently doomed approach in terms of principles of rehabilitation!)

Other aspects of the sociocultural environment are the subject of rather long-term interventions by clinical health psychologists and are perhaps as important when considering the future quality of patient care. Such interventions include the following: (a) contributing to the body of knowledge about effective diagnostic and treatment strategies through clinical research (the foundation for the future of the field), (b) serving as volunteers with public-information groups to defuse myths and stereotypes, (c) working toward behavioral health legislation (e.g., controls on smoking in the workplace and mandatory helmet laws), and (d) participating in governmental policymaking regarding health care reform.

CHOOSING INTERVENTIONS

When choosing an intervention, one must take into account the effects of any given intervention on other targets, the appropriateness of goals for intervention, issues of patient and staff cooperation, and cost–benefit issues.

Interrelationships of Interventions

Just as information obtained about one target of assessment can influence the interpretation of information about another, so can interventions impact targets in other areas. Interventions aimed at one target can have positive or negative effects on other areas of functioning or ongoing treatments. For instance, in the positive realm, a patient who is treated for chronic headaches with relaxation and biofeedback approaches might experience less need for pain medication, less depression, an improvement in family relationships, and an increase in activity level. Thus, a positive adaptive cycle of improvement has been initiated by treatment aimed primarily at the headache problem.

However, one must be particularly concerned about negative effects that any area of intervention might have on other areas. For example, let us assume that the initial decision is made to increase self-management skills (e.g., self-catheterization), to promote more independent functioning. Success in this endeavor is likely to bring with it an increased sense of control over bodily functions, which is usually associated with a reduction in anxiety and a decrease in autonomic nervous system arousal. However, self-catheterization can also be associated with an increase in family members' fears because a professional is no longer performing the technique. Or family members might be repulsed by the nature of the procedure occurring at home and subsequently discourage the patient's attempts. We are aware of one patient in whom self-catheterization training, which involved using mirrors, triggered old memories of sexual abuse and resulted in subsequent phobic responses and increased emotional distress.

In another example, the use of relaxation training to help manage stress in a patient with diabetes can produce shifts in insulin needs that warrant close medical attention so as to not produce unstable diabetes (Rosenbaum, 1983). Inattention to these interrelationships and the potential effects when designing an intervention program can result in treatment failures, unexpected negative side effects, or, at best, short-lived success. In our experience, it is extremely rare that the clinician can focus solely on a single target for intervention.

In summary, a primary factor in choosing a target is the understanding of its interrelationships with other blocks in the model. This understanding is obtained through knowledge of the specific problem area, the empirical bases of the various interventions available, and a firm grounding in the clinical process of behavior change.

Appropriateness of Goals

Another aspect to consider when designing interventions is the determination of a realistic and attainable goal for treatment. This involves taking into account the likelihood that the targeted goal is amenable to treatment within the current situation. For example, the care-seeking behavior of Munchausen and polysurgical patients is notoriously unresponsive to short-term psychological interventions. These patients also tend to elicit a good deal of anger on the part of health care providers. Thus, it is sometimes wiser to target ward interventions toward preventing inappropriate acting out by staff and protecting the patient from unnecessary medical procedures rather than toward the psychological issues related to the help-seeking behavior itself (with appropriate referrals for subsequent care, of course).

It is important to explicitly specify the target(s) of intervention and to operationalize them to permit evaluation of change (e.g., "take medication three times per day with meals" vs. "improve compliance").

Clear articulation of targets for intervention is also critical to obtaining informed consent for treatment. For example, we once saw a young woman in an orthopedic ward who, subsequent to a bicycle accident, had both legs in traction. She was not eating sufficiently to permit bone mending and engaged in constant conflicts with nursing staff about her eating behavior. Psychological evaluation revealed the presence of an eating disorder that the patient denied and for which she refused treatment. However, she did consent to a focused treatment goal of obtaining sufficient nutrients to permit bone growth.

Related to the issue of appropriate goal setting is the importance of understanding whether the goal of intervention is cure or the facilitation of coping. A cure is not unreasonable to expect in some areas, but much of what we do in clinical practice is done to promote coping. The clinician needs to maintain a delicate balance between hope and positive expectations, which can facilitate treatment, and the reality of the situation, which could suggest a poor prognosis.

Cooperation of the Patient and Staff

The choice of a particular intervention often depends heavily on the cooperation of patient, staff, or both, and its feasibility in ameliorating the current problem. One can spend hours designing a powerful treatment program that depends on the staff's executing various components, only to have it fail miserably when an uncooperative (or already overburdened) staff must execute it. We are reminded of a situation in which a relatively straightforward behavioral program was designed to address the acting-out behavior of a girl with a closed-head injury. Theoretically, the program should have worked, but inconsistent application by the staff, lack of commitment, and communication problems assured its failure.

When designing an intervention that requires staff involvement, one must take into account such things as their willingness and ability to participate, the simplicity and ease of treatment administration, and the potential for sabotage or misapplication. Educating staff about the treatment and giving them an understandable rationale for its implementation are especially important.

Cost–Benefit Analysis

As discussed before, in deciding among intervention strategies in clinical health psychology, one must consider not only the information obtained during the assessment process (review Table 3.1) but also aspects of the intervention strategies themselves, specifically their costs and anticipated benefits. The clinician should consider issues of treatment efficacy, efficiency, durability, generality, convenience, cost, side effects, and clinician competence.

First, the clinical health psychologist needs to understand how effective the treatment strategy is in terms of absolute change in the target of intervention. There is no substitute for having a current knowledge of the empirical bases for psychological interventions. For example, relaxation training has been shown to have effects on immune function, but the sustained nature of these effects and their significance in influencing resistance to disease have not been sufficiently documented. Thus, offering this intervention as a primary intervention in immune functioning appears unwarranted. However, it could be offered as a means of enhancing control over some symptoms, increased tolerance for others, decreased anxiety and suffering, and so forth, depending on relevant findings in clinical research.

In general, the clinician should address the following questions in the decision-making process:

1. How efficient is the intervention in terms of time involved and effort expended?
2. For how long are the results expected to last?
3. What percentage of patients with similar problems can be expected to respond using the intervention?
4. How convenient or inconvenient to the patient and to his or her environment (including the therapist) is the treatment?
5. What is the cost of the intervention?
6. What are the side effects of the particular strategies or the program to be used?
7. How competent am I in using the particular intervention strategy?

This type of self-questioning can help in the process of deciding among several alternative intervention possibilities.

INTERVENTION STRATEGIES

In selecting a particular intervention strategy, we encourage flexibility, without rigid adherence to any one or two individual strategies. Historically, the development of psychological interventions for medical–surgical patients has moved from general, broadband techniques to those methods designed to address more narrowly and specifically defined targets. We follow this format in describing the more commonly used therapeutic intervention strategies in the practice of clinical health psychology, giving examples of usage and providing references for further study of the method.

Although the following techniques are discussed in a unitary fashion, it is recognized that in actual practice many of these procedures are used in combination. In fact, the empirical support for some procedures has been established only within the context of a multistrategy treatment program. For this reason, rather than provide evidence of the empirical basis for each strategy, a later section will provide suggested readings for further study of the research relevant to common problem areas in clinical health psychology.

Placebo

The *placebo effect* might be the simplest behavioral change procedure in common use (Agras, 1984). It refers to changes in behavior that occur because of the patient's expectations and faith that a particular treatment will produce the desired change and is thus described as "nonspecific." It can influence all patient and family target domains and is undoubtedly a part of all health care interventions. It is particularly powerful in pain control, where it has been linked to increased circulating endorphins and can be blocked by morphine antagonists. It also can be systematically used in such problems as conversion reactions (e.g., using EMG biofeedback to "shape" movement behavior in nonorganic paralysis). The reader is referred to White, Tursky, and Schwartz (1985) and Sobel (1991) for reviews of literature on the placebo effect.

Supportive Counseling

Physicians have historically attempted to support patients by reassuring them regarding illness and treatment procedures. Prokop and Bradley (1981) used the term *psychological support* to define this rather vague form of psychotherapeutic intervention directed toward amelioration of the patient's psychological distress. This type of treatment can involve individual or family meetings or consist of organized support groups. Furthermore, supportive psychotherapy can be clinician based or network based, depending on the nature of the problem and the availability of community resources. Other health care providers, paraprofessionals, and family members can be trained to provide supportive counseling and thus become valuable resources to the practicing psychologist.

Individual and Family Approaches

These types of interventions are generally based on a short-term treatment model and focus on helping the patient and family cope successfully with psychologically threatening information or procedures. This can be done by encouraging active participation in medical decisions, establishing a good patient–therapist relationship, and assuring the patient that feelings of anxiety or depression are normal (Gruen, 1975). The clinician should never underestimate the power of a pat on the back or a squeeze of the hand, procedures unlikely to be practiced in traditional clinical psychology. Note, however, that these behaviors might be seen as offensive in some ethnic groups.

Support Groups

Group discussion typically allows an opportunity for patients with similar illnesses or problems to meet with one another to discuss their concerns, anxieties, and coping strategies, as well as to obtain information. Examples include preparation-for-childbirth groups, postmastectomy groups, arthritis self-help groups, and groups for AIDS patients and their families. Such groups can have a designated leader or be leaderless, and they typically meet on a hospital ward or in an outpatient clinic. There is a wide range of local and national associations relevant to specific disease populations that can provide information about such groups in the community (see Appendix C). Local newspapers often publish listings of available support groups.

Because the clinical health psychologist frequently uses active approaches to treatment, the clinician might feel that supportive therapy does not represent "real therapy." However, it is important to remember that insufficient support has been related to increased risk of morbidity and mortality (House, Landis, & Umberson, 1988; Pilisuk, Boylan, & Acredolo, 1987), and there are many patients with significant deficits in social support systems.

Education and Information

In clinical health psychology treatment, education about the biopsychosocial model and its specific application to the patient and his or her problem is an essential ingredient. In addition, provision of information is necessary to obtain informed consent for any treatment and to ensure compliance with medical regimens. Information is fundamental to the entire field of health education with which clinical health psychologists often interact.

Information has also been used as a specific intervention to promote coping with stressful medical procedures. There are two types of information: procedural and sensory. *Procedural* refers to information about aspects of the medical procedure itself, and *sensory* refers to information regarding sensations the patient might feel during or after the procedure. Although sensory information appears to be a more important aspect of preparation, interactions among kind of information, individual coping styles, and level of initial anxiety have been found. The belief that more is better is naive; some patients actually do worse with more information. The clinician must have a strong background in this literature, to practice effectively (see Johnston & Vogele, 1993, for a meta-analysis of psychological preparation for surgery studies).

Verbal Psychotherapy

There are a variety of approaches toward verbal psychotherapy (e.g., analytic, cognitive–behavioral, rational–emotive, directive, and systems oriented), some of which are discussed in this chapter. Psychotherapy can be symptom specific, general in focus, or a combination of both. Psychotherapy has been shown to reduce medical utilization, to decrease postsurgery use of narcotics, to reduce symptoms associated with peptic ulcer, and to enhance coping after myocardial infarction (see Agras, 1984; Mumford, Schlesinger, & Glass 1982; VandenBos & DeLeon, 1988). Psychotherapy can occur in individual or group formats. See Belar (1991) and Gentry and Owens (1986) for descriptions of several types of behavioral-medicine groups.

Issues of patient resources and current trends in health reform require that clinical health psychologists be familiar with the practice of brief psychotherapies. There are several excellent references for this work: Austad and Berman (1991); Budman and Gurman (1988); Budman, Hoyt, and Friedman (1992); and Garfield (1989).

Crisis Intervention

Life events that overwhelm the patient's ability to cope or those that reinstate earlier conflicts are apt to create crisis situations. In the practice of clinical health psychology, the psychologist is likely to face a sizable percentage of patients whose lives are in crisis. Often these crises are centered around personal or professional losses from illness or death of a family member. However, the actual crisis is not necessarily related to health issues and could represent any number of developmental or accidental events. Whatever the precipitating event, the psychologist needs to have an understanding of crisis intervention as a therapeutic technique and be aware of the immediate goals of crisis counseling.

Korchin (1976, p. 507) lists three primary goals of crisis intervention: (a) to relieve the patient's present psychological distress (e.g., anxiety, hopelessness, and confusion), (b) to restore the patient to his or her previous level of functioning, and (c) to help the patient and significant others learn what personal actions and community resources are available. In practice, these goals are accomplished by acknowledging the patient's thoughts, feelings, and behaviors; helping the patient to stay problem focused by exploring alternative explanations and solutions; emphasizing the patient's strengths in coping with previous life events; mobilizing additional resources; and providing information and advice, as appropriate. In working with problems of grief, it is important not to build the patient's defenses too quickly, as this might result in a longer term maladaptive grief reaction.

Crisis intervention for the clinical health psychologist often involves working with family members, significant others, and health care providers as well as the identified patient.

Relaxation-Training Procedures

Perhaps the most well-researched clinical health psychology intervention strategy is relaxation training. The literature is replete with studies documenting its usefulness in the treatment of hypertension, tension and migraine headache, insomnia, irritable bowel syndrome, Raynaud's disease, pain tolerance, preparation for stressful medical procedures, and nausea. Because this training is considered the aspirin of behavioral medicine (Russo, Bird, & Masek, 1980), we are hard pressed to conceive of a practicing clinical health psychologist who does not have expertise in several of the techniques to be discussed, all of which have as their goal the reduction of physiological arousal. Although relaxation strategies were originally proposed as interventions in the physiological state of the patient, their effects in affective and cognitive domains are well documented, as they decrease subjective anxiety and enhance a sense of mastery and competence in the patient.

Relaxation strategies have in common that they are all easily learned and administered by the clinician. The procedures to be discussed are diaphragmatic breathing, progressive muscle relaxation, and autogenic relaxation training.

Diaphragmatic Breathing

Diaphragmatic breathing is perhaps the simplest form of relaxation exercise (see Davis, Eshelman, & McKay, 1988, for training instructions in this and the strategies described next). Although frequently used before beginning a more in-depth relaxation exercise, this technique is also commonly used by itself to extinguish a conditioned response to a stressor. Fried (1993) provided a systematic review of respiratory psychophysiology, with a focus on the role of breathing in health and illness.

Progressive Muscle Relaxation (PMR)

PMR is based on the principle that relaxation (relaxed muscles) has physiological accompaniments opposite those of anxiety (i.e., physiological tension). Jacobson (1939) developed this technique by teaching patients to intentionally tense, then relax, various muscle groups throughout the body. Patients could thereby familiarize themselves with the sometimes subtle distinction between relaxed and tense states—a form of discrimination learning. Variations use different muscle groupings in the training process. This particular procedure is widely used in the practice of clinical health psychology and is particularly useful for those patients who are unaware of their levels of body tension. The following example demonstrates the usefulness of PMR in training a patient to relax her neck muscles during conversation.

> Mrs. N. was a 39-year-old woman who experienced muscle tension in her neck with accompanying strained, raspy speech. She entered psychological treatment to learn to decrease the neck cramps she experienced at the end of each workday and to improve the quality of her speech.
>
> Mrs. N. was initially trained in basic PMR exercises. After several sessions of total-body relaxation training, she was instructed to specifically focus her attention on the muscles in her neck and throat. After several additional relaxation-training sessions, Mrs. N. developed awareness of tension cues that signaled to her the need to relax before the tension became problematic. Through increased

sensitivity to physiological processes, she became better able to control her levels of throat and neck tension, and subsequent neck cramping; the quality of her speech also improved.

Although most patients are capable of tensing and relaxing various muscle groups, it might be necessary for the clinician to slightly modify standard procedures to accommodate certain types of patients: those with chronic-low-back pain or spinal fusions, with paraplegia or quadriplegia, or with arthritis or with limited mobility. Poppen (1988) provided a comprehensive approach to training, emphasizing the need to assess.

Autogenic Relaxation Training

Autogenic training (Schultz & Luthe, 1969) can create a very deep state of relaxation through the use of positive self-statements suggesting such sensations as warmth, heaviness, and calmness in various body parts.

Ms. O. was very anxious about an impending gynecologic examination designed to determine the cause of her infertility. She had a history of becoming so upset during even routine pelvic examinations that she subsequently missed work, needing a day to recover from her trauma. Ms. O. was trained in autogenic relaxation techniques that she would be able to use while lying quietly during the exam. In addition, a number of preparatory procedures, including guided imagery and coping self-statements, were used. The patient used the autogenic phrases throughout the procedure and coped successfully without incident.

When considering the relaxation therapies, note that, like aspirin, they have sometimes been used indiscriminately with the naive notion that they are good for everyone and everything. Any technique that has such potential benefit must also be assumed to have potential harm. Although there is insufficient attention in the psychological literature to negative side effects, relaxation training and related procedures have been noted to produce increased anxiety, shifting insulin needs, diabetic instability, hypotension in the elderly, and flooding of intrusive thoughts and impulses (e.g., Heide & Borkovec, 1984; Seeburg & DeBoer, 1980). Careful pretreatment evaluation, proper monitoring, and appropriate modification of procedures are critical to good practice. The reader is referred to the following references for transcripts of various relaxation techniques and related discussions: Bernstein and Borkovec (1973); Davis et al. (1988); Linden (1991); Poppen (1988); and Turk, Meichenbaum, and Genest (1983). Poppen provided an especially good discussion, with guidelines for assessment of relaxation in the patient.

Imagery

Imagery makes use of the private inner world of the patient through created images, imagination, and focused awareness. The use of imagery may be directed at general relaxation and anxiety reduction, symptom treatment, and behavioral change.

Guided Imagery

Samuels and Samuels (1975) described the positive physiological and psychological effects of visual imagery. Patients are asked to visualize, in minute detail, a scene that they consider to be relaxing. As the scene becomes clearer, the patient begins to relax.

Other forms of imagery use all of the body's senses and ask patients to project themselves into the scene being imagined rather than just watching the scene before them. In these exercises, the patient's mind plays a very active role through imagined re-creation of certain sights, smells, sounds, tastes, and touch. We use this technique in pain management as a means of recalling a pain-free episode in the patient's life and of re-creating the associated sense of well-being. We also use guided imagery to prepare for stressful medical procedures.

Covert Sensitization

Covert sensitization is a procedure developed by Cautela (1967) that applies the laws of classical conditioning to imagery. Use of this technique has primarily been directed toward extinguishing previously learned maladaptive behaviors, such as smoking or overeating. This is accomplished by associating a learned habit (e.g., smoking) with very detailed and unpleasant, obnoxious, and repulsive stimuli that are imagined (such as burning eyes, nausea, or sore throat). By pairing the habit with a visualized noxious response, the habit is less associated with pleasure.

Imagery is an ideal relaxation and symptom-reduction treatment for many patients, as it does not require active movement or special equipment. However, the successful use of these techniques also requires a moderate ability to concentrate for a sustained period of time and the ability to implement a certain degree of fantasy. There are some patients who report that they are not good imagers, but this in itself is a skill that can be trained. However, patients who are rigidly controlled or who lack adequate reality testing are probably not good candidates for these techniques. Patients taking medications that impair concentration often find these exercises difficult. In using imagery, it is important to constantly assess the patient's reaction to the image. The standard images of a beach or a mountain scene suggested by the clinician may actually be highly aversive to the patient who has had negative experiences in these settings. Knowledge of the individual patient is important in choosing images, and clinicians must be careful in using mass-produced tapes.

Hypnosis

Hypnosis has been reported useful in the treatment of pain, skin diseases, warts, and coping with chronic disease. Goals are usually to produce direct physiological changes, to change the perception of a symptom, to foster general relaxation, or to facilitate insight related to a particular symptom. Self-hypnosis, as described by LeCron (1970), is quite similar to therapist-cued procedures but transfers responsibility for trance induction and awakening to the patient. Golden, Dowd, and Friedberg's (1987) clinical guidebook for hypnosis includes cognitive–behavioral and Ericksonian methods as well as traditional methods. Hilgard and Hilgard (1994) provide a comprehensive examination of the application of hypnosis to pain relief.

Hypnosis has sometimes been useful for uncovering material that has been out of the awareness of the patient and that could have been associated with the onset of a maladaptive symptom. We are aware of one case in which total body palsy in a young adult was cured through the use of both therapist-based hypnosis and subsequent self-hypnosis. Hypnotic procedures helped the therapist to identify the emotional factors related to onset of the symptom (an urge to hit his father at the onset of an argument with an effort to hold back, resulting in a trembling hand which later spread to the entire body). The patient was then taught self-hypnosis procedures, so that he could voluntarily control the symptoms by being able to both produce the palsy and eliminate it.

Biofeedback

The primary goal of biofeedback training is to teach the patient voluntary control over physiological processes. The reader is referred to a review of the clinical biofeedback literature for further study in this area (Olton & Noonberg, 1980; Ray, Raczynski, Rogers & Kimball, 1979). M. S. Schwartz (1987) wrote a superb guide to practice in biofeedback.

Although biofeedback was originally thought to be a specific intervention in the physiological realm, more recent analyses suggest that it can also be used as an intervention in the cognitive and affective domains. Successful training facilitates the patient's perceived control over physiological events, a belief that might play a significant role in treatment outcome. Perceived control and lower autonomic nervous system arousal are also associated with decreased affective states such as anxiety. The technology associated with biofeedback interventions makes it quite acceptable as a psychological intervention in our technology-oriented society.

The two most commonly used forms of biofeedback include EMG and skin temperature. EMG feedback is useful for educating patients about the level of muscle tension present in selected muscle groups and can thus be useful in musculoskeletal disorders. Fingertip temperature provides an indirect measure of peripheral blood volume and, as such, has been used for disorders associated with vasodilation and vasoconstriction.

In general, these procedures have been used for a variety of stress-related and psychophysiological disorders, including bruxism, tension headache, anxiety, migraine headache, Raynaud's disease, asthma, chronic pain, and essential hypertension. However, other relaxation-training procedures are often as successful with these problems. There is little empirical evidence to support a preference for a particular technique such as biofeedback, hypnosis, imagery, or relaxation training, although sophisticated studies considering individual differences have not yet been completed.

Experienced clinicians engage in complex decision making in their choices. As Belar and Kibrick (1986) noted in their discussion of the use of EMG biofeedback in the treatment of chronic back pain, the clinician might choose this technique for one of three reasons: (a) to produce a specific physiological change such as equalization of muscle tension in the back or reduction of spasm; (b) to train in general relaxation, which is associated with increased pain tolerance and decreased distress; or (c) to facilitate "physiological insight" as the patient learns about relationships between psychological and physiological processes.

More specific uses of biofeedback in clinical health psychology include use of feedback about (a) heart rate to control cardiac arrhythmias; (b) anal sphincter to control fecal incontinence; (c) airway resistance for asthma; (d) muscular functioning for neuromuscular reeducation, dysphagia, and torticollis among other problems; (e) brain wave patterns for epilepsy; and (f) blood pressure for postural hypotension in spinal-cord-injured patients (see reviews in Olton & Noonberg, 1980). A newer application is the use of ear oximetry feedback during pursed-lip breathing to increase blood oxygenation in chronic obstructive pulmonary disease (Tiep, Burns, Kao, Madison, & Herrera, 1986).

Use of these techniques requires specialized training in bioelectric signal processing, psychophysiology, and electrical equipment. The Biofeedback Certification Institute of America certifies therapists for practice in this area.

Systematic Desensitization

Systematic desensitization, as developed by Wolpe (1958), is designed to teach the patient to emit a behavior that is inconsistent with anxiety. In the practice of clinical health psychology, this procedure is often used to reduce patients' fears and accompanying anxiety concerning certain medical or dental procedures. As with modeling, this procedure can be performed either imaginally or in vivo, and it usually involves a combination of both. Consider the following example:

> Ms. P. was a 13-year-old female diabetic with a needle phobia. She was referred by her endocrinologist for evaluation and treatment regarding her inability to self-inject insulin and the problems encountered with other providers. This patient was treated through the use of systematic desensitization, in an effort to help her become less reactive to injections. A hierarchy of progressively anxiety-producing circumstances was first elicited. The patient was then instructed in PMR techniques. While relaxed, Ms. P. practiced imagined scenes of increasing difficulty. Health care professionals and needles were then gradually introduced, allowing the patient to adapt to each set of circumstances before proceeding to the next highest level. After her fears of injection extinguished, she was trained in self-injection through similar procedures.

Systematic desensitization is also used to decrease fears of childbirth, MRI exams, and self-catheterization; to decrease excessive dependence on nebulizers, ventilators, and cardiac monitoring; and to facilitate reentry into public settings by burned or surgically deformed patients.

Modeling

On the basis of the theory of observational learning (Bandura, 1969), modeling provides a means of facilitating the learning of adaptive behaviors. This can be accomplished through either in vivo (direct observation) or imaginal (filmed or covert) techniques. Modeling is an important method for teaching patients necessary skills that might be required to meet the demands of their illness (e.g., self-injection of insulin), and it also reduces patient anxiety in preparation for stressful medical procedures. Melamed and her colleagues have demonstrated that filmed modeling to prepare children for medical and dental procedures, as well as for hospitalization, can be very useful in reducing anxiety and behavioral problems (Melamed

& Siegel, 1980). Additionally, this technique is useful for interventions directed at patient–staff and staff–staff issues. Finally, the clinician himself or herself can model more therapeutic or facilitative interactions.

The clinical health psychologist should be aware of the negative effects of poor models. Consider the following example:

> Mrs. K. was a 59-year-old woman admitted to the hospital for a colostomy. As part of standard procedure, she was interviewed before the surgery and initially appeared to be coping quite well with the information presented to her. On the day of the scheduled surgery (3 days past the planned date, because of a slight elevation in her temperature), Mrs. K. was considerably anxious, fearful of dying, and reluctant to sign the informed consent to the surgery.
>
> On interviewing this patient, the clinical health psychologist learned that the patient sharing Mrs. K.'s room had recently undergone the same operation and was now coping poorly with the pain and discomfort secondary to a postsurgical infection. Given the similarities in age and diagnosis, the patient had been unwittingly provided with an effective, but negative, role model. In this example, staff had failed to consider the impact of one patient on another. A change in the patient's room helped alleviate some of Mrs. K's concerns.

Skills Training and Behavioral Rehearsal

Skills training can incorporate modeling, role playing, and behavioral rehearsal. Patients can learn specific skills that can enhance their psychological and physical adjustment. In the practice of clinical health psychology, the most commonly taught skills are in the area of self-assertion. Whether in a formal or informal manner, we frequently find ourselves helping patients become more assertive, particularly when dealing with medical personnel.

Specific tasks that are taught include learning to formulate and to ask direct questions of physicians, requesting special privileges and giving justifications, requesting privacy during physical exams, learning to appropriately inquire as to alternative treatments, and requesting a second medical opinion. We frequently encourage patients to write down questions to ask their physicians and to obtain written answers if necessary. It is well known that patients can lose up to 50% of the information to which they are exposed during an office visit (see Ley, 1982, for review). We also encourage physicians to request that patients repeat back to them an understanding of the problem and the recommended treatment plan. This simple procedure eliminates many miscommunications and unmet expectations.

Other targets of skills training include the learning of specific behaviors necessary for good health care or rehabilitation. Although clinical health psychologists might not directly teach these skills, they frequently interact with other health care providers (e.g. occupational therapists, physical therapists, speech therapists, and nurses) to address either the emotional aspects or the learning principles associated with acquiring new and often "unnatural" skills. Examples of these skills are proper care of surgical stomas, bowel and bladder care after spinal cord injury, and home dialysis.

Contingency Management

As a treatment strategy, the goal of contingency management is to increase adaptive behaviors and to decrease those that are not adaptive. Positive reinforcement, negative reinforcement, punishment, response cost, extinction, and shaping procedures can all be used to accomplish this goal. Examples of positive reinforcement include the awarding of prizes to children for adherence to dietary regimens while on hemodialysis (Magrab & Papadopoulou, 1977), the insurance industry's reduction of premiums for nonsmokers, and the use of physician time to reward appropriate health care use. Extinction is commonly used to diminish complaining behavior or behaviors designed to elicit attention for the symptom (e.g., grimaces). An example of negative reinforcement includes the work by Malament, Dunn, and Davis (1975), who used the avoidance of an aversive tone to develop habits of postural push-ups in wheelchair patients, so as to avoid the formation of decubitus ulcers.

Although used much less frequently, punishment has been effective in cases of ruminative vomiting in infants. (Whereas Lang & Melamed, 1969, used electric shock, Sajwaj, Libet, & Agras, 1974, were successful with a small amount of lemon juice.) The rapid-smoking technique is another example of aversive conditioning (Grimaldi & Lichtenstein, 1969).

A major advantage to contingency management is that it can be administered by persons other than the clinical health psychologist. Frequently, nursing personnel or family members are educated as to how to change contingencies affecting patient behavior. For example, in attempting to cope with a demanding patient, ward nurses were advised to visit the bell-ringing patient on a regular basis rather than continuing to respond (or not respond) to frequent calls for help. As a result, both nursing personnel and the patient were more satisfied and less frustrated by each other's behavior. Family members can be instructed to increase attention and nurturance for well behavior versus sick-role behavior. Contingency management is a fundamental component of comprehensive pain rehabilitation and is more fully described in Fordyce (1976).

Although contingency management is effective under well-controlled conditions, its efficacy is diminished by poorly detailed instructions or lack of follow-up. Family members often unwittingly abandon recommended treatment suggestions because of a temporary, albeit annoying, exacerbation of symptoms when the patient has been put on an extinction schedule ("the extinction burst"). Additionally, when staff members are implementing a program, it is important to ensure that they are not using contingencies to express their anger at a difficult patient. The failure of a contingency management program is often attributable to the clinician's failure to adequately assess the "ABCs" (antecedents, behaviors, and consequences) of the planned intervention.

Self-Monitoring and the Use of Cues

Because of the reactive nature of self-monitoring, the use of patient diaries can be an effective means of intervention as well as of assessment and tracking treatment progress. Simply recording eating, smoking, and compliance behaviors often brings about changes in the desired directions.

Other means of self-monitoring include the use of external or internal cues as a signal to institute a behavior. Patients with complicated medication regimens have been directed to categorize and separate pills into daily doses, using a weekly pill box to help them remember when the next dosage is due. Another example of external cues for self-monitoring includes using time-of-day or environmental prompts as stimuli to perform relaxation exercises.

In the treatment of obesity, patients are taught to attend to internal rather than external cues for signs of hunger and to self-monitor their food intake. Insulin-dependent diabetics can be taught to recognize early warning symptoms of insulin imbalance and make necessary adjustments.

Family members can also participate in cuing strategies (which must be differentiated from "nagging"). In addition, the health care system uses this technique when sending appointment reminders as external cues for preventive care.

Self-monitoring does require a certain degree of self-discipline and commitment to change. Patients who are ambivalent regarding behavioral change are not likely to do well with this procedure unless it is presented in combination with other forms of intervention. Self-monitoring can be a very useful method to assess commitment to treatment.

Cognitive Strategies

There are a variety of interventions that use cognitive strategies to effect behavioral change. These include the use of distraction, calming self-statements, and cognitive restructuring. In attention-diversion or distraction procedures, patients are taught to direct their attention away from unpleasant events. Use of pleasant imagery, difficult mental tasks (serial 7s backwards; reciting the States of the Union in alphabetical order), counting aloud, and focusing attention on other neutral stimuli (counting holes in ceiling tiles) are examples of this process.

Patients can also be taught to silently or softly talk to themselves using calming, relaxing, and reassuring statements. These statements could emphasize the temporary nature of a discomfort (e.g., "this pain will not last" or "I only have 5 minutes to go"), could be directed at maintaining low physiological arousal (e.g., "stay calm," "stay relaxed," or "breathe"), or could be directed toward preservation of self-image (e.g., "I am a strong and worthwhile person," "It's OK to feel uncomfortable," or "I can cope with this").

Cognitive restructuring is a generic term that describes a variety of procedures, including stress-inoculation training (Meichenbaum, 1977), rational–emotive therapy (Ellis, 1962), cognitive therapy (Beck, Rush, Shaw, & Emery, 1979), and problem-solving training (Goldfried & Davison, 1976). These procedures educate the patient regarding the relationships among thoughts, feelings, and behaviors and help patients replace self-defeating cognitions with adaptive thoughts. McKay, Davis, and Fanning (1981) provide detailed instructions in applying many of these techniques.

Paradoxical Interventions

Although not well researched in many areas of health, paradoxical interventions have received some support in the treatment of insomnia, urinary retention, and encopresis. Jacob and Moore (1984) suggest that paradoxical procedures may be warranted when symptoms are exacerbated by the patient's attempt to decrease them or when the patient is resistant to direct therapeutic instructions. Weeks (1991) provides an excellent collection of readings detailing the theory and use of paradoxical techniques.

The list of intervention strategies we have provided is not exhaustive, yet skills in those procedures mentioned would prepare the psychologist for practice in clinical health psychology. In general, these intervention strategies are not used in isolation. For example, stress inoculation is an example of a treatment package that incorporates a variety of strategies. Furthermore, these "generic" strategies need to be adapted for each patient on the basis of the particular disorder and the presentation of the patient's issues.

Note also that a number of these strategies are not necessarily patient focused but can be used either *for* targets within the family, the health care system, or the social network or *by* these environmental agents of change.

Although the clinical health psychologist cannot be expert in all possible interventions and kinds of problems likely to be encountered in this broad field, there are several categories of problems with which the practitioner should have some basic familiarity. These are listed below, along with related references with which the practitioner should be familiar or might find practically useful.

SUGGESTED READINGS

Adherence to Treatment Regimens

Meichenbaum, D., & Turk, D. C. (1987). *Facilitating treatment adherence: A practitioner's guidebook.* New York: Plenum.

Turk, D. C., & Meichenbaum, D. (1991). Adherence to self-care regimens. In J. J. Sweet, R. H. Rozensky, & S. M. Tovian (Eds.), *Handbook of clinical psychology in medical settings* (pp. 249–266). New York: Plenum.

Arthritis and Rheumatology

Freedman, R. R. (1993). Raynaud's disease and phenomenon. In R. K. Gatchel & E. B. Blanchard (Eds.), *Psychophysiological disorders: Research and clinical applications* (pp. 245–267). Washington, DC: American Psychological Association.

Young, L. D. (1993). Rheumatoid arthritis. In R. K. Gatchel & E. B. Blanchard. (Eds.), *Psychophysiological disorders: Research and clinical applications* (pp. 269–298). Washington, DC: American Psychological Association.

Asthma

Creer, T. L., & Bender, B. G. (1993). Asthma. In R. K. Gatchel & E. B. Blanchard. (Eds.), *Psychophysiological disorders: Research and clinical applications* (pp. 151–203). Washington, DC: American Psychological Association.

Creer, T. L., Reynolds, R. V., & Kotses, H. (1991). Psychological theory, assessment, and interventions for adult and childhood asthma. In J. J. Sweet, R. H. Rozensky, & S. M. Tovian (Eds.), *Handbook of clinical psychology in medical settings* (pp. 497–515). New York: Plenum.

Cancer

Andersen, B. L. (1992). Psychological interventions for cancer patients to enhance the quality of life. *Journal of Consulting and Clinical Psychology, 60,* 552–568.

Tovian, S. M. (1991). Integration of clinical psychology into adult and pediatric oncology programs. In J. J. Sweet, R. H. Rozensky, & S. M. Tovian (Eds.), *Handbook of clinical psychology in medical settings* (pp. 331–352). New York: Plenum.

Cardiovascular Disorders

Rosen, R. C., Brondolo, E., & Kostis, J. B. (1993). Nonpharmacological treatment of essential hypertension: Research and clinical applications. In R. J. Gatchel & E. B. Blanchard. (Eds.), *Psychophysiological disorders: Research and clinical applications* (pp. 63–110). Washington, DC: American Psychological Association.

Shapiro, A., & Baum, A. (Eds.). (1991). *Behavioral aspects of cardiovascular disease.* Hillsdale, NJ: Erlbaum.

Weiss, S. M., Anderson, R. T., & Weiss, S. M. (1991). Cardiovascular disorders: Hypertension and coronary heart disease. In J. J. Sweet, R. H. Rozensky, & S. M. Tovian (Eds.), *Handbook of clinical psychology in medical settings* (pp. 353–373). New York: Plenum.

Chronic Illness

Burish, T. G., & Bradley, L. A. (Eds.). (1983). *Coping with chronic disease.* New York: Academic Press.

Costa, P. T., & VandenBos, G. R. (Eds.). (1990). *Psychological aspects of serious illness: Chronic conditions, fatal diseases, and clinical care.* Washington, DC: American Psychological Association.

Death, Dying, and Bereavement

Dershimer, R. A. (1990). *Counseling the bereaved.* Des Moines, IA: Allyn & Bacon.

Rando, T. A. (1984). *Grief, dying, and death: Clinical interventions for caregivers.* Champaign, IL: Research Press.

Diabetes

Cox, D. J., Gonder-Frederick, L., & Saunders, J. R. (1991). Diabetes: Clinical issues and management. In J. J. Sweet, R. H. Rozensky, & S. M. Tovian (Eds.), *Handbook of clinical psychology in medical settings* (pp. 473–495). New York: Plenum.

Polonsky, W. H. (1993). Psychosocial issues in diabetes mellitus. In R. K. Gatchel & E. B. Blanchard (Eds.), *Psychophysiological disorders: Research and clinical applications* (pp. 357–381). Washington, DC: American Psychological Association.

Gastrointestinal Disorders

Blanchard, E. G. (1993). Irritable bowel syndrome. In R. J. Gatchel & E. B. Blanchard (Eds.), *Psychophysiological disorders: Research and clinical applications* (pp. 23–62). Washington, DC: American Psychological Association.

Shabsin, H. S., & Whitehead, W. E. (1991). Psychological characteristics and treatment of patients with gastrointestinal disorders. In J. J. Sweet, R. H. Rozensky, & S. M. Tovian (Eds.), *Handbook of clinical psychology in medical settings* (pp. 517–537). New York: Plenum.

Whitehead, W. E. (1992). Behavioral medicine approaches to gastrointestinal disorders. *Journal of Consulting and Clinical Psychology, 60,* 605–612.

Habit Management

Brownell, K. D., & Wadden, T. A. (1992). Etiology and treatment of obesity: Understanding a serious, prevalent, and refractory disorder. *Journal of Consulting and Clinical Psychology, 60,* 505–517.

Lichtenstein, E., & Glasgow, R. E. (1992). Smoking cessation: What have we learned over the past decade? *Journal of Consulting and Clinical Psychology, 60,* 518–527.

Health Care Providers and Systems

Maslach, C. (1982). *Burnout: The cost of caring.* Englewood Cliffs, NJ: Prentice Hall.

Moos, R. H., & Schaefer, J. A. (1987). Evaluating health care work settings: A holistic conceptual framework. *Psychology and Health, 1,* 97–122.

Human Immunodeficiency Virus Disease

Kelly, J. A., & Murphy, D. A. (1992). Psychological interventions with AIDS and HIV: Prevention and treatment. *Journal of Consulting and Clinical Psychology, 60,* 576–585.

Landau-Stanton, J., & Clements, C. D. (1993). *AIDS, health and mental health: A primary sourcebook.* New York: Brunner/Mazel.

Temoshok, L., & Baum, A. (Eds.). (1990). *Psychosocial perspectives on AIDS.* Hillsdale, NJ: Erlbaum.

Winiarski, J. G. (1992). *AIDS-related psychotherapy.* Des Moines, IA: Allyn & Bacon.

Insomnia

Morin, C. M. (1993). *Insomnia: Psychological assessment and management.* New York: Guilford Press.

Occupational Health

Weiss, S., Fielding, J. E., & Baum, A. (Eds.). (1990). *Health at work.* Hillsdale, NJ: Erlbaum.

Organ Donation and Transplantation

Rodrigue, J. R., Greene, A. F., & Boggs, S. R. (1994). Current status of psychological research in organ transplantation. *Journal of Clinical Psychology in Medical Settings, 1,* 41–70.

Shanteau, J., & Harris, R. J. (Eds.). (1990). *Organ donation and transplantation: Psychological and behavioral factors.* Washington, DC: American Psychological Association.

Pain

Holzman, A. D., & Turk, D. C. (1986). *Pain management: A handbook of psychological treatment approaches.* New York: Pergamon Press.

Martin, P. R. (1993). *Psychological management of headache.* New York: Guilford Press.

Turk, D. C., Meichenbaum, D., & Genest, M. (1983). *Pain and behavioral medicine.* New York: Guilford Press.

Turk, D. C., & Melzack, R. (Eds.). (1992). *Handbook of pain assessment.* New York: Guilford Press.

Wall, P. D., & Melzack, R. (1994). *Textbook of pain* (3rd ed.). New York: Churchill Livingstone.

Pediatrics

Olson, R. A., Mullins, L. L., Gillman, J. B., & Chaney, J. M. (Eds.). (1994). *The sourcebook of pediatric psychology.* Des Moines, IA: Allyn & Bacon.

Routh, D. K. (Ed.). (1988). *Handbook of pediatric psychology.* New York: Guilford Press.

Surgery/Stressful Medical Procedures

Johnston, M., & Vogele, C. (1993). Benefits of psychological preparation for surgery: A meta-analysis. *Annals of Behavioral Medicine, 15,* 245–256.

Melamed, B. G., & Williamson, D. J. (1991). Programs for the treatment of dental disorders: Dental anxiety and tempomandibular disorders. In J. J. Sweet, R. H. Rozensky, & S. M. Tovian (Eds.), *Handbook of clinical psychology in medical settings* (pp. 539–565). New York: Plenum.

Salmon, P. (1992). Psychological factors in surgical stress: Implications for management. *Clinical Psychology Review, 12,* 681–704.

Prevention and Behavioral Health

Matarazzo, J. D., Weiss, S. M., Herd, J. A., Miller, N. E., & Weiss, S. M. (Eds.). (1984). *Behavioral health: A handbook of health enhancement and disease prevention.* New York: Wiley.

Rehabilitation

Bleiberg, J., Ciulla, R., & Katz, B. L. (1991). Psychological components of rehabilitation programs for brain-injured and spinal-cord-injured patients. In J. J. Sweet, R. H. Rozensky, & S. M. Tovian (Eds.), *Handbook of clinical psychology in medical settings* (pp 375–400). New York: Plenum.

Caplan, B. (Ed.). (1987). *Rehabilitation psychology desk reference.* Rockville, MD: Aspen.

Frank, R. G., Gluck, J. P., & Buckelew, S. P. (1990). Rehabilitation: Psychology's greatest opportunity? *American Psychologist, 45,* 757–761.

Women's Health Issues

Blechman, E. A., & Brownell, K. D. (Eds.) (1988). *Handbook of behavioral medicine for women.* New York: Pergamon Press.

Rodin, J., & Collines, A. (Eds.). (1991). *Women and new reproductive technologies: Medical, psychosocial, legal and ethical dilemmas.* Hillsdale, NJ: Erlbaum.

Travis, C. B. (1988a). *Women and health psychology: Biomedical issues.* Hillsdale, NJ: Erlbaum.

Travis, C. B. (1988b). *Women and health psychology: Mental health issues.* Hillsdale, NJ: Erlbaum.

5

Special Issues in Assessment and Intervention

In the previous chapters, we presented frameworks with which to conduct a thorough psychological assessment and to develop intervention strategies. In the current chapter, we shift focus from the content and methods of assessment and intervention to the barriers and problems encountered while working in the field of clinical health psychology, with suggestions for solutions where possible. Discussion focuses on practical concerns relevant to both inpatient and outpatient settings. Case examples reflect pertinent practice topics and represent actual experiences that we have either encountered or witnessed.

PROBLEMS WITH REFERRALS

It is not uncommon to receive vague, poorly defined consultation requests. In our experience, we have found that many physicians and other referral sources are still unclear as to what services clinical health psychologists provide and what kinds of information are helpful when making a consultation request. As a result, assessment questions are often ambiguous, unclear, too specific, untimely, or inappropriate. Listed next are some common issues encountered in the referral process.

Determining the Reason for the Referral

"Patient recently diagnosed as having prostate cancer, refuses surgery." Given the limited amount of information, it is not clear as to what services are being requested. One could guess that the referring doctor or nurse is frustrated by the patient's refusal of a surgical procedure and wants the psychologist to convince the patient otherwise. In this type of case, it is essential that the clinical health psychologist attempt to garner additional information from a variety of sources, especially the consultee, before actually speaking with the patient. Additionally, the psychologist should be aware that this consultation might reflect conflict between the value systems of the patient and the health care system. Assessment needs to be directed toward both the patient and the staff.

Handling Predetermined Procedures

"Patient is very tense and has migraine headaches. Please give biofeedback." In this example, the referral source is prescribing a type of treatment that might or might not be appropriate or cost-effective for the patient. We have found this to be a frequent problem when a referral source is personally invested in a particular technique.

When a specific form of treatment (e.g., biofeedback) has already been prescribed for the patient by another professional, problems are created for the consultant. First, patients expect the prescribed treatment to be delivered, and the fact that such a treatment might be inappropriate must be addressed explicitly at an early stage. In doing this, it is important to remember that patients could feel that they are getting "something less" if they do not receive the "promised" form of treatment. Or in an attempt to ally with the psychologist, the patient might lose confidence in or disengage from the referral source. This can enlarge the gulf between professionals and result in fragmented, poor quality care for the patient. Thus, a clear rationale for not providing a prescribed treatment should be given along with the alternative treatment plan. Referral sources also occasionally order specific tests, such as the MMPI, that are not the appropriate assessment techniques for the domain in question (e.g., ability to comprehend complicated medical regimen). These instances require similar handling.

In addition to dealing with patient issues when inappropriate procedures are ordered, the clinical health psychologist must communicate the inappropriateness of "prescription" consultations to the referral source. In our opinion, the best way to avert further conflict in this regard is to speak cordially but directly with the referral source and to clarify what represents an appropriate referral and what does not. Often physicians and medical personnel are so accustomed to ordering specific tests and procedures that they are unaware that the same process does not apply between disciplines. Alternatively, it has also been found that physicians prescribe treatments such as "biofeedback" or "stress management" as euphemisms for assessment and intervention with perceived emotional problems. Many believe that their patients are more receptive to this language on the referral form.

It is important to train referral sources as to how to discuss the referral with their patients. For example, one can ask the physician to help make the clinician's job easier by preparing the patient for the referral, or one can suggest that careful preparation might avoid having the patient become angry at the physician. We suggest that physicians explicitly state that the referral is not being made because he or she thinks it's "all in the patient's head" but rather that it is being made because of his or her interest in the whole patient and the awareness that other disciplines have certain skills to offer that have been helpful in similar cases. Physicians need to emphasize that *all* illnesses have psychological components, because mind and body cannot be separated. Exhibit 5.1 is a handout that is useful for educating physicians.

Identifying the "Patient"

In some cases, the identified patient might not be the real target for intervention. Consider this referral request, "Patient is a 17-year-old female student undergoing bone marrow transplant. Patient does not seem to appreciate seriousness of condition." After the clinical health psychologist interviewed this patient, it was apparent that the patient had a clear understanding of her medical condition and possible consequences. Her religious beliefs, general optimistic style, and strong social relations were

Exhibit 5.1

Sample Handout for Referring Physicians

CONSIDERATIONS FOR MEDICAL
PSYCHOLOGY CONSULTATION

Complaints seem out of proportion to organic pathology.

Treatment does not yield expected results despite an improved organic status.

New symptoms arise as old symptoms resolve.

The patient repeatedly raises issues/questions already addressed.

The patient seems to require more time and attention than usual.

The patient does not adhere to prescribed treatments.

The patient takes anxiolytic, sleep, or analgesic medication for a longer period of time than appropriate.

The patient resists the idea of attempting to wean from anxiolytic, sleep, or analgesic medications.

The patient exhibits a great deal of emotional distress.

The patient reports significant family problems in dealing with illness.

The patient overuses alcohol or other psychoactive substances.

Psychophysiological components could exacerbate the medical condition.

interacting in a manner that produced effective coping techniques and a minimum of psychological distress or depression.

This example demonstrates a case in which health care professionals had projected their own fears and emotions onto the patient, who was actually coping with the illness better than the staff was. Consequently, when the patient did not behave in the expected manner, a consultation was gen-

Exhibit 5.1 (cont.)

PHRASING THE REFERRAL

Patients may be resistant to the idea of referral to a psychologist. They may respond by thinking (or saying), "You think the pain (or other symptom) is all in my head" or "I'm being dumped." The following phrases seem to be more palatable to patients:

A referral for pain or stress management

A referral for evaluation for a special symptom-management program

A referral to see if other factors are making your symptoms worse (e.g., stress)

A referral to help prepare you for surgery that might improve outcome

A referral for symptom management, so that the use of medicines can be reduced to a minimum

A referral because of interest in the whole patient, with the recognition that all illnesses have psychological components and that other disciplines have skills to offer that have been helpful in similar cases

A referral with recognition of the stressors that the medical condition has caused the patient (and his or her family)

erated. As a result, the clinical health psychologist needed to refocus attention to acknowledge staff concerns and stressors as the potential targets for intervention. Although it is not always efficacious to attempt *explanation* of psychological defenses (e.g., projection) to staff, recognition of staff concerns and education regarding individual differences in patients can help alleviate some of their anxieties when one does not behave in the typical fashion.

Sometimes the referral comes about because of family reactions to the patient or illness. One referral we received concerned adjustment issues after loss of sight in a 40-year-old man. On further exploration, it was found that the wife's reaction to this loss was the real reason for referral and thus the more appropriate target of intervention.

Dealing With Choice of Inappropriate Provider

"Patient is 49-year-old, single, male status post coronary bypass surgery. Unable to care for self at home during recovery. Please arrange for supportive services." Discussion revealed the confusion that sometimes results from the diversity of services available within an inpatient setting. In this case, the referring resident wanted the patient to receive home nursing care during the early stages of recovery. He contacted an inappropriate provider (psychologist) for an appropriate type of service desired (social work). Division of labor often is not clear among the disciplines of psychiatry, psychology, and social work, which are usually housed in separate departments. In fact, these departments often overlap in services provided (e.g., supportive care), thereby justifying the resulting confusion. We believe disciplines should work collaboratively to clarify related issues within any institution, so as to minimize unnecessary costs and care. However, if the clinician is working within an academic teaching hospital, he or she can expect an especially high incidence of this type of error during times of medical resident rotations and arrival of new residents (July 1 of each year).

Patients as well as referral sources may also be mistaken about the types of services provided by a clinical health psychologist. Much of the public remains poorly informed regarding the traditional differences between psychiatry and psychology. When a profession becomes even more specialized within a given discipline, (i.e., clinical health psychology vs. clinical psychology), it is not surprising that people are perplexed when certain services are not offered. As example, Mrs. M. was a 35-year-old woman with chronic history of severe migraine headaches. She was referred to an outpatient headache-management program by her neurologist for evaluation and treatment. On completion of the initial interview, it became obvious that the patient expected the clinical health psychologist to offer some form of medication treatment and expressed considerable dismay and agitation when this type of "headache management" was not available. In the case of outpatients, sending written materials along with appointment materials that describe the nature of services available can minimize these kinds of problems. In any case, written materials should be available to the patient in accordance with the *General Guidelines for Providers of Psychological Services* (American Psychological Association, 1987).

Dealing With Poorly Timed Requests

Occasionally, the timing of a consultation request is inappropriate. Referrals can be premature or extensively delayed. We have received more than one consultation request asking for evaluation of a patient's mental status and ability to cope within hours of a major trauma (e.g., motor vehicle accident or surgery). In these instances, the patient is often comatose and clearly unable to meet the demands of the assessment process. We have found that it is useful to contact ward staff before making a trip to the hospital and to be sure to respond to the physician's concerns, explaining the best timing for such an assessment. Scheduling follow-up times and coordinating those with the referral source will provide assurance that the request is not being ignored.

Alternatively, we have also discovered that well-meaning health care providers have delayed a consultation request for psychological evaluation or treatment beyond the point of a consultant's ability to provide optimal services. This is particularly true when the referral source has attempted to deal with the patient's problems alone, without seeking a psychologist's opinion. As a result, by the time the clinical health psychologist is consulted, he or she often finds a much more severe problem than what had initially occurred. As an example, consider the following case:

> Mr. S. was a 54-year-old man. He was hospitalized for lower extremity edema and phlebitis in his left leg. On admission to the unit, the patient behaved in a very arrogant, noncompliant, and demanding manner (did not stay in bed with leg elevated), which intimidated the newly arrived medical residents. Mr. S. adamantly denied noncompliance with medical regimen; however, laboratory

results suggested that he had not been taking his medication as prescribed. As Mr. S.'s hospitalization progressed, he became increasingly disruptive. The medical team attempted to independently deal with his behaviors by increasingly confrontational behavior. As a result, the patient became even more agitated and began acting toward medical personnel in a belligerent manner. The psychology service was then consulted.

On arriving at bedside, the psychologist conducted an individual interview with the patient that assessed previous general psychological condition as well as issues associated with compliance. It was revealed that this patient was suffering from a bipolar affective disorder, manic phase, in addition to having long-standing personality problems that included narcissistic features. Given these psychological parameters, it became increasingly clear that this patient would be unlikely to adhere to any complicated medication regimen (he had also been noncompliant with psychotropic medication), especially when feeling pressured by staff to do so. Had the clinical health psychologist been consulted earlier, staff members could have been provided with information to help them in case management that might have had some preventative value.

Dumping and Turfing

Dumping and *turfing* are two terms with which the clinical health psychologist will unfortunately become familiar. These terms represent assessment and intervention requests for patients for which other professionals no longer wish to be responsible. As such, the patients are dumped or turfed to a different department or service. Occasionally patients are referred for psychological assessment because of the physician's inability to determine a medical diagnosis. It is often unfortunately assumed that if the patient is not physically ill and still complains, the patient *must* be psychologically ill. This is especially true in cases where patients have a previous history of psychological problems.

Medical personnel are not the only professionals to turf patients. In mental health practices, patients who present with frequent and multiple medical complaints are often viewed as less desirable clients and are referred out as "not amenable to psychotherapy; needs stress management." This type of referral implies that the consultee is differentiating *stress management* from *psychotherapy*, reserving the latter term for those treatment approaches that are perceived as more insight oriented in nature (and sometimes more valued). Consequently, outpatients who present with somatization issues and who are not YAVIS (young, attractive, verbal, intelligent, and successful) might be referred to a clinical health psychologist. That is, because the primary therapist has no professional interest in dealing with this kind of patient problem, he or she "turfs" the patient to the clinical health psychologist. The patient might then experience a sense of rejection or diminished self-worth from the initial mental health contact and be less amenable to work with a psychologist. Although we deplore the discrimination against these patients, we believe it to be true that the clinical health psychologist often has services more useful to them than traditional mental health service providers.

ISSUES IN THE CONDUCT OF CONSULTATIONS

Adequacy of Background Information

Throughout this book, we have described key resources for background information on the patient and his or her illness. In the actual course of obtaining information, the clinical health psychologist is likely to encounter a number of roadblocks. Ultimately, the amount of time and energy channeled into pursuing background information will be based on the clinician's judgment concerning the necessity and utility of the sought-after information. Difficulties in gathering background information include lack of medical expertise, inability to obtain releases of information, unavailability of records, and poor handwriting.

Lack of medical expertise. Although the clinical health psychologist will have studied basic medical terminology and will have a general understanding of common medical disorders, many technical reports focus solely on the medical aspects of disease and do not address behavioral or emotional ramifications of the illness. We have found it extremely helpful to ask our medical colleagues to explain various aspects of specific diseases, and their implications, in terms that are understandable to nonmedical professionals. It has been our experience that most physicians are not only willing to provide this information but also respect our judgment and efforts in attempting to understand these issues.

Inability to obtain releases of information. Patients might be unable or unwilling to release information concerning previous psychological or medical treatments. It is not uncommon for patients to forget, or to be too ill to recall, the names of previous health care providers. This is especially true when they have been in treatment with multiple providers over the course of many years. Alternatively, some patients prefer not to disclose information concerning past treatments, as they fear it could be perceived in a negative manner or be damaging to them in some way. Over the past 2 decades, we have practiced in a variety of independent, institutional, and managed care settings. Clearly the best system for access to history has been that at Kaiser Permanente, where medical charts available to clinicians are kept on all members, sometimes dating back 40 years!

Inability to obtain releases of information also limits with whom the clinician can speak. That is, except under extreme or urgent circumstances, it is unethical to speak with family members, friends, previous treatment providers, or employers regarding the patient without first having the patient's consent to do so. If the patient is not willing to provide releases of information, the clinician needs to consider the ramifications for treatment and to determine whether or not to proceed given these circumstances.

Unavailability of records. Assuming that a release of information has been provided, the clinician will quickly discover that medical and psychological records are not easily obtainable. Records are occasionally lost or unavailable at time of assessment. The clinical health psychologist might need to be very persistent in obtaining previous treatment histories from a variety of sources and to continue the process of gathering information throughout the first few sessions. Note also that when obtained, records can also be surprisingly noninformative. It is often wise to communicate by means of telephone with previous providers to ensure a thorough understanding of previous diagnoses and treatments and the provider's subjective impressions that might otherwise be unrecorded.

Poor handwriting. It is a joke that the sine qua non of a good physician has been the degree of impairment of his or her handwriting. In actual practice, poor handwriting is no laughing matter. Review of medical records is unavoidably hampered by the inability to read medical personnel's description, diagnosis, or treatment of the patient. Not only is poor handwriting frustrating to read, but it can also lead to misdiagnosis or mismanagement of the patient. From our perspective, one is only as effective as one's ability to communicate.

Of course, there can be times when gathering background information is not possible. In these cases, we have found it useful to tell the patient of our efforts to do so, because this communicates a high level of professionalism and caring and elicits cooperation in yet another request for history.

Problems in the Initial Contact

It is crucial that the clinician be knowledgeable about the nature of the medical problem and relevant treatments *before* seeing the patient. For example, it would be useless to interview a candidate for penile prosthesis surgery (in which it is critical to assess how realistic the patient's expectations are) without being aware of the probable outcomes of this type of surgery. It would be unethical to assess whether a patient could withstand the stressors of heart transplant surgery without having knowledge of what those stressors are. The clinician also needs to know the potential psychological concomitants of the patient's disease and pharmacological therapies before interviewing the patient.

In addition to considering possible interactions among the person, the disorder, and the treatment, the consultant should have an understanding of the patient's preparedness, if any, for the psychological consultation.

Before actually making initial contact with the patient, the clinical health psychologist should consider the following questions to enhance the probability of adequate rapport building:

1. Does the patient know that a psychologist has been consulted?
2. What might a psychological consultation mean to the patient?
3. Given background information obtained, what is the best way to approach this particular person?

The first question addresses a very common problem. Physicians frequently request a psychological evaluation without advising the patient. One study noted that 68% of hospitalized patients had not been informed by their physicians that a psychiatric consultation had been requested (Bagheri, Lane, Kline, & Araujo, 1981). The primary reason given by physicians for not advising the patient was the fear that the patient might view the consultation as an insult. Other common reasons were that the physician did not think of it, the physician was too busy, the physician thought the patient might become belligerent or refuse consultation, or the physician feared that the patient might lose faith in him or her. Note that many of these reasons reflect anxiety responses on the part of physicians. The information in Exhibit 5.1 can be helpful in avoiding this problem.

With respect to the second question, we find it critical to deal with the *reason* for referral at the beginning of the interview. A good opening question is to ask the patient about his or her own understanding of the process. A problem frequently uncovered is that the physician has indicated to the patient that he or she has "nothing further to offer medically." This, especially when associated with referral to a psychologist, is then interpreted by the patient as meaning that the problem is thought to be "in my head." On numerous occasions, this is not what the referral source meant (e.g., the patient might have documented medical problems accounting for the symptoms reported, but there is no available treatment other than "learning to live with it"). Because both patients and physicians often subscribe to mind–body dualistic philosophies, there are many opportunities for misinterpretations.

The third question serves as a reminder that each patient is unique with his or her own idiosyncratic expectations, fears, coping mechanisms, abilities, and medical problems. Patients should not become a "label" or a "diagnosis," a tendency we have seen among some providers in discussing "pain patients."

Problems with settings. With today's soaring costs of medical care, many hospitals have fewer private rooms. As a result, the patient's privacy is often quite limited, and the clinician needs to be acutely aware of confidentiality issues. If the patient is feeling well enough, and there are no medical contraindications, it might be possible to request to meet in the clinician's office. However, this is usually not feasible, particularly for the initial contact. The persistent clinician might be able to locate a family, conference, or waiting room that is not in use. Generally, if such rooms are available, there is little objection to allowing the psychologist access.

Unfortunately, many patients require bed rest or are housed in specialized units (e.g., burn units or cardiac care units [CCUs]), thereby eliminating the possibility of complete privacy. Under these conditions, the clinician should, at a minimum, close the curtain around the patient's bed and talk in a lowered voice, checking with the patient on occasion as to the extent that limitations on privacy are affecting self-report. Sometimes roommates can be requested to leave temporarily. In our experience, roommates are usually agreeable to facilitating others' privacy.

Problems with scheduling. Although scheduling the patient for an initial evaluation session seems like a simple task, it can prove to be very difficult. Working in a hospital poses several problems that the outpatient psychologist might never face. Medical procedures take precedence over all other procedures. As a result, patients are frequently off the ward for laboratory work and treatment. Scheduling an appointment with the patient through either the ward clerk or the charge nurse can alleviate this difficulty. However, the clinical health psychologist needs to have sufficient flexibility in his or her schedule to allow for variation in hours.

Scheduling the medical outpatient poses the same difficulties as scheduling any psychological outpatient, with a few additional considerations. Depending on the patient's health status and stamina, it might be better to schedule a shorter appointment than what is customary. Physical limitations of patients often necessitate special considerations in parking arrangements, wheelchair access, and restroom facilities. Additionally, many medical patients prefer appointments in the morning or afternoon, because of medication regimens and other treatments (e.g., radiation, occupational therapy, or physical therapy) or because of personal needs (e.g., transportation, sleep habits, availability of significant others, or work schedules). If the clinical health psychologist can remain flexible in scheduling patients, he or she will be more able to capitalize on the optimum performance of the patient. Depending on the nature of the outpatient service, it is often desirable for the clinical health psychologist to schedule patient appointments in the outpatient medical clinic in conjunction with other medical visits so as to facilitate professional communication.

A common problem in outpatient settings is the lack of follow-through by the patient in scheduling an appointment after referral. One means of overcoming this problem is for the clinical health psychologist to contact the patient initially, not waiting for the patient to call. Alternatively, the clinician can educate the physician in how to make "strong" referrals and can provide the physician with multiple copies of professional brochures. Common referral sources might also be given a specially tailored videotape on relevant issues that the patient can view in the physician's office. Provision to hospitalized patients of business cards and materials, describing services and location, is also useful.

The reluctant or hostile patient. Clinical health psychologists, probably more so than those in traditional practice, must often deal with reluctant or hostile patients in the initial visit. The reasons for this can be numerous, but we have found four common ones:

1. The patient was not told about the referral to a psychologist.
2. The patient has negative perceptions about psychological intervention for what the patient has defined as a medical problem (as previously noted, most patients are mind–body dualists also).
3. The patient is being asked to shift from a biomedical model of un-

derstanding disease (with its passive, external locus of control) to a biopsychosocial model of understanding disease, with different responsibilities and a more internal locus of control.

4. Patients are rarely self-referred to a clinical health psychologist and thus tend to be more skeptical about the initial session than those patients who have self-initiated contact with a psychologist.

Of these, the most typical source of reluctance is patients' focus on the medical aspects of the problem and anger about their doctors' implying it might be "all in your head."

As mentioned earlier, it is imperative to gauge a patient's reaction and emotional state related to the referral for psychological evaluation. If this is not done adequately, with appropriate adjustment in interviewing style, the assessment can yield invalid data, the patient might not commit to any type of treatment, or the patient might sabotage treatment attempts.

We and others (see DeGood, 1983; Weisman, 1978) have observed several early warning signs of patient reluctance or hostility related to psychological assessment, including the following:

1. Refusal to schedule an appointment or to show up for return visits.
2. Anger and bewilderment in the initial session as to why the referral was made, or being closedmouthed in discussing his or her problem.
3. Interest in the initial session, then "yes, but-ing" and taking personal exception to what has been discussed.
4. Statements implying that the patient wishes to pursue other medical treatments first.

The clinical health psychologist must be very alert to these cues, given the challenging task of establishing rapport in a relatively short time. We find DeGood's and Weisman's suggestions of ways in which to facilitate reduction of patient reluctance and hostility toward psychological intervention very helpful:

1. *Establish rapport.* Self-introduction of name and position is of course required. Establish eye contact with the patient. When possible, sit

down while talking. If you do not tower over a person in bed, who might already feel inferior because of role issues, he or she might feel less threatened. Ask the patient what he or she understands was the reason for the referral.

2. *Avoid asking yes–no questions.* Yes–no questions are usually not questions but statements in disguise. The reluctant patient quickly assumes that the assessing psychologist has already determined a diagnosis without listening to his or her comments or questions.

3. *Defuse the organic-versus-functional myth.* Depending on how the primary physician made the referral, this can be more or less of a problem. It can be useful to simply state overtly that many patients have concerns about referral to a psychologist for medical problems. Further discussion should include the patient's feelings and thoughts about this and some mention of the interaction between physical illness and psychological state. Allow the patient to present physical symptoms for a short time. Acknowledging the real aspects of the medical condition is crucial and reduces patient anxiety.

4. *Avoid "psychologizing" the patient's symptoms.* Many patients referred to a clinical health psychologist are not psychologically minded and are not interested in insight. It is important to meet some of the needs of the patient and to provide something concrete in the first interview. This could entail some explanation of psychophysiological aspects of the medical problem, a rationale for treatment, and perhaps some diary forms for self-monitoring of troublesome symptoms.

5. *Shape adequate beliefs rather than challenge misconceptions.* The initial contact should involve mostly listening and encouragement. Acknowledging but not overly challenging the patient's reluctance to participate can facilitate patient willingness to return. We find it useful to both elicit and negotiate the patient's health belief model. Exhibit 5.2 illustrates with a miniscript one method of approaching a patient with chronic pain.

6. *Present treatment strategy in a positive fashion, rather than as a last resort.* Unfortunately, referral to the clinical health psychologist is sometimes a last resort after traditional medical management has failed. Distressed patients perceive this communication from the physician as "you

Exhibit 5.2

Sample Script of Reluctant Patient Interview

Interviewer: Mr. Jones, what is your understanding about why you are here to see me today?

Patient: Well, my doctor, he told me to come here.

Interviewer: Why do you think he suggested that?

Patient: I don't know. I guess he thinks it would help, but I don't see how, not unless you can give me something that will help with this pain in my back. That's the only think that's bothering me.

Interviewer: Well, I'm not sure what we have at this point that might be helpful for your pain, that's what we'll try to find out. But I was wondering if you had any thoughts about why you're here to see a psychologist?

Patient: No, my doctor told me to come.

Interviewer: Well, sometimes patients think that they get sent to see me because their doctor doesn't believe that their pain is real. Have you ever felt that way?

Patient: Well, I should know, I feel my pain, I know it's real.

Interviewer: Well, of course it is, and you're right—you are the only one who can feel it. No doctor can. Which I guess might feel a bit lonely sometimes, if it seems no one else can feel what you feel.

Patient: Well, that's true. You know they've done all these tests, and they can't find anything wrong.

Interviewer: What do you mean by "wrong"?

Patient: Well, they can't operate, they say it would just make my back worse.

(exhibit continues)

Exhibit 5.2 (*cont.*)

Interviewer: So maybe what your doctor meant was that he didn't have any medical treatments that might be useful.

Patient: Yes, that's right. I guess I'm a lost cause. But I think I'm managing as best I can, I mean I'm not ready for the nuthouse yet.

Interviewer: Well people don't get sent to me because they're ready for the nuthouse. I get to see patients just like you because their doctors understand that there have been developments in the field of psychology that have sometimes been useful to patients with chronic-pain problems.

Patient: Oh, come on, you mean that I could just talk myself out of this pain?

Interviewer: Well, I'm not sure, but it might be possible that you could learn to live with it without suffering so much. Learning is sometimes a big part of pain and coping with pain, you know.

Patient: Now I didn't learn this pain; I hurt my back at work lifting a sack of cement.

Interviewer: Of course, and you know we can't do anything about that original injury. But you know it's very normal for a pain that has been going on for a while to get affected by other things. You know, bodily processes can be conditioned. Let me give you an example.

If I hold up a bright, yellow lemon in front of you, now imagine this in my hand here, and then I cut it with a knife so that you can see the juicy pulp inside. And then I hold it here and begin to squeeze. Now imagine those drops running down and the squishing sound it makes as I squeeze the lemon tight. By the way, do you feel anything in your mouth? Sometimes people do, they actually feel saliva forming under their tongues. And that is real, not imaginary, although of course it was a learned response, I mean you never really felt the lemon itself.

Exhibit 5.2 (*cont.*)

Patient: Yeah, I felt that. So how does this relate to my pain? My pain is caused by that squished disc I have, not some lemon.

Interviewer: Well, I think of pain as a big pie we can divide into pieces. Some of those pieces we might actually be able to take out, like pieces of your pain that could be due to not managing your activity level well or due to having been conditioned—affected by learning. And some pieces could be affected by your mood. We all know that if we have the flu after a bad day at work, we feel a lot worse than if we have the flu and it's been a good day. And you can't have pain without it having affected your life in some way. How has it affected yours?

Patient: Well, I have been more depressed—and my family is about fed up with me—you know they don't understand—I think they think I'm faking this sometimes . . . but I know I hurt.

Interviewer: Yes, you do, now tell me more about it. . . .

---

have failed" and as a rejection. Providing a clear rationale and more positive explanation of treatment (e.g., next logical step) can help increase motivation and compliance.

7. *Foster realistic expectations about treatment.* Patients generally do not understand the process or time commitment required in psychological treatment. Providing the patient with an outline of how psychological treatment differs from medical treatment is important. Issues of special importance include the facts that there is no sudden cure, that the patient is likely to be a more active participant than in previous medical treatments, and that there will be ups and downs in the course of treatment. Such a discussion can prevent premature therapy termination due to unmet expectations or frustration.

8. *Clarify other treatment roles.* The patient will want to know how the psychological treatment will interface with ongoing medical management.

The clinical health psychologist must be familiar with other treatments and be able to provide a clear explanation of how the various treatment procedures could interact and the communication that will be conducted among professionals. Be sure the patient understands that this is not an either–or situation.

In general, the psychologist must be vigilant to the overt or covert presentation of concerns by the patient and must facilitate open discussion to dispel myths and to reassure the patients that their concerns are not unusual. The task is not to *coerce* the patient into obtaining the service, but to dispel misconceptions that prove to be barriers to obtaining help. Protection of the patient's right to consent is paramount, except when contraindicated by law. In rare cases, the consultation might be terminated until the patient has the opportunity to discuss it in more detail with the referring physician.

New Information

It is often the case that the psychologist is the first professional to listen extensively to what the patient has to report. Hence, he or she might actually obtain more information than previous health care professionals. The patient might relish the opportunity to tell his or her story by detailing specific events leading up to the referral. Given the chance, patients sometimes tell the psychologist details that had either escaped their memory in the time-pressured discussions with their physicians or were withheld in the absence of sufficient rapport, especially if the information did not appear relevant to the patient. We had one patient reveal for the first time that she had never been adequately treated for a past episode of syphilis because she was afraid her physician would reject her if he knew of this disease. It is important to document symptoms and history, so that appropriate information becomes available to other health care providers.

Boundary Issues

When working with medical–surgical patients, the clinical health psychologist is likely to encounter special boundary issues that are not as salient in traditional outpatient services. In fact, clinical health psychologists can find themselves involved in a variety of behaviors that are not part of traditional therapeutic practice (e.g., closing a tracheotomy tube so that the patient can speak). As a result, a more traditionally trained clinician might need to make adjustments in professional identity, to provide certain services.

Nudity. It is not uncommon within inpatient medical settings for the clinician to encounter patients in various states of undress. For example, as part of a heart transplant team, regular attendance on patient rounds might be required. During these rounds, patients are physically examined, which necessitates partial nudity. Not being socialized into the profession with these experiences, psychologists often wrestle with their sense of intrusiveness on patients' rights. Identifying and processing practice issues for different settings and reframing professional interests as *health care* rather than *psychotherapy* can help alleviate this initial discomfort. We hope that we will not become insensitive to patients' discomfort with nudity and our potential for intrusiveness, however.

Touching. In the course of practice of clinical health psychology, therapists might need to touch their patients, a behavior most unusual except for the greeting handshake in traditional practice. As an example, touching occurs in the application of electrodes for biofeedback treatments. Other forms of contact might include gently holding a patient's hand to offer reassurance or a gentle pat on the shoulder. These acts of touching differ dramatically from traditionally established taboos and can cause a certain amount of anxiety for the psychologist.

PITFALLS IN ASSESSMENT

Professional concerns regarding the use of psychometric assessment devices and evaluation procedures include lack of normative data on medical–surgical patients, misuse of psychological data by nonpsychological personnel, and applicability of standard interpretive rules. These are discussed more thoroughly in chapters 6 and 7. In addition to those concerns, however, there are other issues and pitfalls in the assessment process.

Dealing With Limitations of Knowledge

Even when good normative data for medical–surgical patients are available, the answers to many diagnostic and treatment questions are not easily answered with available tests. That is, psychological assessment techniques typically do not yield "clean" interpretations of a patient's problem. Our inability to specifically state that the problem is one thing or another is often quite frustrating to a physician who is hoping to establish a definitive diagnosis. The clinical health psychologist needs to feel comfortable furnishing sometimes ambiguous results and not succumb to pressures to go beyond the data to solve a problem.

Failing to Gather Background Information

Sometimes clinicians accept at face value patient reports that previous treatments have been unsuccessful. For example, patients have reported a lack of success with "biofeedback" or "relaxation," but when questioned in more detail it became obvious that they lacked understanding of the procedures, had not had either an appropriate type or trial of such treatment, had not complied with homework, or had just been told to relax rather than provided with systematic training. Failure to gather thorough information on past treatments can lead to erroneous conclusions and recommendations. In another example:

> Dr. Young was a 4th-year psychiatric resident completing his training in a general medical hospital. He received a consultation to assess depression in a patient who had undergone surgery for cancer. When Dr. Young arrived on the ward, the patient's medical records were being used by another service provider. In his rush to complete the consult, Dr. Young interviewed the patient without reviewing the medical record or speaking with nursing staff, making the assumption that the patient was suffering from an adjustment reaction. During the interview, the patient spoke rarely and frequently stared off into space, apparently ignoring the resident's questions. The physician concluded in his report that the patient was severely depressed and exhibiting signs of catatonia.

Unfortunately for Dr. Young, he later learned that the patient was almost completely deaf and unable to comprehend many of his interview questions. Gathering adequate background information could be the first thing to be ignored by the rushed and time-pressured clinician. However, it is an important aspect of accurate evaluation and treatment and in fact must be explicitly acknowledged in writing a consultation report according to hospital guidelines. Also, malpractice litigation suggests one is responsible for being aware of what is in a patient's past records (*Jablonski by Pauls v. United States*, 1983).

Neglecting the Impact of the Environment

Put yourself in the following situation:

> Two days ago, you had a mild heart attack. As a result, you had to end all work responsibilities and are now lying in a bed in the CCU. There are no clocks, calendars, or windows in your room. You are dressed in a hospital gown, are confined to bed, and are required to use a bedpan. A nurse observes you through a window and another nurse checks your vital signs every hour; you are not told the results. You have been given a sedative to help you rest but have not been told of potential side effects. There is an intravenous tube in your arm, but you are not aware of its purpose. Every once in a while a beeper goes off in your room, and nurses come in to make adjustments to your equipment. You have never been hospitalized before and are unsure as to how to behave. The doctor has not seen you today, and you do not know the extent of damage to your heart. Your family, also being unfamiliar with the situation, is acting in a very anxious manner. You hear that far away relatives are making plans to visit you. A clinical health psychologist then enters your room, introduces himself, and advises you that your physician has requested an evaluation for depressed mood.

In interpreting data obtained from patients, we have repeatedly mentioned the importance of considering the impact of the immediate setting. In the example just given, the psychologist must take into consideration the effect of environmental and situational events (e.g., new role as patient, unfamiliarity with hospitals, or intensive care unit [ICU] stressors) when assessing potential causes of anxiety and depressed mood. According to attribution theory, observers (particularly clinicians because of their person-focused training; Jones & Nisbett, 1971) overestimate the role of dispositional (trait) factors when inferring causes of behavior. As a safeguard, the clinical health psychologist should pay particular attention to environmental cues that could precipitate maladaptive behavior and should be aware of common environmental stressors in health care. Failure to do so will result in erroneous conclusions about the causality and permanence of the patient's condition.

Underestimating Psychopathology

Clinical health psychologists sometimes underestimate the impact of psychopathology and its relationship to the medical–surgical problem. The clinical health psychologist must have as strong a background in psychopathology as any clinical psychologist. Although obviously not all medical–surgical patients are disturbed, a National Institute of Mental Health study suggested that around 20% of all American adults suffer from psychiatric disorders (Leo, 1984). Thus, it is likely that any clinical health psychologist will have to deal with psychopathology. Indeed, 20%–25% of medical–surgical patients have been diagnosed as suffering from depression severe enough to warrant treatment (Shevitz et al., 1976). Clinical health psychologists must be especially skilled in the management of depression and anxiety, as well as how personality disorders and other psychopathologies interface with medical–surgical problems and treatment.

Coping With Competing Agendas

In providing clinical services, the psychologist might have to deal with competing agendas with respect to a particular case and be quite clear as to *who* is the client. For example, in one presurgical screening of a kidney donor, we became very much aware of the referring physician's desire for a "clean bill of psychological health," so that the kidney could be obtained for his own patient. (This was his third psychological consultation in an effort to clear the donor for surgery.) The potential donor was also extremely eager to undergo the operation, because it gave him the opportunity to atone for perceived sins within the family. The hospital's agenda was for written confirmation of no psychological risk to the donor, so as to avoid malpractice liability. Given the nature of the case, none of these parties were satisfied with the results and recommendations of the psychological evaluation, which could not provide unqualified clearance. Although the potential donor demonstrated a clear understanding of the procedure, he also had a long history of poor impulse control and instances in which he manifested very poor judgment in decisions related to self-care. (The organ donation did occur after the patient obtained a court judgment, which satisfied the hospital's malpractice lawyers, that he was not *legally* incompetent to make this decision. Indeed the psychologist had insufficient evidence to conclude that the patient was legally incompetent.) Psychologists must be acutely aware of any temptation to please referral sources or employers by modifying interpretations of data obtained.

Coping With the Hostile Physician

As in any profession, there are hostile and arrogant physicians. Strategies for coping include a task-oriented focus on the patient's needs as a mutual goal, consistent assertiveness, confrontation as necessary, and a wealth of good humor. If the goal is to change physician behavior toward the patient, emphasizing benefits that would accrue to the physician is critical to laying the groundwork for change.

SPECIAL ISSUES IN INTERVENTION

Determining an Adequate Trial

It is important for the clinical health psychologist to understand what constitutes an adequate trial of treatment for any given approach, because there are significant ethical problems with persisting in an ineffective treatment regimen. In making this decision, the clinician should consider both patient variables (e.g., motivation, attendance, consistency, and acceptance of the biopsychosocial model) and treatment variables (e.g., what procedures have been attempted, what revisions in protocol have occurred in response to lack of improvement, and what the limitations of the strategy are).

Understanding the nature of previous treatment attempts and reasons for failure can also help the clinician decide when to pursue other forms of intervention or when to cease treatment. We cannot underscore enough the need to obtain numerous details about previous treatments. When closely scrutinized, the relaxation therapy or biofeedback treatment previously obtained may have been very inadequate in terms of design and implementation.

In the therapist's zeal to help patients learn to cope with various medical and psychological problems, he or she should not lose sight of the fact that not all problems are treatable, at least by methods currently available. The experienced clinician will accept the limitations of interventions, thereby avoiding a failure experience that could have negative effects on the patient and be nonrewarding for the clinician.

Maintaining the Therapeutic Contract

Medical–surgical patients can be in multiple psychological treatments. For example a patient might be referred by another mental health professional for an adjunctive intervention for tension headache. These patients often begin relating material that is also appropriate to the primary psychotherapy. It is necessary for the clinical health psychologist to deal with this material in the context of the focused treatment, to be aware of potential risks to the primary therapy, and to ensure a collaborative approach to treatment. Alternatively, the therapist might need to renegotiate the existing contract with both patient and referral source.

Interrupting Psychological Treatment

Interruptions can occur because of either planned or unplanned circumstances. It is not uncommon for patients to take a hiatus from psychological treatment while attending to acute medical problems. Patients also request interruption of treatment for financial reasons or for personal reasons.

A common reason for treatment interruption has to do with premature discharge, which can occur for a variety of reasons, including pressures to adhere to diagnosis-related groups (DRGs) and to shorten inpatient stays. As a result, physicians could discharge their patients as soon as they were medically cleared, not considering psychological intervention a reasonable cause for extending hospitalization. Consequently, the clinician might begin an intervention procedure that he or she is unable to complete.

When the clinical health psychologist has had insufficient time to establish adequate rapport with the patient before discharge, it is unlikely that the patient will continue with treatment on an outpatient basis. Furthermore given that most psychological interventions take time, the patient could be discharged believing that interactions with the psychologist had little or no effect or hope of effect. This colors the patient's perceptions of the relevance of psychology in the future, and may do more harm than good in the long run.

An additional source of premature termination or separation is created by faculty-attending schedules and student-training rotations. In large teaching institutions, psychological interns and postdoctoral residents typically rotate through various psychological subspecialties. To help eliminate some of the problems associated with this issue of "temporary therapists," we have found it helpful to clearly state early in the therapy process the time limits imposed by these conditions and to offer the patient reasonable alternatives (e.g., delay onset of treatment, transfer to another trainee, or transfer to staff personnel). The potential for interrupted treatment, and the possible consequences, should be considered in treatment planning.

COMMUNICATION OF RESULTS

Within an inpatient setting, the goal of the initial interview is to obtain sufficient information to respond to the consultee's request. This does not mean that the consultation will necessarily be answered in full, but it does mean that the consultee is *responded* to in a timely fashion. In practicing within an outpatient setting, the consultant is more likely to base case disposition on a number of interviews; thus, the initial communication might reflect a more complete workup of the case.

When physicians consult one another, the consultant typically responds with some objective data and then an opinion. This holds true for lab results, X-ray interpretations, and physical exams. The same expectations are made of psychologists. However, because we often do not have the same type of diagnostic tools available, we find ourselves limited in the type of information we can provide the referral source. Often, our opinion rests on an extensive interview with the patient and a detailed history.

At other times, our opinions are based on psychometric evaluation, data from which is often not appropriate to share with other professionals as it could be easily misunderstood. When testing is involved, we do not provide the physician with scores, offering, instead, a summary of interpretations. Our statements and opinions need to be presented in a sound manner, reflecting an understanding of the patient and the relevant issues.

Written Reports

In an inpatient setting, whether or not the initial contact results in a case conceptualization, the clinician must record the contact in the medical chart. Ideally, communication is also done verbally, but given the frequent unavailability of staff due to conflicting schedules and shift changes, it is often impossible to communicate directly. Consequently, the written report becomes paramount to good communication.

Whether the patient is seen in an inpatient or outpatient setting, a note is either placed in the Progress Notes section of the patient's medical records or written on a separate Consultation Report and placed in the patient's ward chart. Although settings can differ, the following are some typical medical record department rules:

1. Chart entries must be made only in black ink.
2. It is prohibited to leave spaces between entries.
3. It is prohibited to black- or white-out errors.
4. Errors are marked through with a single line, accompanied by the writer's initials.

5. Only approved abbreviations may be used and then not in discharge summaries.
6. Inpatient progress notes require not only date and name of service but also time and duration.

Although such regulations appear picayune at first, they have developed over time in response to specific needs or problems. They are codified in either JCAHO standards or local rules and regulations; infractions are monitored by special committees and can provide bases for suspension of hospital privileges.

If the clinician attempted to meet with the patient and was unable to complete the assessment, a note so indicating would also be placed in the medical chart. Although this could initially appear to be a trivial exercise, it is important to communicate to the referral source that an attempt was made to respond to the consultation request.

Failure to chart interactions with patients and staff can result in professionally embarrassing situations. Once we encountered a politically difficult situation in which a mental health professional, who usually did not see medically ill patients, continued to see one of his patients at bedside during a difficult hospitalization. Because the clinician was unfamiliar with protocol, he had not been documenting these contacts in the medical record. The attending physician was unaware of the patient receiving these services and requested psychological evaluation and treatment for depressed mood and anxiety. Although duplication in services was avoided, professional embarrassment was not.

Of course the content of the report largely depends on the referral question. As previously emphasized, however, "psycho babble" tends only to infuriate medical personnel and fosters the belief that psychology has nothing of practical value to offer. The report should be brief, succinct, relevant, and practical and have explanatory value. It is customary to include an overview of the presenting problem, behavioral observations and mental status information, relevant biopsychosocial interactions, patient strengths and problem areas, impressions, and recommendations. See Exhibit 5.3 for several report formats we have used over the years.

Exhibit 5.3

Sample Report Formats

I. PRESURGICAL EVALUATION

Referral information

Assessment procedures

Brief background information

Family of origin

Education–occupation

Marital–family history

Psychological–behavioral health history

Social support network

Current issues–stressor

Findings

Behavioral observations–mental status

Test results

Features specific to the surgical–treatment procedure

Attitudinal–motivational features

Informational and cognitive features

Affective features

Family issues

Coping strategies

Recommendations

Exhibit 5.3 (*cont.*)

II. CONSULTATION REGARDING PAIN MANAGEMENT

Referral information

Assessment procedures

Background information

Presenting problem

Other medical history

Behavioral health history

Psychosocial factors

Family history

Occupational history

Marital history

Leisure time

Psychotherapy history

Findings

Behavioral observations

Test results

Factors impacting pain management

Sensory

Affective

Cognitive

Behavioral

Compliance issues

Medication issues

Recommendations

Recommendations should include a specific treatment or management plan. Even when no treatment is indicated, the clinician should indicate, when appropriate, *the implications of the findings for medical management and for the behavior of health care providers.* Psychiatric diagnosis might or might not be included in the written consultation, depending on the nature of the consultation, the rules of the setting, and personal preference. In general, diagnostic labels, in and of themselves, are of little value to the consultee and are sometimes viewed with disdain by nonpsychiatric physicians. Also, they can be inadvertently used by other health care professionals in such a manner that the patient becomes defined by his or her diagnosis.

There is always concern as to how much and what type of information to reveal in medical charts, written reports, and through verbal communication. It is not uncommon for medical personnel to fix their attention on key words in an assessment summary and miss or de-emphasize important subtleties. The following example of a poorly written summary demonstrates this issue:

> The patient was a 49-year-old man with recent onset of cardiac arrhythmias. Psychological testing reveals that this patient does not have limited intellectual abilities. This patient behaves in a manner consistent with type A behavior and is likely to react in a hostile, competitive manner when his goals are thwarted.

First, it is likely that the reader will miss the *does not* that precedes a description of intelligence. Consequently, this patient might be perceived to have limited intellectual understanding. Second, it is quite possible that the reader will not focus on the fact that type A behaviors are elicited *under certain conditions* and not under all circumstances. As a result, staff could attribute to this man qualities that do not exist or be unduly defensive in response to a perceived risk of general hostile behavior.

ISSUES OF DISPOSITION

Knowing When to Refer

Being alert to possible changes or oversights in medical conditions is a responsibility of the clinical health psychologist. When the clinician suspects that the patient is behaving in a manner suggestive of organic disease, or

132

symptoms described by the patient point to such a case, it is imperative that the psychologist pursue medical evaluation. Consider the following example:

> The patient was a 34-year-old, single woman who self-referred to a clinical health psychologist for treatment of her bruxing problem. She specifically requested hypnosis and biofeedback to stop the clenching and associated pain. The patient described symptoms of tension and pain in the jaw muscles and of congestion in the nasal passages and stated that her palate felt like a "piece of hard steel." Her dentist had found no abnormality. The psychologist insisted on an examination by an otolaryngologist before beginning treatment. A nasopharyngeal tumor was discovered on this exam and radium-implant therapy was begun immediately.

This example illustrates how important assessment of biological targets can be. Patients often do not want to complete medical and dental evaluations because they desire to get on with treatment and are convinced that they are so stressed that this is what is producing their symptoms. It is imperative that this issue be routinely addressed, and, as indicated previously, the clinician might need to take on an advocacy role to be sure that this is accomplished.

In other circumstances, the patient might have had a thorough medical workup that yielded negative physical results yet continued to report symptoms suggestive of an undocumented organic disease. This type of situation requires the clinical health psychologist to carefully document the patient's symptoms while pursuing further medical evaluations. The psychologist should not be intimidated by medical personnel or hard data attesting to lack of organic disease. In more than one case, the insistence on repeated medical evaluations has resulted in diagnosis of initial stages of disease.

Follow-Up and Follow-Through

Rarely is the single interview or single assessment process sufficient to answer the referral question. As a result, the clinical health psychologist typically allows for follow-up procedures. Usually this contact involves additional assessment procedures, some form of intervention, and evaluation as to the effectiveness of an intervention. Unfortunately, follow-up procedures are not always completed. This happens for a variety of reasons, including premature discharge of the patient, failure of the clinician to recognize the need for follow-up, and reluctance by the patient to provide further information.

In some packaged treatment programs, there is no provision for outpatient follow-up after discharge from the program. This occurs if follow-up is not viewed as necessary, if follow-up procedures are seen as not cost-effective, or if follow-up sessions are not defined as treatment and thus hold little interest for both patient and clinician.

Follow-through refers to ensuring that necessary or recommended procedures have been executed. It is not uncommon for the clinical health psychologist to recommend that another service, such as social work or psychiatry, also be consulted on behalf of the patient. Although this information is typically related through medical chart progress notes and consultation forms, it is not adequate to assume that the recommended action will automatically occur. Thus, the clinician needs to make direct contact with allied services and continue to follow progress in that department, sometimes coordinating types of services.

ALTERNATIVES

Clinical health psychologists should abide by the following well-known saying: "Stay open-minded but not so open that your brains fall out." Sometimes rather nontraditional types of assessment and intervention are suggested, as highly novel approaches might be required. For example, when attempting to assess a patient for possible self-infection of an open wound (Munchausen's syndrome), one strategy used was to tape the patient's hands (with consent) to determine if reinfections would decrease. In another case, spot fingernail cultures were ordered to more definitively assess the source and means of infection.

An example of unusual intervention is illustrated by the clinician who suggested to a patient facing laryngectomy (and who had a booming baritone voice, which he used regularly in a barbershop quartet) that he tape various messages to his family as a means of preserving his voice (much like a family photo album). Thus, his young grandchildren would have a record of what he sounded like before surgery. Guided by scientific knowledge base of behavior, the clinicians are limited only by their creativity in devising innovative solutions to difficult problems.

Obviously not all special issues and problems have been discussed in this chapter. However, the information presented should alert the reader to common pitfalls in practice.

6

Ethical Issues in the Practice of Clinical Health Psychology

B ecause of the special settings and patient populations encountered, the practice of clinical health psychology brings with it unique ethical issues. The "Ethical Principles of Psychologists and Code of Conduct" (American Psychological Association, 1992) are, of course, still applicable. In clinical health psychology, it is just as important to be knowledgeable of the ethical principles as in any other area of practice. Ethical Standard 8.01 (Familiarity With Ethics Code) states the following:

> Psychologists have an obligation to be familiar with this Ethics Code, other applicable ethics codes, and their application to psychologists' work. Lack of awareness or misunderstanding of an ethical standard is not itself a defense to a charge of unethical conduct.

DEVELOPMENT OF ETHICAL PRINCIPLES

An understanding of the development of the ethical principles can be very helpful in applying them effectively to the area of health psychology.

The ethical principles of psychologists have been revised many times since their initial formulation in 1952 (American Psychological Association, 1953). Pope and Vetter (1992) provided an excellent review of their initiation and evolution. The authors noted that the method for formulating the original ethical code was markedly different than any method previously used by other professions. Traditionally, professional ethical codes were developed by committee, in which ethical codes from other professions, the wisdom and experience of the most mature clinicians, and the available literature were used to construct ethical guidelines. These would then be submitted to the membership for approval. This is the so-called "armchair" or rational approach to ethical guideline construction.

In making a significant departure from this process, the American Psychological Association decided to use an empirical method to develop an ethical code. A representative sample of member psychologists involved in a wide variety of professional activities were assessed for ethical dilemmas they encountered. On the basis of these data, the original ethical code was developed. In addition, it was planned that future revisions would be based on not only recommendations from ethics committees but also data collected from the membership about the dilemmas experienced in everyday practice.

ETHICAL DILEMMAS

It is important to be familiar with categories and frequencies of various "ethically troubling incidents" (Pope & Vetter, 1992, p. 399), because they indicate the areas of greatest ethical challenge in actual day-to-day practice. As is discussed shortly, many areas of greatest ethical concern in general psychology practice could be even more pertinent to the area of clinical health psychology.

Pope and Vetter (1992) conducted the most recent national survey of American Psychological Association psychologists to assess ethical dilemmas. Details of their data-collection methodology and complete results can be found in the original publication. Table 6.1 is a summary of their findings as they pertain to the present discussion. Confidentiality, dual relationships, and payment sources are among the categories with the highest frequencies of report. Other areas particularly applicable to health psy-

Table 6.1

Relevant Categories of Ethically Troubling Incidents

Category	% of incidents
Confidentiality	18
Blurred, dual, or conflictual relationships	17
Payment sources, plans, settings, and methods	14
Academic settings, teaching, and training	8
Forensic psychology	5
Questionable or harmful interventions	3
Competence	3
Medical issues	1
Treatment records	1

chology are assessment, questionable interventions, competence, advertising, medical issues, and treatment records.

Additional important information about ethical behavior can be gleaned from the Report of the American Psychological Association Ethics Committee (1993). This report documents such things as the number of ethical inquiries received, complaints filed, formal cases opened, and active cases during the year. An *inquiry* is simply a letter asking about or indicating intention to file a complaint; a *complaint* constitutes an actual filing. A *formal case* occurs when an office investigator and the chair of the Ethics Committee determine that there are grounds for proceeding. Table 6.2 summarizes some of the data relative to the present discussion. As can be seen, dual relationships, competency, confidentiality, test misuse, fee problems, and advertising are the areas of highest frequency. All of these issues are discussed in the following sections as they relate to the practice of clinical health psychology.

REVISION OF THE ETHICAL CODE

Since our previous discussion of ethical principles in the book, *The Practice of Clinical Health Psychology* (Belar et al., 1987), the ethical principles

Table 6.2

Relevant Ethical Cases Opened in 1992

Category	% of cases
Dual relationships	
Sexual	21
Nonsexual	11
Inappropriate professional practice	
Practice outside competence	3
Confidentiality	6
Inappropriate follow-up/termination	2
Test misuse	5
Insurance/Fee problems	6
Inappropriate public statement	
False, fraudulent, or misleading	6

have been revised. The revision process of the previous code (American Psychological Association, 1981) was started in 1986 and was completed in 1992 (American Psychological Association, 1992). The revision was done to ensure that the ethics code continued to be relevant to the most current issues in professional practice, research, and training. The revision included many substantive changes, including the organization of the document as well as a narrative introduction and overview. During the course of developing the revised code, the ethics committee had to address problems with the earlier ethics code that had been the subject of an investigation by the Federal Trade Commission (FTC). This primarily focused on the language used to prohibit referral fees and advertising claims. The 1992 code of ethics dealt with these objections by the FTC.

SPECIAL ETHICAL PROBLEMS IN CLINICAL HEALTH PSYCHOLOGY

The following discussion examines the most current ethical principles, as relevant to the practice of clinical health psychology. The discussion will focus around the first five of the six principles, because the ethical standards are generally subsumed within these principles. The principles discussed are competence (A), integrity (B), professional and scientific responsibility (C), respect for people's rights and dignity (D), and concern for others' welfare (E). The reader is referred to the original source for complete documentation (American Psychological Association, 1992).

PRINCIPLE A: COMPETENCE

Psychologists strive to maintain high standards of competence in their work. They recognize the boundaries of their particular competencies and the limitations of their expertise. They provide only those services and use only those techniques for which they are qualified by education, training, or experience. Psychologists are cognizant of the fact that the competencies required in serving, teaching, and/or studying groups of people vary with the distinctive characteristics of those groups. In those areas in which recognized professional standards do not yet exist, psychologists exercise careful judgment and take appropriate precautions to protect the welfare of those with whom they work. They maintain knowledge of relevant scientific and professional information related to the services they render, and they recognize the need for ongoing education. Psychologists make appropriate use of scientific, professional, technical, and administrative resources.

There are several issues relevant to clinical health psychology subsumed under the principle of competency. These include competency in training, recognition of boundaries of competence, maintenance of current knowledge, work with people of different backgrounds, use of appropriate assessment and interventions, computerized psychological testing, and recognition of personal problems that could interfere with practice.

Competency in Training

Since the 1983 Arden House Conference, there have been guidelines for training practitioners in health psychology. Of course, these are ideals at present; many of the senior health psychologists today did not have such a training background themselves. Even so, it is well recognized that weekend workshops do not produce a clinical health psychologist. As discussed in detail in chapter 2, core training and preparation for clinical health psychology practice should include specific graduate-level courses in the area as well as supervised practical experience. A psychologist should not present him- or herself as a "clinical health psychologist" unless training criteria have been adequately satisfied. A psychologist will not be eligible for a diploma in health psychology from the American Board of Professional Psychology unless certain educational requirements have been met.

Recognition of One's Boundaries of Competence

A psychologist must ensure the best interests and welfare of the patient who presents with a problem of psychological factors related to a medical problem. Consider the following example:

> Dr. Smith, a clinical psychologist, works in private practice setting, serving mostly adults. In the course of her work, she began therapy with a 22-year-old man who was suffering from muscle contraction headaches. Dr. Smith had done some reading about the treatment of muscle contraction headaches but had never actually treated a person with this problem. She continued treating the patient but received supervision by a clinical health psychologist experienced in the treatment of chronic headaches.

Dr. Smith acted appropriately and ethically in this example. Had she not received the outside supervision, she could have been acting unethically in not providing "only those services and use only those techniques for which they are qualified by education, training, or experience" (American Psychological Association, 1992). This is especially true in cases of psychophysiological disorders, because there are often clearly specified and empirically validated treatment approaches available for use. Another option might have been for the psychologist to have referred the patient to a colleague for concurrent treatment of the headache problem. (Although data are not available, in our experience, cross-consultation does not appear to be as frequent in the independent practice of psychology as it does in medicine, other than referrals for neuropsychological and learning disabilities evaluations.)

Related to this issue, it is unlikely that a psychologist could be proficient in all areas of practice that fall within the field of clinical health psychology. As indicated in chapter 1, clinical health psychology includes such diverse problems as eating disorders to headaches and such diverse assessments as neuropsychological evaluations to chronic-pain patient workups. The skills necessary for these different clinical tasks are extremely varied. As in the preceding example, the clinical health psychologist must be aware of his or her limitations even *within* the field of clinical health psychology and take steps to assure ethical professional behavior.

Maintenance of Current Knowledge

In a field as rapidly changing as clinical health psychology, it is essential to keep abreast of current literature. This is addressed in the principle of competence as well as in Ethical Standard 1.05 (Maintaining Expertise). Attending continuing education workshops, belonging to professional organizations, and subscribing to health psychology journals can facilitate this continuing education process. It has been said that the half-life of a PhD in clinical psychology is about 10 years when no further postgraduate education is sought (Dubin, 1972). In the area of clinical health psychology, this estimate may be much less, because of the high level of research and clinical activity.

Work With People of Different Backgrounds

Ethical Standard 1.08 (Human Differences) states that

> where differences of age, gender, race, ethnicity, national origin, religion, sexual orientation, disability, language, or socioeconomic status significantly affect psychologists' work concerning particular individuals or groups, psychologists obtain training, experience, consultation, or supervision necessary to ensure the competence of their services, or they make appropriate referrals.

Although we know of no data on this, it may be that clinical health psychology patient populations represent more of a cross-section of society than the populations presenting to services at mental health clinics. We find that to meet this ethical guideline in the practice of clinical health psychology, an understanding of patients' health belief models is essential. Furthermore, it is important to have an appreciation for cultural and other factors that influence patients' explanatory frameworks for medical problems. The following is an overview of a conceptual model useful in accomplishing these goals.

A conceptual distinction among *disease, illness,* and *sickness* is helpful for understanding patients presenting to clinical health psychologists (Engel, 1977; Fabrega, 1974; Kleinman, Eisenberg, & Good, 1977). *Disease* is an abnormality in physical structure or bodily function; it is the focus of biomedicine. *Illness,* on the other hand, is the human experience of sickness and is influenced by interpersonal, social, and cultural variables (Landrine & Klonoff, 1992; Mechanic, 1972). Illness entails explanation of the disease and how one is supposed to act when ill. It is how we perceive, experience, and cope with disease. In keeping with this model, there is rarely a one-to-one relationship between disease and illness (Beecher, 1956; Melzack & Wall, 1983; Zola, 1966). The combined influences of disease and illness yield what we ultimately observe clinically as *sickness.* Patients are generally much more concerned with the treatment of their illness than with simply the "cure" of the disease.

The ethical principle of competence as well as Standard 1.08 (Human Differences) dictates that the clinical health psychologist have an understanding of the model discussed above. The domain of clinical health psychology treatment is often illness behavior, explanatory beliefs, and sickness. When there is a significant discrepancy between the doctor's and patient's explanatory models, problems in treatment can occur.

> Mrs. A. B. was 56-year-old woman who was recovering from pulmonary edema secondary to atherosclerotic cardiovascular disease and chronic congestive heart failure on a general medical unit. Her physical status was improving, but she was frequently inducing vomiting and urinating into her bed. She became very angry when told by the staff to stop these behaviors. Psychological consultation re-

vealed that the patient had been told by her physician that part of her medical problem included "water in the lungs." Because of her family's occupation as plumbers, her conception of her anatomy consisted of a pipe connecting her mouth and urethra. She was therefore attempting to remove as much water from her body as possible through vomiting and urinating. She was hesitant to share this belief model with her physician because "he was so rushed" and she felt embarrassed. A sharing of the doctor's and patient's explanatory models, including a careful didactic session about her anatomy, resulted in a resolution of the problem behaviors and feelings of anger. (Case example adapted from Kleinman et al., 1977)

Other common examples of patients' misconceptions about medical treatments include the following: (a) If one pill is good, then two or more must be better; (b) if symptoms are not occurring, then the pills are not necessary (often seen in medication usage for hypertension and diabetes); and (c) continued use of *any* medication is "overdependence." As can be seen, any of these beliefs will have serious consequences for medical treatment.

Kleinman et al. (1977) suggested that in addressing a patient's belief model, one should attempt the following: (a) to elicit the patient's belief model with simple, straightforward questions; (b) to formulate the physician's model in terms the patient can understand and communicate this to the patient; (c) to openly compare models to identify contradictions; and (d) to help the physician and patient engage in a negotiation toward shared models related to treatment and outcome. Awareness of cultural and social issues related to a patient's belief model is crucial in guiding this process. It must also be realized that subgroups other than identified minority cultures may have beliefs about illness that affect behavior (as portrayed in the above example). It may be unethical to fail to address these issues.

Psychological Assessment

In psychological assessment with medical patients, the clinical health psychologist must be acutely aware of using the proper standardization data for medical patients when available (Standard 2.04a: Use of Assessment in

General and With Special Populations), differences in test interpretation with a medical–surgical patient population versus a psychiatric population (Standard 2.04), increased risk of inappropriate use of test results by nonpsychologist health care professionals (Standard 2.06: Unqualified Persons), the language of the test interpretation and risk of misinterpretation (Standard 2.05: Interpreting Assessment Results), and systemic issues hampering the patient's right to be informed of the test results (Standard 2.09: Explaining Assessment Results). Consider the following relatively common example:

> The patient was a 34-year-old woman who presented to her primary physician with diffuse and vague somatic complaints, including pain. The patient also expressed that she had been recently experiencing some significant life stressors, and the physician hypothesized that these might be contributory. Initial physical evaluation was negative, in keeping with the physician's hypothesis, and the patient was referred for psychological evaluation, including psychological testing. The consultation request was to "determine if the symptoms might have a functional rather than organic basis." On the MMPI, scored using standard normative data, the patient obtained a classic "conversion V" profile with Scales 1 and 3 primed and all other scales below a T-score of 70.

The psychologist gave the following interpretation for the MMPI and sent the recommendations to the physician without discussing them with the patient. (Informed consent had been obtained to release the test results to the physician.)

> Patients with similar profiles present themselves as normal, responsible, and without fault. They make extensive use of such defenses as projection, denial, and rationalization and blame others for their troubles. They prefer medical explanations for their symptoms, and lack insight into the psychological basis for their symptoms. These patients are generally considered to be converting personally distressing problems into somatic complaints, which are more socially acceptable. Although these patients are resistant to change, because

of firmly entrenched defense systems, a course of psychotherapy targeting the patient's actual source of distress may be useful. (Interpretation based on Graham, 1977; Greene, 1980, 1991)

The physician referred the patient for psychological treatment, on the basis of the above evaluation. The psychological treatment was successful in resolving the stressful life circumstances with which the patient was having trouble, but the physical symptoms persisted. The patient was ultimately diagnosed as having multiple sclerosis when further diagnostic work was done.

This example illustrates a major ethical issue related to psychological assessment in health psychology. First, the psychologist used standard normative data to derive the patient's profile. Although this can be adequate if the use of such norms is taken into account in the interpretation, a more useful approach would be to use both the standard norms and those for medical patients (either norms generated in one's own clinic or those published in the literature, e.g., Greene, 1980, 1991) and compare the difference.

Other issues in this example, and more important ones as they influenced the course of the patient's treatment, were the consultation request itself and the interpretation of the results. First, the physician requested an inappropriate use for psychological testing. Although this type of request is commonly received from medical personnel, recent reviews of the literature suggest that psychologists who use the MMPI to assess pain patients should "not attempt to classify patients as organic, functional, or mixed" (Prokop & Bradley, 1981, p. 96; see also Bradley, McDonald-Haile, & Jaworski, 1992). Second, the psychologist used a standard interpretation developed on psychiatric patients. This included conjecture as to the etiology of the physical symptoms as well as several personality labels that might be cast as pejorative by a non-mental health professional.

Another problem with the response to this referral was that the language of the interpretation might not be in keeping with ethically guarding against the misuse of assessment results and promoting the best interests of the client. Without further explanation, the physician may well have changed his or her opinion of this patient and have tended to see the patient as somehow volitionally controlling the presentation of symptoms or consciously malingering—while there was no evidence bearing on this.

The last ethical issue related to this case is that the psychologist did not "ensure that an explanation of the results is provided using language that is reasonably understandable to the person assessed" (Ethical Standard 2.09: Explaining Assessment Results). Although Standard 2.09 does not state that the explanation must be done directly by the psychologist, he or she must ensure that an adequate and understandable explanation is given. We believe that this can be done most effectively if the explanation is done directly by the psychologist. This explanation and feedback process, however it is accomplished, is ethically mandated (Standard 2.09: Explaining Assessment Results) unless explicitly waived as part of the informed-consent process.

Related to this issue, sometimes the consultant will discuss findings with the referring physician and not directly with the patient. However, this can be problematic, and we recommend that where possible, follow-up with the patient should be provided. It should at least be offered as an option if the patient would like further clarification after feedback from their physician. It is also prudent to inform the referral source of the importance of the feedback process with the patient. Pope (1992) provides guidelines for providing psychological test feedback to patients—including feedback as process, clarification of tasks and roles, informed consent, framing the feedback, documentation, and follow-up.

In summary, in this case, the test results were not used in the best interests of the patient. Even if the patient had not ultimately been found to have multiple sclerosis, psychological evaluation should rarely preclude thorough medical evaluation. Exception to this guideline might include extreme cases, such as somatic delusions or factitious disorders, in which there is a documented history of unnecessary extensive medical evaluations and procedures. Even in these cases, it is important to have an open line of communication with the physician. It is important to remember that people with these types of psychological problems (e.g., somatization or symptom amplification) get sick just like everyone else.

Clinical health psychologists must be aware of special psychological assessment issues in working with medical patients, because general-practice assessment skills are not always applicable. When the psychologist is not familiar with current literature in the area, he or she is at higher risk for unethical practice. A complete discussion of assessment issues in health psychology can be found in chapter 3.

Computerized Psychological Testing

Although there has been controversy over the quality of computerized psychological testing (Fowler & Butcher, 1986; Matarazzo, 1983, 1986), it is prevalent and on the increase. The ethical principle of assessment (2.08) and the *Standards for Educational and Psychological Tests* (American Psychological Association, 1985b) address issues related to computerized testing. Specific and practical guidelines for users have also been discussed in such published works as the *Standards for the Administration and Interpretation of Computerized Psychological Testing* (Hofer & Bersoff, 1983). Hofer and Bersoff's recommendations continue to be applicable and are discussed in the following paragraphs.

With respect to administration, Hofer and Bersoff (1983) emphasized the need for the computerized format to be valid and that "factors affecting test scores related to the computer presentation and recording of items that are irrelevant to the purposes of assessment should be eliminated" (p. 30). Thus, one needs to be aware of the influence on results of computer hardware, test-item display, understandability to the user, ability to change responses, and availability of a proctor. It is important to assure that the computer-testing situation conforms to standardization guidelines, if available. Familiarity with research on conventional versus computerized testing, human factors, and ergonomics is certainly helpful.

So far as computerized psychological test scoring and interpretations, note two major concerns: (a) the adequacy of the scoring algorithms and the classification system used to assign statements to particular test scores and (b) the validity of the interpretations inferred from test results. First, the user should satisfy himself or herself that the computer-generated scores (raw or scaled) are in keeping with those derived through the traditional methods. Although, computer hard copy looks accurate, such is not always the case even after extensive field testing by the company. Second, the user should have available data on the decision rules used to match test scores with interpretative statements. When this is not possible, the user should be aware of existing research on the computer programs being used. Unfortunately, this is often not available. Third, it is important to know which interpretive statements are linked to which test scores. Many computer-generated interpretations do not provide such information, making this guideline difficult to satisfy. Often one can scan the interpretative reports, comparing interpretations with test scores, to help assure validity. Once again, application to clinical health psychology requires use of appropriate norms in interpretation.

Fourth, it must always be kept in mind that computerized interpretive reports are *tools* of the qualified professional. The clinician is ultimately responsible for the report's validity and use. This means that the clinician might need to edit or amend the computer-generated psychological report to take into account sound clinical judgment.

Clinical health psychologists are often involved in computerized psychological testing in the context of a medical center, a comprehensive treatment program (e.g., a chronic-pain program), or on an individual clinical treatment level. Matarazzo (1986) voiced concern that "the tremendous advances during the past five years in microcomputerized psychological testing hardware and software have made it possible and economically seductive for a psychologist, a physician, another health service provider or a hospital administrator to offer such testing to unprecedented numbers of patients and clients" (p. 17).

Aside from being used by psychologists, computerized interpretive reports are being used by other health care professionals, who are often accustomed to ordering lab tests from technicians. It is difficult enough for psychologists to force themselves to scrutinize the "slick" computer report. Those professionals untrained in psychometric assessment and unaware of the special ethical issues related to computerized psychological assessment are even less likely to be able to make adequate judgments. It would be easy for these reports to become just another piece of data, without interpretation by any psychologist familiar with the case. One negative effect of this might be the physician's prematurely ascribing symptoms to emotional distress on the basis of psychological testing and doing an inadequate diagnostic workup. Cummings (1985) was able to empirically demonstrate this in showing that the number of missed diagnoses by physicians increased significantly in proportion to the amount of psychological assessment information rendered to them.

The American Psychological Association (1986) published the *Guidelines for Computer-Based Tests and Interpretations* to help guide professional behavior. The clinical health psychologist should be aware of these, and in our opinion should "watchdog" how these systems are being used (or abused), assuming advocacy roles when appropriate.

Recognition of Personal Problems

As with any area of professional practice, the clinical health psychologist must be aware of any personal problems that could impact his or her ability to perform duties adequately. This problem is addressed in the principle of competency as well as Ethical Standard 1.13 (Personal Problems and Conflicts):

> (a) Psychologists recognize that their personal problems and conflicts may interfere with their effectiveness. Accordingly, they refrain from undertaking an activity when they know that their personal problems are likely to lead to harm to a patient, client, colleague, student, research participant, or other person to whom they owe a professional or scientific obligation.
>
> (b) In addition, psychologists have an obligation to be alert to signs of, and to obtain assistance for, their personal problems at an early stage, in order to prevent significantly impaired performance.
>
> (c) When psychologists become aware of personal problems that may interfere with their performing work-related duties adequately, they take appropriate measures, such as obtaining professional consultation or assistance, and determine whether they should limit, suspend, or terminate their work-related duties.

The unique settings (e.g., the acute-care hospital) and environments (e.g., working with medicine) in which clinical health psychologists find themselves add to the stress of the work. The health psychologist may tend to deny the impact of the work and deal with the stress in a destructive manner. For instance, Pope, Tabachnick, and Keith-Spiegel (1987) found that 5.9% of psychologists acknowledged doing therapy sessions while under the influence of alcohol. In the same research survey, 59.6% of psychologists reported working when too distressed to be effective. The characteristics of the work and its impact on the professional have been discussed in previous chapters.

Important recent research suggests that a practitioner's beliefs about whether it is unethical to practice in a state of burnout will affect whether steps are taken, such as decreasing one's weekly caseload, when impairment is realized (Skorupa & Agresti, 1993). In the settings where clinical health psychologists are more likely to practice (e.g., an acute-care medical hospital), it may be easier to "get away with" practicing while impaired and providing substandard care, because of diffusion of responsibility issues, which are discussed shortly.

PRINCIPLE B: INTEGRITY

Psychologists seek to promote integrity in the science, teaching, and practice of psychology. In these activities psychologists are honest, fair, and respectful of others. In describing or reporting their qualifications, services, products, fees, research, or teaching, they do not make statements that are false, misleading, or deceptive. Psychologists strive to be aware of their own belief systems, values, needs, and limitations and the effect of these on their work. To the extent feasible, they attempt to clarify for relevant parties the roles they are performing and to function appropriately in accordance with those roles. Psychologists avoid improper and potentially harmful relationships.

The issue of integrity concerns imposition of values onto the patient, advertising for one's own services, endorsing psychological services or related products, clarification of roles, avoiding improper and potentially harmful dual relationships, and providing mental health services to those served by others.

Imposition of Values Onto the Patient

In keeping with this ethical principle, the clinical health psychologist is not justified in imposing rigid criteria for "healthy behaviors" onto patients. Working within the patient's health belief model and expectations for treatment is necessary to the formulation of treatment goals. For example, the Mexican-American patient who suffers from ulcers may be willing to modify his or her spicy diet but may outrightly reject an admonition to switch to bland food. The clinical health psychologist could be doing an injustice by holding to the latter treatment goal. This course of action would be not only risking a treatment failure but also decreasing the probability that a future intervention would be successful.

Advertising for One's Own Services

Guidelines for advertising by psychologists are addressed in the ethical standards of Avoidance of False or Deceptive Statements (3.03), Media Presentations (3.04), and Testimonials (3.05) as well as in Statements by Others (3.02) and In-Person Solicitation (3.06). Advertisements may contain such accurately presented information as name; highest relevant academic degree earned from a regionally accredited institution; type of certification or licensure; diplomate status; American Psychological Association membership status; services offered; fee information; foreign languages spoken; scientific or clinical basis for, or results or degree of success of, their services; and policy with regard to third-party payments.

The clinical health psychologist might include in advertising that he or she specializes in the treatment of psychological issues related to health problems or a particular subcategory of practice (e.g., chronic headaches, stress disorders, eating disorders, or smoking cessation). Because the FTC has loosened guidelines on professional advertising, most simple factual information about one's services are probably reasonable (Koocher, 1983,

1994). What is prohibited in advertising is exaggeration of the uniqueness of services offered. Unwarranted claims such as "hypnotherapy will end smoking and overeating in 1 day" or "10 sessions of biofeedback will eliminate your headache problem" would be considered unfounded and unethical.

Endorsements

Beyond advertising for one's own services, care must be taken in the endorsement of products or printed materials. In clinical health psychology, there has been an explosion of technology related to practice (e.g., relaxation tapes, hypnosis tapes, self-help manuals, and biofeedback equipment). Unfounded claims related to the efficacy of these procedures might include such statements as the following:

> In this manual, you will learn to subliminally reprogram yourself to lose weight, eliminate pain, and quit smoking in a short amount of time using these proven audiotapes.
>
> These tapes will produce a positive restructuring of self-image, alleviate depression, and increase self-esteem.
>
> These relaxation methods are proven to inhibit postoperative swelling, pain, and bleeding and to produce rapid healing. They are also used for all pain management.
>
> The real cause of smoking is stress, and you'll learn to control it through this proven and tested home biofeedback system.

These hypothetical statements could be considered unfounded and unethical, because they go beyond what has been validated. Furthermore, they do not specify the context within which these technologies have been tested (e.g., as used in a comprehensive psychological treatment package). The psychologist is ethically bound to protect how his or her name is used, even when production or publication rights have been transferred to a marketing company (Standard 3.02: statements by others).

Clarification of Roles

The principle of integrity dictates that psychologists clarify the roles they are performing for all relevant parties and function in accordance with those roles. In clinical health psychology practice, this issue usually arises in clarifying one's role within the context of medical treatment. In the hospital setting, patients are often seen by a variety of providers, and they will often become confused about "who does what." The patient could mistake the psychologist for a physician or expect a similar type of care. These roles should be clearly identified for the patient. For the patient who is unfamiliar with psychological interventions, the process of explanation of roles may proceed over several sessions.

Another area that requires very clear clarification of roles is forensic activities (Ethical Standards 7.01-7.06) and third-party requests for services (1.21). These issues are covered more fully under informed-consent guidelines.

Avoid Improper and Potentially Harmful Dual Relationships

Dual relationships have been divided into sexual and nonsexual categories. Sexual relationships with patients are prohibited in the ethical standards and in many laws. This area is relevant to clinical health psychology, as in any other area of practice. One issue that might be unique to the practice of clinical health psychology is the frequent interactions with other professions (e.g., physicians, dentists, and attorneys), which have different ethical codes. In some of these other professional ethical codes, there is no prohibition against sexual relationships with patients or former clients. The psychologist must beware of influences from other professionals, who could be behaving in an ethical manner for their profession but whose behavior would reflect a clear ethical violation for the psychologist.

Nonsexual dual relationships can occur in a number of ways. One area that appears particularly relevant to clinical health psychology is that of financial incentives provided by a third party for either hospital or outpatient services. This is specifically covered under Ethical Standard 1.27 (referrals and fees). Recently, there has been wide media coverage of this type of abuse by for-profit hospital corporations and medical corporations specializing in workers' compensation cases. For instance, one news story described a psychiatrist who did what the nursing staff had termed *wave therapy* on his inpatient cases. He would literally walk through the hospital corridor either waving or saying hello to his patients. These "sessions" were billed as full sessions of psychotherapy treatment. In this same situation, the hospital corporation was paying the doctor's overhead expenses (e.g., rent and secretarial) in exchange for the unwritten understanding that he would keep the census high in the hospital.

Other similar situations have also been common in the workers' compensation area, in which financial arrangements had been developed among doctors, insurance adjusters, and attorneys to form lucrative referral networks. These types of arrangements would be in violation of ethical standards and constitute harmful dual relationships (one with the patient and the other with an institution). In these situations, treatment decisions might be based on incentives other than patient needs.

Providing Mental Health Services to Those Served by Others

Ethical Standard 4.04 dictates the following:

> In deciding whether to offer or provide services to those already receiving mental health services elsewhere, psychologists carefully consider the treatment issues and the potential patient's or client's welfare. The psychologist discusses these issues with the patient or client, or another legally authorized person on behalf of the client, consults with the other service providers when appropriate, and proceeds with caution and sensitivity to the therapeutic issues.

In the practice of clinical health psychology, it is not uncommon to be referred a patient who is already in psychotherapy for other issues. It would not be unethical for the clinical health psychologist to proceed with one intervention while a different psychological intervention continues with another mental health professional. However, this can be a potentially confusing and conflictual situation if not managed correctly. Proper management includes clearly informing the patient as to the nature of the intervention and, with appropriate releases, discussing with the other professional how the treatment focuses will be kept distinct yet not work at cross-purposes. The guideline of putting the patient's welfare first is of absolute importance in making these types of clinical decisions.

PRINCIPLE C: PROFESSIONAL AND SCIENTIFIC RESPONSIBILITY

Psychologists uphold professional standards of conduct, clarify their professional roles and obligations, accept appropriate responsibility for their behavior, and adapt their methods to the needs of different populations. Psychologists consult with, refer to, or cooperate with other professionals and institutions to the extent needed to serve the best interests of their patients, clients, or other recipients of their services. Psychologists' moral standards and conduct are personal matters to the same degree as is true for any other person, except as psychologists' conduct may compromise their professional responsibilities or reduce public's trust in psychology and psychologists. Psychologists are concerned about the ethical compliance of their colleagues' scientific and professional conduct. When appropriate, they consult with colleagues in order to prevent or avoid unethical conduct.

This principle suggests that professional responsibility extends to personal, social, organizational, financial, and political involvements. For the clinical health psychologist, the principle of responsibility includes issues of quality assurance, increased responsibility for physical health, the risk of diffusion of responsibility for aspects of patient care in a large health care institution, cooperating with other professions, consulting with colleagues to avoid unethical behavior, and personal behavior.

Responsibility, Accountability, and Quality Assurance

There are three basic rights that determine the integrity of an independent profession (Jacobs, 1983). These include the following:

1. self-determination of the qualifications of candidates for entry into the profession

2. autonomy of professional functioning within the bounds established by social, moral, and legal responsibilities

3. self-regulation, exercised through peer review and based on a self-promulgated code of ethics, as well as self-promulgated standards of practice. (Jacobs, 1983, p. 20)

For psychologists, these aspects are reflected in the *General Guidelines for Providers of Psychological Services* (American Psychological Association, 1987) and the "Ethical Principles of Psychologists and Code of Conduct" (American Psychological Association, 1992). More specifically, the ethical principles of professional and scientific responsibility mandate the assurance of quality services. As part of this directive, psychologists should engage in quality assessment (a measurement of quality of care; Stricker, 1983), in which peer review and accountability are often essential elements.

Clinical health psychologists are governed by the same principles as those in general practice, thus, it is important that the psychologist obtain periodic review of his or her services. If one is working in a larger health care institution, peer review systems are often already in place, because they are a basic requirement for accreditation by the JCAHO. Models of peer review may differ as long as the goal of quality assurance is achieved (see Miller, 1981).

As an example, in a large health care organization with which we are familiar, a multidisciplinary peer review committee functions to review all mental health services. Membership on the committee rotates at regular intervals. All mental health staff members are required to submit to periodic chart review of cases, with feedback provided by the committee and appearances required as necessary. Cases are selected in a somewhat random fashion by choosing an arbitrary date and requiring the clinician to submit the first appointment seen or new case opened. The chart is reviewed in terms of assessment, diagnostic formulation, and treatment plan. Other considerations include documentation of treatment and relevant legal–ethical issues. The peer review committee is completely separate from administrative structures (although department administration also reviews a random sample of clinicians' charts on an annual basis). In another institution, a weekly case conference is held in which faculty present their own clinical cases for peer review, critique, and discussion in a group setting.

It is important for the clinical health psychologist that there be a reviewer who is qualified to assess the particular services delivered. For example, the child clinical therapist might not be competent to provide adequate peer review for a clinical health psychologist working on a coronary care unit and vice versa. The psychologist must work toward developing competent review of one's services.

The clinical health psychologist in independent practice has a difficult task in obtaining adequate peer review. Although there is nationwide peer review of services offered by psychologists built into many third-party payment systems (see Stricker, 1983; Stricker & Cohen, 1984; Theaman, 1984), these offer only cursory assessment of treatment, often guided primarily by insurance reimbursement policies. It can be useful to begin study groups or to contract for mutual peer review with colleagues in the community. This not only provides for quality assurance but also increases the probability that one is practicing in keeping with prevailing community standards. (See chapter 7 for a discussion of malpractice issues.)

Responsibility for Physical Health

One unique aspect of clinical health psychology is an increased responsibility for physical health. More so than in traditional practice, the clinical health psychologist deals with psychological factors associated with medical conditions. Therefore, such things as concomitant medical evaluation and management must be assured.

Related to the above, the clinical health psychologist is more often interacting with the medical care, both on an individual and an institutional level. This interaction can be intimately tied to patient care (for instance, being sure a particular medical evaluation is completed or helping a patient to confront health care systems problems). To successfully assume this responsibility for patient care, we have found that one must have many of the personal attributes discussed in chapter 2.

Risk of Diffusion of Responsibility

Another area relevant to the responsible practice of clinical health psychology is what Zerubavel (1980) called the "bureaucratization of responsibility." He held that within the hospital context, there was an ever-increasing segmentation of responsibility for patients. Hospital patients are cared for by a myriad of specialized clinicians. Thus, the responsibility for the patient does not lie with any one clinician but rather with a collective entity such as "the hospital" or "the team." (As Zerubavel pointed out, the legal responsibility for the patient lies ultimately with the attending physician.) With such a complex organizational structure, the likelihood of diffusion of responsibility or "floating responsibility" becomes very great. Under these conditions, passivity on the part of the clinical health psychologist can go unnoticed, because so many aspects of care are occurring simultaneously. For example, such things as treatment planning, record keeping, follow-up, communication with other professionals, and informed consent might not be responsibly completed. The psychologist must take care to provide responsible care to patients even when the structure of the system allows for a diffusion of responsibility or passivity.

Consult, Refer, and Cooperate

As indicated previously, patient care in both inpatient or outpatient settings is often provided by multiple clinicians of varying specialties. The psychologist usually provides only one aspect of the complete treatment package. It is imperative that regular communication occur among professionals. This is often achieved in team meetings but many times is accomplished chiefly through chart notes. One of the most common complaints we hear from our physician colleagues is that they have referred a patient to a psychologist (or other type of clinician) and have received no feedback on the evaluation or course of treatment. It is helpful to maintain written as well as verbal contact with other professionals to be sure treatments are coordinated in an appropriate manner.

Enhancement of professional relationships and good patient care is facilitated by having a working knowledge of what competencies are encompassed by other professions. For instance, on one case there could be a surgeon, infectious disease specialist, nutritionist, physical therapist, nursing staff, and clinical health psychologist. Having an understanding of what each profession does will help the psychologist communicate more effectively, gain respect, and be aware of treatment needs of the patient that are not being met adequately. As noted before, it is also important to be aware of varying ethical principles by which different professions abide.

Consult With Colleagues to Avoid Unethical Behavior

It is important to have colleagues to consult with regarding ethical dilemmas that occur in daily practice. Although these relationships can be established with those in general practice or other specialty areas, some of the consultants and colleagues should also practice in the area of clinical health psychology. Documentation of these consultations should be completed to substantiate the decision-making process if necessary. In addition, one can find assistance from local ethics boards.

Personal Behavior

The clinical health psychologist might need standards of behavior beyond those inherent in general psychological practice. As an extreme example, the clinician who is a heavy smoker, very overweight, drinks an excessive amount of coffee, and consumes more than a moderate amount of alcohol often has special problems in relationships with professional colleagues (physicians and psychologists) and patients, as well as in representing health psychology to the public. Although this could appear to be an infringement on one's personal freedom of choice, Principle C states clearly that personal behavior can come under ethical scrutiny as it impacts professional practice. The clinical health psychologist must be aware of personal health habits and make decisions about acceptable, ethical public behavior. These behaviors cannot be rigidly defined, nor should they be, but rather a range of acceptable behaviors must be decided on individually.

PRINCIPLE D: RESPECT OF PEOPLE'S RIGHTS AND DIGNITY

Psychologists accord appropriate respect to the fundamental rights, dignity, and worth of all people. They respect the rights of individuals to privacy, confidentiality, self-determination, and autonomy, mindful that legal and other obligations may lead to inconsistency and conflict with the exercise of these rights. Psychologists are aware of cultural, individual, and role differences, including those due to age, gender, race, ethnicity, national origin, religion, sexual orientation, disability, language, and socioeconomic status. Psychologists try to eliminate the effect on their work of biases based on those factors, and they do not knowingly participate in or condone unfair discriminatory practices.

This principle primarily deals with issues of privileged information and confidentiality. It also addresses the issue of human differences and avoiding the impositions of one's values onto patients, as previously discussed.

Privileged Versus Confidential Information

Privileged communication refers to the legal confidentiality between psychologist and patient. The limits of this privilege are determined by state statutes and vary from state to state. The privilege of confidentiality lies with the patient, and except in special circumstances, the psychologist must abide by the patient's determination.

Confidentiality is an ethical concept, but it is influenced by legal guidelines (e.g., mandates to breach confidentiality to prevent self-harm or harm to others; see chapter 7). The psychologist must maintain a confidential relationship with the patient and obtain permission before releasing information. As can be seen in Tables 6.1 and 6.2, confidentiality issues are paramount ethical challenges in clinical practice.

Special Confidentiality Problems in Clinical Health Psychology

Earlier chapters noted some of the special confidentiality problems in clinical health psychology, including providing information to the referral source, charting treatment notes in a more circulated medical record versus a less available psychological record, and releasing medical records that contain psychological treatment notes to an outside source. Other problems arise in providing services to multiple-bed hospital rooms, case discussion within the context of a multidisciplinary team approach, and discussion of the patient's psychological status with members of the patient's family.

Generally, the clinical health psychologist should strive to maximize confidentiality. One should also inform the patient of the limits to confidentiality set either by law or by institutional organization. For instance, finding a setting to conduct confidential psychological services on a medical–surgical unit can be very difficult. Patient consultation rooms are sometimes available, but these are often heavily scheduled. If the patient is nonambulatory and is in a multiple-bed room, it may not be possible to maintain confidentiality (unless services can be scheduled when other patients are out of the room). The patient should be *explicitly* given the option of declining services if not comfortable with the situation; otherwise, the pressure from an "authoritative" professional may induce the patient to engage in behavior without true consent. Similarly, when a patient's psychological status is to be discussed in the context of a team-treatment approach, the patient should be informed of what material will be discussed.

Last, we have found that pressure from family members to discuss the patient's psychological status often arises in the case of brain dysfunction; "conversion" disorders; and compliance problems, which can be closely related to family-systems issues (e.g., eating disorders, compliance with insulin-treatment regimens, or chronic-pain management). If the patient is not able to make informed decisions, such as in brain dysfunction cases, legal and ethical guidelines may allow release of confidential information to an appointed person as necessary. Except in these instances, the process of obtaining a written release of confidential information should be followed, as in any traditional psychological case.

PRINCIPLE E: CONCERN FOR OTHERS' WELFARE

Psychologists seek to contribute to the welfare of those with whom they interact professionally. In their professional actions, psychologists weigh the welfare and rights of their patients or clients, students, supervisees, human research participants, and other affected persons, and the welfare of animal subjects of research. When conflicts occur among psychologists' obligations or concerns, they attempt to resolve these conflicts and to perform their roles in a responsible fashion that avoids or minimizes harm. Psychologists are sensitive to real and ascribed differences in power between themselves and others, and they do not exploit or mislead other people during or after professional relationships.

A primary purpose of Principle E is to safeguard a consumer of psychological services against exploitation. The psychologist must be aware of such issues as informed consent, conflicts of interest between treatment of the patient and employing institutions, providing services at the request of a third party, and patients who do not benefit from treatment.

Informed Consent

The doctrine of informed consent was developed so that patients could weigh the risks and benefits of a treatment and determine for themselves if they wanted to participate (Barton & Sanborn, 1978; Knapp & Vande-Creek, 1981). The patient should understand the nature of the proposed treatment, the risks and likelihood of success, and available alternative treatments. Ideally, the procedure of informed consent is meant to force the health care professional to make the patient more of an equal bargaining partner in treatment decisions (A. A. Stone, 1979). There has been an increase in interest in informed consent for medical and psychological treatments with the consumerism movement among patients and judicial involvement in this area (Widiger & Rorer, 1984). Although informed consent had not been specifically addressed in previous ethical codes, it is addressed in the most recent revision. Informed consent is contained under Ethical Standards 4.01 and 4.02. These are summarized in the following:

> Psychologists discuss with clients or patients as early as is feasible in the therapeutic relationship appropriate issues, such as the nature and anticipated course of therapy, fees, and confidentiality (4.01a); information about the psychologist's supervisor if supervision is being done (4.01b); and, if the therapist is an intern (4.01c).

Psychologists make reasonable efforts to answer patients' questions and to avoid apparent misunderstandings about therapy. Whenever possible, psychologists provide oral and/or written information, using language that is reasonably understandable to the patient or client. (4.01.d)

Psychologists obtain appropriate informed consent to therapy or related procedures, using language that is reasonably understandable to participants. The content of informed consent will vary depending on many circumstances; however, informed consent generally implies that the person (1) has the capacity to consent, (2) has been informed of significant information concerning the procedure, (3) has freely and without undue influence expressed consent, and (4) consent has been appropriately documented.(4.02a)

The legal concept of informed consent includes *capacity, information,* and *voluntariness. Capacity* means that a patient must have the ability to make rational decisions (this tenet often excludes children and the developmentally disabled from being able to give informed consent and necessitates proxy consent by a guardian). *Information* consists of both the substance of the material presented and the manner in which it is given. It is gauged by demonstrated understanding by the patient. *Voluntariness* means that the patient was able to exercise free choice, without coercion, in making the decision.

Inadequate informed consent is unethical and has been grounds for malpractice in medicine (Cohen & Mariano, 1982). A significant problem is how much to actually disclose about treatment (Halperin, 1980; B. M. Schutz, 1982). Adequate disclosure is legally determined by the community standard (telling patients what other practitioners in the community would tell their patients under similar circumstances) and "the reasonable person" statute (telling the patient what a reasonable person would need to know to make an informed decision). However, these guidelines actually offer the practitioner little guidance (A. A. Stone, 1979).

Other problems are revealed by demonstrations that informed-consent procedures are often inadequate when patient understanding and retention of the material are assessed (see Ley, 1982, for review). Such problems are sometimes related to readability of consent forms. For example,

Grunder (1980) found that each of five surgical-consent forms analyzed from major Eastern hospitals were written at the upper undergraduate or graduate level of language; four of the five were at the level of a scientific journal. In addition, it has been found that although a majority of patients report that "just the right amount" of information has been given, they often remember very little (Cassileth, Zupkis, Sutton-Smith, & March, 1980). Research findings in this area present serious problems for the practitioner in obtaining informed consent. Because of legal pressures, many medical professionals have gone to what might be considered the extreme position of providing all possible risks in graphic detail to ensure completeness. Problems with this approach and suggestions for a process of informed consent are discussed later.

Clinical health psychologists may be involved in several aspects of informed consent in the medical setting. In our work, we are often involved in (a) helping the physician to explore the patient's health belief model about aspects of treatment and determining the extent of the patient's understanding or possible misconceptions; (b) working with patients to encourage behaviors that will increase the likelihood of "true" informed consent (including determining what questions the patient has about the medical treatment and teaching the patient how to obtain the information from the physician); and (c) helping patients deal with the increase in feelings of uncertainty about treatment, which often occur after explicit informed-consent procedures are carried out.

Clinical health psychologists must also deal with the issue of informed consent in the course of service delivery of psychological services. Many practitioners view the informed consent with contempt and rarely provide information about alternate treatments. Gutheil, Bursztajn, Hamm, and Brodsky (1983) suggested that the informed-consent process was a double-edged sword. The positive aspect is that it clarifies options and stimulates understanding. The negative aspect is that it can increase the patient's having to accept more uncertainty about treatment and decrease belief in the doctor's ability to cure. We agree with Gutheil et al. (1983) that the informed-consent procedure should be entered into as a process of mutual discovery rather than as a formality. We outline the rationale for service, treatment plan, and goals in an atmosphere of open negotiation. Once a plan is formulated, it is useful to have the patient paraphrase their understanding of the treatment (or evaluation), so that misperceptions can be corrected.

We have found that the process of informed consent can often be difficult with patients referred to a clinical health psychologist. Many times, the physician has not given the patient much information about our services, or the physician has given incorrect information. Furthermore, the patient is being expected to shift from a biomedical orientation to a biopsychosocial approach. Overwhelming the patient in the first session with details of a treatment plan and expectations can result in premature termination. The informed-consent procedure can extend over many sessions, in fact, over the entire course of treatment. Skills in working with people of different backgrounds (competency) facilitate the informed-consent process.

Conflicts of Interest

When one interacts with the medical system, conflicts of interest can arise. There can occur a basic, unacknowledged, antagonistic relationship between patient and hospital or employee of the institution (Bazelon, 1974). As Noll (1976) stated, "whenever the mental health professional is employed by an agency or by an institution, the institution needs will almost invariably supersede those of the patient" (p. 1451). Thus, the clinical health psychologist may have a "hidden agenda" when consulting to a medical–surgical unit—depending on the needs of the staff and the reason for the consultation request.

> The patient was a 37-year-old, married woman, who had been diagnosed as having lung cancer with multiple metastases. The prognosis was very poor. She had been through several courses of chemotherapy without significant benefit. A more experimental drug had been suggested, but the patient refused, stating that she would rather be discharged to home. A referral for psychological evaluation of the patient's mental status was made. When the clinical health psychologist arrived on the unit, it was verbally commu-

nicated to her by the staff that "the patient needed to be convinced to stay in the hospital for further treatment because it was her only hope of survival." The psychological evaluation revealed that the patient had carefully considered her options in treatment, was fully informed about risks and benefits of each alternative, and had made a decision with a clear sensorium and intact mental status. The psychologist reported the results of her evaluation to the staff and subsequently dealt with the anger and frustration staff had toward both her and the patient.

In this example, the psychologist might have easily been influenced by staff issues and have thus seen the patient with a goal of convincing her to have the experimental treatment. Psychologists must remember to be responsible to the patient, to take into account the needs of the patient versus those of the staff, and to clarify the nature of their loyalties and responsibilities.

Services at the Request of a Third Party

The services of a clinical health psychologist are often requested by a physician to provide either an evaluation, treatment, or both. The psychologist must always determine the extent of the patient's understanding as to why the consultation was requested and whether services are actually necessary. We find that many times the physician has not told the patient a consultation had been ordered. As with any other case, informed consent must be acquired before proceeding. Furthermore, many consultation requests are found to result from projection on the part of providers, who are experiencing frustration, anger, depression, or some other emotional response to the patient. Intervention is sometimes more appropriately targeted at the staff rather than the patient. A thorny ethical problem that then arises is determining who is going to pay for the staff intervention.

Other areas in which the services of a clinical health psychologist are often requested by a third party include neuropsychological assessment, psychological evaluation for a specific treatment program or procedure, and evaluation as part of filing a workers' compensation or disability claim.

Patients are often not aware that in requesting these programs to pay for services, they must agree to release their psychological evaluation as a condition of reimbursement. In any of the above situations, the psychologist must fully inform the patient as to the nature of the assessment, the purpose, what the results will be used for, who requested the evaluation, and who will pay for it (Cross & Deardorff, 1987).

Patients Who Do Not Benefit From Treatment

If a patient does not benefit from treatment after a reasonable trial, the psychologist is ethically mandated to terminate the treatment and to help with an appropriate referral. The clinical health psychologist will often receive referrals who are "last-option" treatments, in that all previous traditional medical treatments have failed (e.g., chronic-pain syndromes, tinnitus, blepharospasm, or atypical facial pain). In these cases, the psychological referral is to "give it a try," because there appear to be no other options. These cases represent clinical challenges in which the therapist must gauge carefully, in realistic negotiation with the patient, when an adequate trial of treatment has been accomplished without significant benefit. The following case illustrates such a decision:

> The patient was a 78-year-old married woman with a post-herpetic neuralgia secondary to having herpes zoster several years before. The pain, as well as an excoriated skin surface, was distributed in a dermatomal pattern on the right side of the face and neck. Extensive dermatological treatments had failed to provide relief, and the patient was referred for pain management. Evaluation indicated that the symptoms did fluctuate, with stress and tension being related to an exacerbation of the condition and relaxed states being associated with symptom relief. A treatment plan was formulated, including relaxation training with suggestions for hypnotic analgesia. After the patient had gained the ability to relax across all settings and had practiced routinely with the auto hypnosis, no pain relief, as documented by symptom charting, had occurred. It was decided that the patient would not benefit from further treatment with that thera-

pist and that an adequate trial had been given. The patient was referred for evaluation for a trial of an antidepressant and pheno-
thiazine combination (found useful in some cases by Loeser, 1986).
She was also given a referral to another psychologist experienced in
hypnotic analgesia, to see whether a different approach might be
beneficial.

In this example, the psychologist had to make a decision, with the patient's
full participation, as to when an adequate trial had been attempted. The
psychologist must also provide a referral if other treatments are available.
The termination process in these cases must be handled carefully to prevent iatrogenic deterioration effects (e.g., patient being left with a "failure
experience") and to capitalize on the positive effects, however small, of the
treatment experience.

UNDERSTANDING VERSUS APPLYING THE ETHICAL PRINCIPLES

An important aspect of professional ethics that is just now being researched is the difference between understanding and implementing ethical principles. This is the "should" versus "would" discrepancy. Most research suggests that clinicians generally have high-quality ethical
decision-making capacity but that this is put into practice to a lesser degree (see Smith, McGuire, Abbott, & Blau, 1991; Wilkins, McGuire, Abbott & Blau, 1990, for review).

For instance, Wilkins et al. (1990) conducted a survey of a random
sample of American Psychological Association members. Research participants were presented with four scenarios that reflected ethical dilemmas
in the areas of alcohol-related impairment, dual-role sexual abuse of a
client, confidentiality, and need for referral related to competence limits.
Participants were asked what they should do according to the American
Psychological Association Ethical Principles and what they would do if actually faced with the situation. These were rated on a scale from *do nothing* (least restrictive) to *report the individual to the ethics board* (most restrictive). Results confirmed that respondents were generally able to

recognize ethical conflicts that required action. However, significant differences were found when the "should" ratings were compared with what the respondents "would" do (the "should" results were more restrictive than the "would" results). One important finding was that when the ethical violation was more clear-cut (e.g., misconduct related to sexual abuse or impairment due to substance abuse) and there was a consensus as to what to do vis-à-vis the ethical principles, there was increased congruence between what should and would be done.

These findings are relevant to all areas of psychological practice. All clinicians need to be aware of the likelihood of experiencing the should/would difference. Especially applicable to clinical health psychology is the finding that practitioners will have increased difficulty applying the ethical principles that are defined in a more ambiguous fashion. This might include such principles as those of confidentiality, nonsexual dual relationships, and informed consent. As discussed in previous sections, the clinical health psychologist might be presented with challenges in these areas more frequently than other areas of practice.

SUGGESTED READINGS

American Psychological Association. (1985). *Standards for educational and psychological testing.* Washington, DC: Author.

American Psychological Association. (1986). *Guidelines for computer-based tests and interpretations.* Washington, DC: Author.

American Psychological Association. (1987). *General guidelines for providers of psychological services.* Washington, DC: Author.

American Psychological Association. (1992). Ethical principles of psychologists and code of conduct. *American Psychologist, 47,* 1597–1611.

Keith-Spiegel, P., & Koocher, G. P. (1985). *Ethics in psychology.* New York: Random House.

Pope, K. S. (1990). Ethical and malpractice issues in hospital practice. *American Psychologist, 45,* 1066–1070.

Pope, K. S., & Vasquez, M. J. T. (1993). *Ethics in psychotherapy and counseling.* San Francisco: Jossey-Bass.

7

Malpractice Risks in Clinical Health Psychology

I deally, malpractice law serves three important social functions (Klein & Glover, 1983). First, it protects the public from professional wrongdoing by providing aversive consequences for misconduct. Second, it transfers the "loss" from one party to another who more so deserves to pay. Third, it distributes the cost of a professional's negligent conduct across the profession at large through insurance premiums. In these ways, the threat of malpractice provides constant pressure on professional communities to self-regulate and self-scrutinize while giving the public a mechanism to recompense when this does not occur.

As evidenced by spiraling medical costs, partially related to increased malpractice litigation, it appears that the social function of malpractice law has been disrupted by consumers' propensity to initiate litigation. This may either be where negligence has occurred or, increasingly, where no

---

This chapter provides an analysis of some legal issues that may arise in the practice of clinical health psychology. It does not provide legal advice; nor should it substitute for the assistance of legal counsel, should a practitioner encounter legal issues in his or her practice. The proper handling of any particular situation depends on the facts unique to that situation and the applicable laws. Those laws may differ from state to state and also may change with some frequency. Psychologists who encounter legal issues in their practices should consult with a competent attorney familiar with laws in their state.

negligence is ultimately determined. We speculate that skepticism about health care treatment and heightened angry affect over medical costs combined with an increase in the number of attorneys per capita have fostered the likelihood of malpractice litigation occurring (VandeCreek & Stout, 1993). Costs are incurred in such legal actions, even if the professional is exonerated. Often, the case will be settled out of court in an effort to avoid the higher expenditures regardless of whether there was misconduct, thus reinforcing suit-filing behavior independent of the merits of the case (VandeCreek & Stout, 1993). There is a societal cost for such freedom of action, and this is ultimately passed back to consumers.

Mental health professionals have not been threatened by malpractice in the same magnitude as physicians. This is thought to be due to the nature of the therapist–patient relationship as inhibiting such action (Charles, 1993) and to the difficulty in proving the four malpractice standards to be described below. However, along with a greater public awareness of psychologists' professional behavior (Wright, 1981), malpractice claims in psychology are on the increase—a trend that is likely to continue (Stromberg & Dellinger, 1993). Although the American Psychological Association's Insurance Trust had relatively few claims filed in the first 27 years of operation, between 1955 and 1982 (Fisher, 1985; Wright, 1981), there was a dramatic rise in claims from 1982 to 1986. This increase in litigation against psychologists was reflected in a 700% rise in insurance premiums in the 2-year period from 1984 to 1986 (Fisher, 1985; Turkington, 1986). Although premiums remained fairly constant from 1986 to 1989 (Dorken, 1990), they again have increased from 1990 to the present.

Beyond public scrutiny of general psychological practice, psychologists working in the area of clinical health psychology open themselves to a myriad of new malpractice liability risks of which they should be aware (Knapp & VandeCreek, 1981). First, because clinical health psychologists practice in close concert with the medical profession and deal more often with physical problems, they run the risk of inadvertently practicing medicine without a license. Second, the nature of the therapist–patient relationship, often thought to protect the traditional psychotherapy practitioner against malpractice, can be very different in many clinical health psychology cases. Third, physical harm may be much more likely in the practice of clinical health psychology than in more traditional psychological treatment. This chapter delineates general concepts of psychological malpractice and focuses on those high-risk areas pertinent to clinical health psychology.

PSYCHOLOGICAL MALPRACTICE

Psychological Malpractice Defined

Malpractice is a professional error of commission or omission. Malpractice suits have been generally founded in tort or contract law as opposed to criminal law. The difference is that the former pertains to acts damaging to a person whereas the latter applies to transgression against society (Schutz, 1982). To make a successful case of malpractice, the plaintiff must prove, by a preponderance of evidence, the following four elements (Deardorff, Cross, & Hupprich, 1984; Feldman & Ward, 1979; Furrow, 1980; Harris, 1973): (a) that the defendant/practitioner owed a "duty" to the patient, (b) that the defendant/practitioner's behavior fell below the acceptable standard of care or that the "duty" owed to the plaintiff was breached, (c) that the defendant/practitioner's act or omission was the proximate cause of the plaintiff's injury, and (d) that an injury was actually sustained by the plaintiff. Each element is discussed below, with its implications for clinical health psychology. Each of these must be demonstrated by a preponderance of evidence. They are summarized by the 4D mnemonic: Dereliction of–Duty–Directly causing–Damages (Rachlin, 1984). Each of these areas are discussed more fully below.

Owing a Duty to the Patient

The first of these allegations, that the practitioner owed a duty to the patient, is usually the easiest to prove (Schutz, 1982). This basically involves proving that a professional relationship existed between the psychologist and patient; such things as a contract or bill for services, or chart notes, are sufficient evidence. Related to this contract, when a professional accepts a case, he or she owes a duty to possess the level of skill to treat commensurate with that possessed by the average member of the profession in good standing in the community. Furthermore this skill and learning must be applied with reasonable care (Deardorff et al., 1984; "Professional Negligence," 1973).

Proving a Breach of Duty

To prove a breach of duty, the plaintiff must show that the practitioner did not have the proper knowledge to treat or that this knowledge was misapplied. Outrageous actions such as beating a patient (*Hammer v. Rosen*, 1960) or engaging in sexual contact with a patient as part of treatment (*Roy v. Hartogs*, 1975) can provide a prima facie case of malpractice (Cross & Deardorff, 1987; Knapp, 1980). Other than cases of this nature, proving a breach of duty has, historically, been difficult in an ambiguous practice such as psychotherapy. However, this may not be as true in the area of clinical health psychology. As discussed by Knapp and VandeCreek (1981), clinical health psychologists may have to adhere to more specifiable standards of care than traditional psychologists, because the techniques used can often be more explicitly delineated. Many treatments used in the practice of health psychology arise from behavioral, cognitive, and social learning frameworks that have a strong empirical base; thus, aspects of treatment are often more measurable than in more psychodynamically oriented approaches. In the area of psychodiagnosis, techniques such as neuropsychological assessment are more open to validation and verification than more traditional projective techniques.

Generally, the standard of care against which the practitioner's behavior can be judged in malpractice litigation is established by expert testimony. In the past, it has been difficult to get members of a profession to testify against one another (Markus, 1965), but this is less problematic since the courts abandoned the "locality rule" (which required the expert witness to be from the same geographical area as the defendant/practitioner). This change in court practice has had two important implications. First, it has successfully diminished the "conspiracy of silence" related to expert witness testimony (Slovenko, 1978). Second, it means that a reasonable standard of care for psychological practice may be set at the national standard instead of a community standard and that the practitioner may have malpractice liability where state standards are below those of the national level (Pope, Simpson, & Myron, 1978). This may be especially relevant for the practice of clinical health psychology, because it is a relatively new and expanding area. Because there are likely to be fewer clinical health psychologists in a community, the court would be forced to draw expert witnesses from a more national geographical territory (Knapp & VandeCreek, 1981). Therefore, the standard of care may be set commensurate with a national, rather than a state, average minimum level of practice expertise. With this in mind, "psychologists who expand their practices into this specialty should obtain appropriate training and expertise before presenting themselves to the public as specialists" (Knapp & VandeCreek, 1981, p. 680).

Proving Proximate Cause of Patient's Injury

The next allegation to prove is that the plaintiff's injury was either directly caused by the practitioner's action or a reasonably foreseeable consequence of such behavior. Where the practitioner's behavior is not outrageous, proving this essential causal link between professional conduct and mental injury can be very difficult (Tarshis, 1972). However, if the injury is physical, proof is much easier (Dawidoff, 1966). In the practice of clinical health psychology, the injury is more likely to be physical, because the patient is often being treated for psychological factors affecting a physical condition. An example of this might be a psychologist encouraging a cardiac patient to engage in an inappropriate amount of exercise without medical clearance and thus inducing a myocardial infarction.

Establishment of Injury

The last element the plaintiff must demonstrate is that harm or injury was suffered. Where physical harm has been sustained, it is easier to establish injury and specify monetary compensation; where the injury is emotional or psychological, it can be very difficult to establish compensation amounts (Klein & Glover, 1983). For instance, in the example of the cardiac patient, it would be relatively easier to estimate compensation on the basis of medical costs, physical disability, lost wages, and pain–suffering than in an emotional injury case.

AREAS OF MALPRACTICE RISK IN CLINICAL HEALTH PSYCHOLOGY

It is important to be familiar with high-risk areas for psychological malpractice. This is best done by investigating trends in claims made as well as losses incurred by the malpractice insurance carrier. Table 7.1 shows the frequency and severity of claims made against psychologists as of 1991. These data were adapted from VandeCreek and Stout (1993).

As can be seen in Table 7.1, sexual misconduct, incorrect treatment, evaluation, confidentiality, incorrect diagnosis, and suicide-related cases are areas of high-frequency claims. By far the greatest area of loss in terms of malpractice claims and awards is sexual misconduct. The following sections discuss areas of malpractice risk with a particular focus on the practice of clinical health psychology.

Table 7.1

Frequency and Severity of Claims Against Psychologists as of 1991

Malpractice area	% of claims	% of costs
Sexual misconduct	19	50
Incorrect treatment	15	13
Evaluation	11	5
Confidentiality breach	7	3
Incorrect diagnosis	6	6
Suicide-related	6	11
Countersuit for fee collection	4	<2
Defamation, libel–slander	4	<2
Loss of child custody/visitation	3	<2
Improper death of patients	2	<2
Failure to protect/warn	<1	<2

Practicing Medicine Without a License

One of the primary increased malpractice risks one encounters in moving from general clinical work to clinical health psychology involvement is practicing medicine without a license. Several authors (Cohen, 1979; Furrow, 1980; Knapp & VandeCreek, 1981) addressed this increased malpractice liability, and their discussions are summarized below.

The practice of medicine can be generally defined as "persons who diagnose or treat disease, or who represent themselves as healers of disease" (Knapp & VandeCreek, 1981, p. 678). Although the practice of medicine is clear in such things as surgery or chemotherapy, in other areas it becomes much less definable. These less clear areas relevant to "drugless healers" (e.g., psychologists) include diagnosing and treating patients within the bounds of one's own discipline and not crossing over into medical practice. Consider the following example:

> A. J. was a 37-year-old woman, who presented with a complaint of headaches that had occurred daily over the past year. The headaches were characterized by a bandlike pain encircling the head. The pain began in the suboccipital region and radiated to posterior cervical areas. A. J. reported no associated visual or gastrointestinal symptoms. She also stated that the headaches were exacerbated by "stress," typically gaining in intensity over the course of the day. A. J. had not had a recent physical exam. The psychologist performing the evaluation diagnosed the case as stress-related muscle-contraction headaches and began treatment.

There are two problems with this case from both liability and ethical standpoints. First, A. J. had not had an appropriate medical workup related to the chief complaint. Within the practice of clinical health psychology, medical evaluation is almost always necessary. Second, she had not received a diagnosis of muscle-contraction headaches from a physician. Even though the symptom pattern was certainly suggestive of this disorder, from a legal viewpoint the psychologist could be diagnosing a disease that would be considered within the realm of medical practice. This is because the "practitioner gave an opinion as to the origin or cause of the patient's physical ailments" (Knapp & VandeCreek, 1981, p. 678). However, it would be perfectly appropriate for the health psychologist to make a diagnosis on Axis I of the *DSM–IV* system (American Psychiatric Association, 1994), such as psychological factors affecting physical condition, because the psychologist would not be diagnosing the physical etiology of the problem.

Another problem is the legal implications of making a diagnosis on Axis III of the *DSM–IV*. The nonphysician (or the psychiatrist who has not done a physical workup) must be careful not to give an Axis III diagnosis that he or she is either unqualified or unprepared to make. When recording an Axis III diagnosis, we find it most prudent to state where the physical diagnosis originated (e.g., "migraine headache per the patient"; "per the medical record"; "per the referral"). One must also take care in stating the source of the physical diagnosis in the text of the evaluation report. We have often seen statements that suggested that the psychologist was making physical diagnoses.

Beyond diagnosing, clinical health psychologists must take care in treating physical disease. In the practice of clinical health psychology, the practitioner is often involved in the psychological or psychophysiological treatment of a physical problem. When the psychological treatment interferes or takes the place of appropriate medical treatment (without informed consent), it could be grounds for malpractice. There is a legal case history of nonphysician practitioners encouraging their patients to leave standard medical treatment and being held liable (see Cohen, 1979; Knapp & VandeCreek, 1981). Consider the following two examples:

B. J. was a 45-year-old man referred for adjunctive psychophysiological treatment of his borderline hypertension (HTN). He was taking dyazide, which was controlling his HTN adequately, but he was excited about learning self-control techniques, because of the aversive side effects of the medication. As the biofeedback and psychotherapy progressed, B. J. was becoming increasingly able to decrease his blood pressure while relaxing in the clinic. He incessantly asked his therapist about reducing his medication with continued successful training. The psychologist suggested this was an appropriate goal, and he was encouraged to carefully experiment with lower medication dosages while monitoring his HTN with a home-monitoring unit.

The patient was an 82-year-old woman with congestive heart failure (CHF), who was referred for treatment of a psychophysiological disorder. The patient was on a complex medication regimen consisting of diuretics, potassium, and valium as needed (PRN) for anxiety and sleep. The patient was seen for an evaluation and then scheduled for a psychophysiological baseline assessment. She was instructed not to take the valium before the appointment, so that an accurate baseline assessment could be done. The patient came in the next week, having not taken any of her medications for the day. Her legs were slightly edematous due to water retention. The patient had thought the clinical health psychologist prescribed that she not take any of her medications a day before the evaluation.

These two cases present clear examples of a psychologist practicing medicine. This is not because reducing medications as the psychological techniques became more effective was an inappropriate goal, but because these treatment directives must be done by the primary physician on the basis of mutual consultation. Even more difficult decisions involve patients who are referred for treatment and are on PRN medications. For example, we see many patients referred for psychophysiological treatment of their intractable chronic headaches who are on PRN analgesic medication. Although there is no legal case history of whether a nonphysician health care practitioner can be held liable for problems resulting from encouraging a patient to reduce PRN medications as treatment proceeds, the most prudent approach is to discuss this strategy with the physician and to document the results of this consultation.

Furthermore, the clinical health psychologist must be careful to ensure that the patient does not mistake him or her for a physician. If this occurs, the practitioner may be held accountable for practicing medicine if a problem arises. In many medical centers, the likelihood of this occurring is increased by the "dress code" of the institution. Psychologists on both inpatient and outpatient services often wear traditional white lab coats. This can be confusing to patients—a confusion which can be readily ascertained by the nature of the patient's questions. In keeping with informed-consent procedures, on initial contact, we make a concise statement about the psychologist's realm of expertise, which helps to avoid many problems in this area.

In general, on the basis of case law involving other nonphysician health care professionals being sued for practicing medicine without a license, certain recommendations for practice are given: First, in providing psychological treatment for medical patients, one must work closely with the medical specialist. A joint treatment plan should be established; furthermore, this plan should be explicitly stated to the patient, so that he or she understands which aspects of treatment will be handled by each professional. Second, when a self-referred patient seeks treatment for a problem involving a physical complaint, a medical evaluation should be insisted on before treatment ensues. Third, one should communicate and consult, in both verbal and written form, with the primary physician on a periodic basis, so that both medical and psychological treatments can be jointly adjusted as appropriate. These consultations should be documented.

Failure to Refer or to Communicate

This area of malpractice risk is closely associated with practicing medicine without a license. We address this issue as it relates to working with a physician or providing treatment for a physical disorder. As we discussed in chapter 6, the clinical health psychologist is in a position of having increased responsibility for physical health. Malpractice issues can arise when this responsibility is managed in a negligent fashion not in keeping with a community standard.

The issue of psychologists being involved with health and medical problems is being vigorously debated in state and federal legislative arenas. The concern (voiced primarily by medicine) is that psychologists are nonmedical providers and therefore cannot accurately diagnose mental disorders, will misdiagnose physical conditions as psychological problems, will fail to recognize medical problems, and will fail to refer to physicians for needed medical care. It appears that these concerns are ill founded. Dorken (1990) reviewed the claims experience of the American Psychological Association Insurance Trust (APA–IT) from 1976 to 1989. He found that, "there has never been a court decision/award for a medical malpractice or failure to diagnosis/refer a medical problem by a psychologist" (Dorken, 1990, p. 152)

Even so, other cases suggest this may be an area of increasing malpractice risk for the clinical health psychologist. For instance, in one case, a psychologist failed to conduct an adequate mental status examination of the patient and then failed to adequately report any results of the evaluation to the psychiatrist also working on the case. As a result, the psychiatrist prescribed medication that "injured" the patient (*Chambers v. Ingram*, 1988). Stromberg and Dellinger (1993) discussed that "this case represents a good lesson in how psychologists, although they cannot usually prescribe medications, may have liability relating to the patient's use of medications" (p. 7). In another case, a psychiatrist failed to rule out a physical cause for the patient's symptoms. The patient was involved in 11 years of psychotherapy before the condition was traced to a brain tumor (*Russo v. Ascher*, 1988; Stromberg & Dellinger, 1993). The psychiatrist was found negligent for not having ruled out a serious physical etiology for the presenting symptoms.

The two examples above can easily be extrapolated to the practice of clinical health psychology. As we discussed in the previous section, if the psychologist is treating a physical problem, it is imperative that a physician is also involved. In addition, open communication is important to discuss problems and progress. For instance, the patient may be seeing the psychologist much more frequently than the physician. In this situation, the psychologist may be the first to discover such things as side effects to medications or occurrence of additional physical symptoms. On the basis of the cases above, the psychologist may have a duty to encourage the patient to return for medical evaluation or to communicate these concerns and findings to the physician. These actions must be carefully documented. Of course, this is in keeping with good clinical practice anyway.

Duty to Prevent Patients From Harming Themselves

Whenever a suicidal patient presents to a mental health professional, action must be taken to prevent self-harm. Where suicidal threats are not taken seriously or where an inadequate (commensurate with the community standard of care) evaluation is done, the practitioner may be liable in malpractice action (Deardorff et. al., 1984).

The suicidal patient may present a special risk for the clinical health psychologist working in a medical setting. More so than in traditional outpatient practice, clinical health psychologists evaluate suicidal patients in the emergency room and as medical inpatients. Thus, the evaluation and diagnosis of suicidality must be done rapidly and, typically, outside the context of a longer term treatment relationship. The clinical health psychologist must be familiar with the assessment of the suicidal patient and precautionary measures that are appropriate (see Guggenheim, 1978, for review). When a therapist follows accepted evaluation and diagnostic procedures and these do not reveal suicidality in a patient who subsequently commits suicide, there are no grounds for malpractice (*Baker v. United States*, 1964; see also Hogan, 1979, for a review of 38 cases involving suicidality). As concluded by the court in a recent case, "a doctor is not a . . . guarantor of the correctness of his diagnosis; the requirement is [merely] that he use proper care and skill. . . . The question is not whether the physician made a mistake in diagnosis, but rather whether he failed to conform to the accepted standard of care" (*Schuster v. Altenberg*, 1988; Stromberg & Dellinger, 1993).

In addressing the process of managing the suicidal patient, Exhibit 7.1 depicts several questions that the clinician should ask him- or herself to guide the decision process (Bursztajn, Gutheil, Hamm, & Brodsky, 1983; Gutheil, Bursztajn, Hamm, & Brodsky, 1983). The questions are in keeping with sound clinical practice and are derived from legal standards of care against which professional behavior is judged. As can be seen in Exhibit 7.1, these standards include the following: what a reasonable and prudent practitioner would do under similar circumstances, what the community standard of care is, and whether treatment benefits were maximized in relation to possible costs or risks. The first two of these standards are essentially equivalent to the first two malpractice guidelines discussed earlier (that the practitioner owed a duty to the patient and that the practitioner's professional behavior fell below an acceptable standard of care). The last guideline is summarized by Cross and Deardorff (1987) in the following way:

> This is a cost benefit analysis in making treatment decisions. Related to the suicidal patient, the courts have not made it an ultimate goal that all suicides be prevented at any cost. Rather, the risks of certain treatment decisions (e.g., loosening the restraints on a suicidal patient or deciding to treat a suicidal patient on an outpatient basis) must be weighed against the therapeutic benefits to be gained (e.g., an increase in functioning). Thus, a practitioner does not have to be proved "right" by outcome, but rather that clinical judgment and decision-making fell within the three standards of care. (p. 68)

If a practitioner determines a patient to be suicidal, precautionary measures such as involuntary or voluntary commitment for observation may have to be invoked. Although, in some cases, using sound clinical judgment, the suicidal patient may be most appropriately managed on an outpatient basis. As long as the standard of care is commensurate with community standards and the treatment decision is in the best interests of the patient, there would be no grounds for negligence (see Bongar, Maris, Berman, & Litman, 1992, for a review). If a patient is already in the hospital on a medical–surgical unit, other special issues arise. These include determining specific suicide precautions, which must be taken, and making sure the staff carries them out.

Determination of the suicide precautions that must be taken is guided by a thorough assessment and evaluation of the patient. Exhibit 7.2 depicts suicide precautions that can be used, on a medical–surgical unit, listed from most restrictive to least restrictive alternatives. Suicide precautions must be specified precisely in written form either in the progress notes or in the doctor's orders section of the chart (depending on hospi-

Exhibit 7.1

Questions Derived From Legal Standards to Facilitate Management of the Suicidal Patients

Reasonable and Prudent Practitioner

What is my implicit philosophy of science, the set of standards by which I judge my clinical reasoning to be 'scientific'?

Am I focusing on a single cause of the patient's illness (or behavior) to the exclusion of other possible causes?

Am I being as sensitive as I can to the effects that my own feelings may have on the assessment and treatment of this suicidal patient?

Did I adequately document my decision-making process?

Does the literature suggest methods of assessment and treatment that have been shown effective that I am not using?

Community Standards

Would anyone else take into account these same factors (in making the treatment decision)?

Would other clinicians feel as I do toward the patient?
That is, do my reactions tell me something about the way the pa

tal guidelines). The psychologist must keep in mind that the staff is a nonpsychiatric one and, hence, that they are generally not accustomed to implementing such procedures. The psychologist must also be prepared to deal with the staff's emotional response to the suicidal patient. On medical–surgical units, where saving life is the primary goal, the staff will often express anger and frustration toward a suicidal patient in indirect ways (e.g., not administering pain medications on time or not speaking with the patient).

In making sure that the staff carries out the suicide precaution orders,

---

Exhibit 7.1 (*continued*)

tient affects others (especially those closest to him or her) rather than simply about myself?

Would one of my colleagues or, particularly, supervisors, remind me of other considerations that I am overlooking?

Maximization of Benefits in Relation to Costs

Is this a situation in which it is relatively safe to rely on the data that I have)?

Am I overlooking objective data such as the statistical probability that someone with this patient's diagnosis will attempt suicide?

What if I am right about the consequences? What if I am wrong?

What will be the impact on the patient's immediate safety? On the patient's ultimate well-being? On the therapeutic alliance?

Am I sure enough of a high probability of small gains to risk a very low probability of a large loss?

Have I involved the patient as much as possible in the consideration of costs and benefits through the process of attempting to obtain informed consent? Are there any factors (costs or benefits) that I am not considering?

Are there any data that I have not considered (e.g., past medical/ psychiatric records, significant others, staff input, or patient input)?

---

the psychologist would be wise to initiate a staff intervention aimed at education and open communication about exactly what precautions are being taken, who is responsible for carrying them out, and what to do if problems arise. Of course, all information should be documented in the medical or nursing record. One must be particularly careful that adequate communication occurs across different nursing shifts. Where this is done inadequately, negligent professional behavior may be found if litigation were to occur.

Exhibit 7.2

Examples of Suicide Precaution to Be Used on an Inpatient Medical Unit

Patient is in restraints (2 to 5 point) with a 24-hr "sitter," who observes constantly.

Patient is not restrained but has a 24-hr sitter, who observes her or him constantly, including when in the rest room.

No sitter but dangerous objects removed from the room—including sharp objects, belts, combs, writing pens/pencils, glass objects, plastic bags (including wastebasket), and eating utensils. If the patient is on medication, one might consider liquid form to avoid "mouthing" or pill hoarding (especially where antidepressants are involved). Nursing checks every 15 to 30 min (or some time interval). In setting check intervals, one should consider such things as whether patient has access to clothes and whether there are bars on the windows of the room. A suicide contract should be sought.

Nursing checks per unit standards with no special suicide precautions. A suicide contract should be obtained, which specifies that patient understands how to request help if suicidality increases.

Duty to Protect

Increasingly, mental health professionals are being held responsible for protecting the public from violent acts of their patients. The duty-to-protect doctrine received great publicity in the case of *Tarasoff v. Regents of University of California* (1976), a case with which all mental health professionals should be familiar (see Kamenar, 1984). The court's ruling means that although there may be no special relationship between a therapist and victim, the relationship between a therapist and patient is sufficient to impose special legal responsibility on the therapist for the patient's actions if the therapist knows the patient poses a serious threat or the therapist negligently fails to predict such dangerousness (Southard & Gross, 1983). The court's ruling also stated that where a danger to others exists, the confidential doctor–patient relationship must yield.

Since Tarasoff, there has been much confusion in the mental health professions as to the specific implications of the ruling. Schindler (1976) noted that the courts offered no practical guidelines to follow. Southard and Gross (1983) and others (Beigler, 1984; Kamenar, 1984; Monahan, 1993; Quinn, 1984; VandeCreek & Knapp, 1993; Wettstein, 1984) provided a thorough discussion of the misunderstanding surrounding the Tarasoff decision while articulating the responsibilities of therapists related to the duty to protect.

Briefly, this case is often cited as "duty to warn," but the actual court decision was based on a "duty to care" or to protect. The courts did not rule that warning potential victims was a reasonable course of action in all cases but rather that the therapist is to take "reasonable care" to protect the potential victim (Knapp, 1980; Southard & Gross, 1983). Protective action may involve many different possibilities.

Southard and Gross (1983) presented several cases that occurred after Tarasoff, which facilitate the understanding of the "duty-to-protect" doctrine. These findings include the following: that Tarasoff does not apply to suicide or property damage (Schwitzgebel & Schwitzgebel, 1980), that it does not apply to nonspecific threats against nonspecific persons, and that imminence of danger is necessary for a duty to protect to exist. On the basis of these cases, Southard and Gross (1983, p. 41) provided a "Tarasoff Decision Chart" to guide clinical decision making in executing a duty to protect (see Figure 7.1).

As can be seen in Figure 7.1, the initial steps (A–B) involve determining whether a "serious" threat exists. In these first two phases of assessment, a specific threat is not always the only criterion for invoking Tarasoff. If the professional "should have known" that a patient was dangerous to someone as determined by standards of practice, then there is a Tarasoff responsibility (*McIntosh v. Milano*, as cited in Kamenar, 1984). Step C deals with identifiability of the potential victim. Although there are no clear guidelines regarding identifiability, a discussion by Kamenar

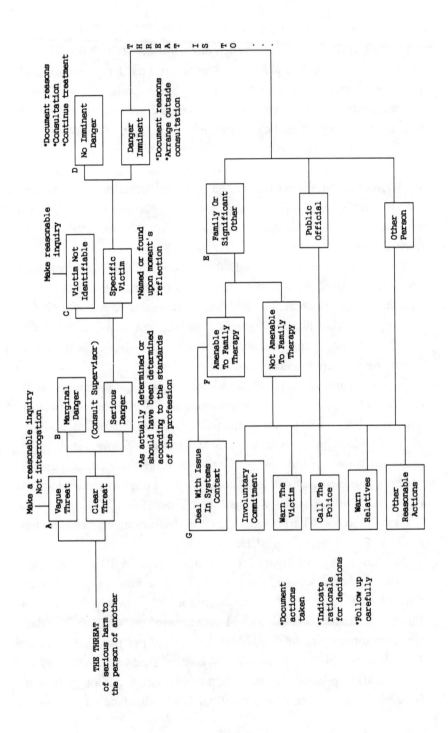

(1984) of several cases suggests that even where the potential victim is not identifiable, the professional may have a duty to "protect" a foreseeable but unidentifiable third party. This might include "detaining the patient, inquiring further as to the identity of the possible victim, warning his or her family or law enforcement officials, or taking some other precaution" (Kamenar, 1984, p. 265). Steps D through E involve determining whether danger is imminent and within what grouping of people the intended victim falls. Throughout this process of decision making, documentation and consultation are of the utmost importance because the clinician's actions will be judged by the reasonable and prudent practitioner guidelines and community standard of care. Steps F and G are possible actions indicated, based on assessment in the previous steps. Thus, warning the victim is not the sole possibility. In fact, some authors feel that the action taken by the therapists in the Tarasoff case was "rash" because, although threats were made, danger was not imminent in that Miss Tarasoff was out of the country. In having the patient who made threats against Tarasoff committed immediately, the therapists may have destroyed any therapeutic alliance, which might have worked against the violent action that took place (Sadoff, 1979; Southard & Gross, 1983).

Although such decision-making trees are helpful, there is much concern that the courts are extending the "duty to protect," related to the prediction of dangerousness, beyond what the scientific level of the profession is capable of delivering (Goodstein, 1985). A therapist's best defense is careful documentation, clinical reasoning, and consultation. Of course, these behaviors are all consistent with sound clinical practice.

The clinical health psychologist working in a hospital setting has a difficult task related to assessment and management of homicidality. He or she is most likely to be confronted with a "Tarasoff" situation while con-

Figure 7.1

Tarasoff decision chart. From Making Clinical Decisions After Tarasoff by M. J. Southard & B. H. Gross, 1982. In B. Gross & I. Weinberger (Eds.), *New Directions for Mental Health Services: Vol. 16. The Mental Health Professional and the Legal System* (p. 98), San Francisco: Jossey-Bass. Copyright 1982 by Jossey-Bass Publishers. Reprinted with permission.

sulting to the emergency room or in the assessment of injured patients. Questions regarding perceived causation of the injury and possible motives for revenge are important. However, the health psychologist will usually not have had a previous relationship with the patient, thus adequate assessment is often difficult. In these situations, hospitalization may be used more frequently.

In summary, VandeCreek and Stout (1993) gleaned three general principles that could be taken from Tarasoff and subsequent cases. These include foreseeability of harm, identifiability of the victim, and the ability of the therapist to protect the potential victim. First, the courts have not found liability when therapists could not have foreseen the danger. Second, the courts have generally found that there is no liability if the potential victim is not identifiable. Third, the courts have generally found that the therapist need only take fairly easy and reasonable steps to warn the potential victim, to fulfill the duty. Thus, the guidelines presented by Southard and Gross (1982; Figure 7.1) appear still applicable.

Duty to Protect and HIV-Positive Patients

The acquired immune deficiency syndrome (AIDS) is caused by the human immunodeficiency virus (HIV). AIDS is an epidemic and presents a special issue related to the duty to protect within the context of a psychotherapeutic relationship. Specifically, what is the psychologist to do if a patient discloses that he or she is HIV positive and also has a sexual or needle-sharing partner who is not aware of the infection? This issue may be more likely to confront clinical health psychologists because of their closer association with the medically ill.

The question is whether the situation above entails a necessary invocation of the Tarasoff duty to protect. The Tarasoff decision was based on long-standing precedents involving physicians' duty to warn third persons about infectious diseases (see Knapp & VandeCreek, 1990; Totten, Lamb, & Reeder, 1990, for review). As such, legal precedent for a duty to warn in HIV cases antedates the Tarasoff decision. Still, one is not expected to invoke the duty to warn in every case of a patient disclosing HIV-positive status and also having uninformed persons within his or her psychosocial environment. The breaking of confidentiality in fulfilling the duty to warn must be done with caution after careful consideration of many factors, just as in cases discussed above under the Tarasoff section.

Legal guidelines for the duty to protect in HIV-positive cases have been developed in many states. It is beyond the scope of this discussion to give each state's guidelines, if guidelines actually exist in a particular state. In addition, these guidelines are often changing rapidly. Knapp and Vande-Creek (1990) provided a useful presentation of these issues as well as general guidelines for the duty to protect in HIV-positive cases. They take into account such things as the three general Tarasoff guidelines as applied to the HIV-positive case, how to assess the level of risk the HIV-positive patient is posing, and clinical management of the HIV dangerous patient. They conclude that psychologists should be aware of state law, consult with colleagues, consult with legal authorities, and document the decision-making process, to deal with these cases in a sound clinical and legal fashion.

Confidentiality

Communication between patient and psychologist within the context of a professional relationship is considered confidential (American Psychological Association, 1992). As with traditional psychological treatment, the clinical health psychologist is mandated to breach confidentiality under special circumstances (e.g., endangerment to others, child abuse, elder abuse, or endangerment to self). Where there is an inappropriate breach of confidentiality, it is grounds for malpractice (*Berry v. Moench*, 1958; *Furniss v. Fitchett*, 1958).

As previously noted, the practice of clinical health psychology can present special problems related to confidentiality. One issue has to do with how much information related to the patient's psychological status, history, and condition should be disclosed to the referral source, who is often the primary-care physician with whom the clinician is working closely in the management of the patient.

Another issue involves the practice found in most medical centers in which patient files are relatively open for access to all professional staff. This, of course, presents problems for confidentiality of psychological services. Many departments of psychiatry and behavioral sciences maintain separate records, a policy that provides more control over access. One procedure we use for responding to a referral involves writing a detailed intake evaluation for our own records and then excerpting relevant parts to comprise a more general evaluation to be sent back to the referral source. In most cases, this general report is also sent to the medical chart. The evaluation that is sent to the referral source is more symptom focused and treatment plan oriented. It does not include a detailed family history, particularly sensitive information, or a *DSM–IV* diagnosis. This practice is in keeping with Ethical Standard 5.03a, which states that psychologists include in oral and written reports only information "... germane to the purpose for which the communication is made" (American Psychological Association, 1992, p. 1606). Psychological material even of this general nature should be released only with the patient's knowledge. In many large health care systems, complete confidentiality cannot be promised, and the limits of confidentiality must be outlined to the patient in the informed-consent procedure.

Inpatient psychological treatment of medical patients presents problems with confidentiality similar to those above, as well as others. A major problem is how much information to document in the unit chart, which is perhaps more widely read than clinic charts. It is most prudent to follow the guidelines presented above in recording the most general and necessary information in the medical chart. It should be kept in mind that the psychological–behavioral information recorded in the unit chart can often affect how the staff interacts with the patient. When there is information particularly relevant to the treatment of the patient but not appropriate to put in the medical chart, conveying the information verbally to the necessary health care professionals is indicated. However, the fact that the patient's care was discussed should be documented in the medical chart.

Problems with confidentiality also occur when there is a release for medical information to an outside source and psychological treatment progress notes or evaluations have been recorded in the medical chart (either inpatient or outpatient). General medical release of information forms are not sufficient to release psychological information, even when this information appears in the general medical record. This may appear obvious, but in large medical systems, this issue is often overlooked. If the standard medical-information release does not specify psychological information, it is important that the medical records department take appropriate precautions (such as "blacking out" psychological progress notes when copying medical records). It may ultimately be the psychologist's responsibility to be sure this is done.

Psychological Evaluation

Psychological evaluation has been an area in which psychologists have been more likely to get sued for malpractice, and this pattern has continued (VandeCreek & Stout, 1993; Wright, 1981). The typical scenario is that the recommendation resulting from the psychological evaluation causes the patient–client to initiate a malpractice complaint concerning misuse of the test or test data. Wright (1981) concluded that in "most instances the filing of the grievance is a retaliatory expression of disappointment because something that the client wanted was denied or the client felt himself or herself to have been presented unfairly" (p. 1490). Stromberg and Dellinger (1993) discussed that the courts have generally not been sympathetic to these suits because they understand that they are often of a retaliatory nature. Still, even the process of being faced with a malpractice action can be traumatic for the psychologist, and everything reasonable should be done to avoid it.

Clinical health psychologists, practicing within the limits of their specialty, would probably not be involved in areas of psychological evaluation that have more frequently resulted in malpractice litigation. These areas include evaluations for employment decisions (hiring, firing, and promotion), child custody issues, and probation. However, clinical health psychologists are involved in psychological evaluations related to medical treatment or disability decision making (e.g., neuropsychological assessment, evaluation for inpatient pain programs, workers' compensation assessments related to occupational injury, or evaluation for penile prosthesis or cardiac transplant), which may have increased malpractice risks.

For instance, if a patient is denied access to a treatment program or surgery, or is given the opportunity for an alternative treatment that is more appropriate but not desired by the patient, a malpractice suit could be precipitated. In initiating the suit, the patient can deny the validity of the findings and express disagreement with the recommendation. Consider the following case example:

> The patient was a 60-year-old married man who was referred for psychological screening in conjunction with evaluation for a penile prosthesis. For the past 5 years, the patient had suffered from erectile dysfunction, which had precluded sexual intercourse. Medical evaluation had shown that blood flow and hormonal studies were within normal limits and that no physical etiology could be established. Nocturnal erections during sleep were intact. The patient was not informed about the implications of the psychological evaluation relative to his surgery nor about the feedback process before being interviewed. The psychological evaluation revealed there were a number of significant marital problems at the time of the onset of the sexual dysfunction. In addition, the patient had been involved in an extramarital affair about which he felt very guilty. Recommendations included a course of behavioral sexual dysfunction therapy and marital counseling. The results of the evaluation were given to the surgeon, who subsequently met with the patient and gave him feedback as to the treatment decision. The patient stated adamantly that he was not interested in psychotherapy, that the problem was physically based, and that he wanted it resolved with the prosthesis. The patient brought a malpractice suit against the surgeon and the psychologist, stating that he was denied the surgical procedure based on unjustifiable reasons.

Of course, clinical health psychologists should not formulate recommendations resulting from evaluations based on attempting to avoid a malpractice suit. However, in the preceding example, the professionals made several errors in handling the informed consent, which may have contributed to the patient's ultimate legal action. In general, the ways to minimize the risk of malpractice stem from what would be considered sound clinical practice, regardless of the malpractice issues. First, the patient should be fully informed about the nature of the evaluation; for instance, who requested it, who will receive copies of the results, where the results will be documented (psychiatric or medical chart), the ramification of the results, and who will pay for it. After receiving information on the evaluation process, some check of the patient's understanding should be conducted, and then a consent for the evaluation should be obtained (see chapter 6). Second, after the evaluation, some discussion of the findings should be completed with the patient. This may occur before or after consulting with the referring physician depending on the case, the psychologist's role as a consultant, and the relationship between the psychologist and the physician. This feedback session with the patient should include an opportunity for the patient to discuss his or her reactions to the results and to ask any questions about "where do we go from here?" Often, when there is a treatment team involved, it is advisable for the team or various members of the team (e.g., the physician and psychologist) to meet with the patient simultaneously for feedback. In doing this, all questions that the patient may have can be addressed while reducing the risk of miscommunication or misinformation. Third, as suggested by Wright (1981), evaluation instruments should be given in the manner in which they were standardized, in keeping with the standards for psychological testing. Fourth, careful documentation of informed-consent procedures, findings, the patient's response to the feedback session, consultation to the referral, and so forth is necessary.

Although the recommendations from psychological evaluations are not always in keeping with patient desires, these guidelines can help reduce the risk of "retaliatory" or successful malpractice actions without having to equivocate evaluation results to the point of uselessness.

Supervision of Trainees

The clinical health psychologist working in a supervisory capacity must be aware of increased malpractice liability. As the area of health psychology expands, increasing numbers of practitioners will be seeking supervision. In general clinical work, ethical issues related to supervision have been articulated in the literature as well as in the ethical principles (American Psychological Association, 1992; Newman, 1981). It is essential for supervisors to be aware of ethical and legal aspects of supervision beyond their theoretical orientation and teaching skills (Harrar, VandeCreek, & Knapp, 1990). Certainly, one of the most important principles is that the clinical health psychology supervisor be competent to supervise in the specific area of practice. The following discussion assumes such a competence. Also, the supervisor is expected to know the skill level of the supervisee and gauge assignment of tasks and supervision accordingly (VandeCreek & Stout, 1993). Harrar et al. (1990) summarized the duties and responsibilities of the supervisor as follows:

1. The supervisor should have sufficient knowledge of each patient to be able to develop and monitor effective treatment plans and countersign written reports.
2. The supervisor should be available for emergency consultation and direct contact with patients.
3. The supervisor should not supervise more trainees than can be responsibly managed.

Conceptually, the most important thing for the supervisor to bear in mind is that "the relationship of an assistant to a licensed professional is, legally, akin to an 'extension' of the professional himself" (Cohen, 1979, p. 237). Although, both parties must understand that the trainee should not function so that the public would be led to believe that he or she is a fully licensed professional or expert specialist if that is not the case.

Another issue is that the amount of supervision must be based on the needs of the supervisee and the patient (Cohen, 1979; Pope, 1990). The supervisor is frequently confronted with this issue in training institutions. As Pope (1990) pointed out, it is important that the needs of the institution or the training rotations do not supersede those of the patient. Setting up a structured schedule of supervision is reasonable, and commonly practiced, but it should be flexible enough to accommodate clinical issues or problems as they arise. In addition, the needs of the patient and the supervisee must be constantly monitored and addressed.

Related to schedules of supervision, a record of the supervisory activity should be kept. This is most easily done in the patient's chart and need not be done at every supervisory session. Rather, the supervisor should periodically document that there is agreement with the supervisee's diagnostic formulation and treatment plan. This guideline should also be followed if the trainee is doing inpatient work and charting in the medical record. In fact, most medical facilities require the supervisor to countersign all charted information.

The recommendations listed above afford increased legal protection for the supervisee as well as the supervisor. Although the supervisory relationship creates supervisor liability for the professional behavior of his or her trainees, the supervisee is not totally absolved of responsibility in malpractice action. Thus, documenting supervision times and following the previously suggested guidelines offer protection of both parties and provide for more high-quality supervision. It should always be kept in mind that, "courts have generally followed the principle 'What has not been written has not been done' " (Harrar et al, 1990, p. 38).

Sexual Victimization and Malpractice

Although sexual misconduct is not unique to the area of clinical health psychology practice, no discussion of ethical and malpractice issues would be complete without addressing this area. Between 5% and 10% of psychologists have acknowledged erotic contact with one or more of their patients (Pope, Keith-Spiegel, & Tabachnick, 1986). Sexual misconduct is by far the most common reason for ethical and malpractice complaints. It also accounts for the largest costs in malpractice expenses and is generally excluded from coverage in most malpractice insurance policies. As discussed in the ethics chapter, clinical health psychologists may be more often associated with other disciplines, which have different ethical and legal guidelines on sexual relationships with patients and ex-patients. As Stromberg and Dellinger (1993) discussed, "one court explained that therapist–patient sex incurs liability while that sex between lawyer and client, minister and parishioner might not, because only the first professional group offers 'a course of treatment and counseling predicated upon handling the transference phenomenon' (*Simmons v. United States*, 1986; Stromberg & Dellinger, 1983, p. 8). This court decision makes it clear that it is important to not be influenced by guidelines for behavior of other disciplines.

Other important court decisions give further instruction in this area. First, the initial consent of the patient to a sexual relationship will not be a defense against a later malpractice claim. Second, even in the case of sex with a former patient, the courts do not easily accept the view that the therapy relationship has ended. The current ethical standards (4.07; American Psychological Association, 1992) provide guidelines in this area that are in keeping with many state laws (e.g., "psychologists do not engage in sexual intimacies with former therapy patients and clients even after a two-year interval except in the most unusual circumstances," Ethical Standard 4.07b). Even so, the most prudent course of action is to avoid sexual intimacies with a patient or ex-patient altogether.

Billing, Collection, and Financial Issues

Countersuits related to fee collection represent an area of increased malpractice risk. Psychologists can avoid many problems in this area by making clear arrangements with patients in advance. This is most often done in writing as part of the informed-consent process. In their article entitled, "Legal and Ethical Issues in Billing Patients and Collecting Fees," Knapp and VandeCreek (1993) discussed guidelines for effectively managing this aspect of clinical practice. Their guidelines will be summarized here.

First, the clinical health psychologist should keep in mind that he or she is "under no obligation to accept all patients who request service" and that "psychologists may refuse to accept any patient for any reason, including the perception that the patient is unable or unwilling to pay for services" (Knapp & VandeCreek, 1993, p. 25). Ethical Principle F (Social Responsibility) encourages psychologists to "contribute a portion of their professional time for little or no personal advantage," which might include seeing patients on a reduced or no-fee basis. This is a choice to be made by the psychologist. In certain cases, deciding not to accept a patient into one's practice for the above reasons may actually avoid antitherapeutic problems, which could occur if treatment were to ensue.

Second, the clinical health psychologist should use a written informed-consent procedure, which includes financial information among other things. An example of a detailed informed-consent form is presented in Exhibit 7.3. As can be seen, it includes financial information as well as other information, in keeping with ethical standards (4.01–4.02) and legal suggestions (Stromberg & Dellinger, 1993; VandeCreek & Stout, 1993). This form may be more detailed than some practitioners would be comfortable using, and each professional must decide what important issues to include. Financial information to be addressed should include fees, insurance billing, notification that insurance may not cover all of the charges, expected payment schedules, interest charges on balances, and collection procedures. Not allowing the bills to accumulate can help avoid problems at a later date. If an account is turned over to collection, the psychologist must first give the patient notification and opportunity to make restitution (Ethical Standard 1.25f).

Obtaining informed consent related to financial issues can be particularly challenging for the clinical health psychologist who sees a patient in the hospital. Physicians do not commonly address these issues when they do inpatient consultations and treatment. In our experience, it is awkward (and usually countertherapeutic) to walk into a patient's room for a first-time consultation and present a detailed consent form to be signed before beginning. In these cases, the informed-consent procedure may be done over several sessions, and the patient may be asked if he or she has questions about the financial arrangements. In addition, the psychologist may want to be more understanding in dealing with any subsequent financial issues that arise for patients seen under these circumstances.

Managed Care

Health care reform and managed care are impacting virtually all aspects of psychological practice, including that of clinical health psychology.

Exhibit 7.3

Example of a Written Consent Form

CLINICAL HEALTH PSYCHOLOGY SERVICES

This is to provide you with general information about health psychology services including biofeedback treatment.

EVALUATION AND TREATMENT SERVICES

The cost of the initial evaluation is _____. The evaluation fee includes the clinical interview, review of available medical records, treatment planning, and a narrative report. This initial evaluation might also include psychological testing or biofeedback assessment. Charges for these services are in addition to the evaluation fee and will be discussed with you. The cost of the treatment sessions is _____, and these typically last from 45 to 60 minutes. The following are goals for the treatment program:

1. _____

2. _____

3. _____

The following techniques will be used in an effort to achieve these goals:

_____ Pain management   _____ Homework exercises

_____ Relaxation training   _____ Symptom/medication
                                              monitoring

_____ Biofeedback training   _____ Couples/family sessions

_____ Psychotherapy   _____ Hypnosis

_____ Other _____

_____

_____

(exhibit continues)

Exhibit 7.3 (cont.)

It is understood that this treatment contract can be renegotiated or canceled at any time. The patient understands that this contract does not guarantee the attainment of these goals but that Dr. _____ will apply her professional skills in good faith at all times. It is understood that the sessions are completely confidential. However, it may be necessary to reveal information when any of the following circumstances exist: (a) if you threaten bodily harm to yourself or another person, (b) if you report firsthand incidents of child abuse, or (c) if a court of law issues a legitimate subpoena.

INSURANCE, BILLING, AND COLLECTION POLICIES

You will receive a statement for services on a monthly basis. As a courtesy to you, we will bill your insurance company for you and help you to get the benefits you are entitled to receive. If you are part of a managed-care insurance plan, your benefits may be limited (either number of visits or payment amount allowed), or you may need to have prior approval for treatment. We can help you to obtain this information. We must emphasize that as health care providers, our relationship is with you and not with your insurance company. All charges are the responsibility of the patient. It is important to make regular payments (e.g., co-payments) on the account balances each month whether insurance has paid or not. Balances over 60 days will be subject to an interest charge (1% per month) to cover the cost of carrying the account as well as continued billing. If no payment has been made within a 60-day period, the account may be sent to a collection agency. You will be notified before this action is taken, so that you can make other arrangements. You will be responsible for any costs incurred if collection proceedings are required. Generally, insurance companies do not pay for missed appointments. If an appointment is canceled with less than 24 hours' notice there will be a charge, unless it is an emergency. Psychological services of this nature are a Medicare benefit, and I am a Medicare provider. Workers' compensation

(exhibit continues)

Exhibit 7.3 (cont.)

cases must be preapproved by the insurance carrier. Medical–legal liens are not accepted.

_____'s signature affirms that he or she has been informed in simple, nontechnical terms of the likely benefits and material risks of this treatment plan, the risks of no treatment, and the available alternative treatments. His or her signature also affirms voluntary assent to the treatment plan.

We further stipulate that this agreement become part of the record, which is accessible to both parties but to no other parties without the patient's written consent. If you have any questions about the above, or about any other aspect of the evaluation and treatment, please feel free to ask at any time.

I have read, understand, and agree with the information presented above.

Patient name _____ Signature _____ Date _____

Witness _____

Managed care relates to malpractice issues in two important ways (Stromberg & Dellinger, 1993). First is whether the "standard of care" under managed care is measured differently than fee for service. The argument is that if a patient is enrolled in a health plan that reimburses at a lower rate or has limited psychological treatment benefits, then the therapist should not be liable for providing a lower quality of care or terminating the treatment after the "allowed" number of sessions. According to Stromberg and Dellinger (1993), the courts have not recognized any lower standard of care based on insurance coverage or managed-care guidelines. The same rules (ethical and legal) apply for all patients regardless of these issues. Of course, the psychologist can deal with such things as a limited number of allowed treatment sessions in an effective manner by being aware of such issues for each patient at the beginning of treatment, using informed-consent procedures, and anticipating other options if necessary.

Second is the issue of whether a clinician can be held liable for decisions to limit treatment made by the managed-care company. This issue began in the courts with the *Wickline v. California* (1986) decision, in which the plaintiff suffered the loss of her leg because of the failure of the health plan to provide treatment. Subsequent legal cases (e.g., *Wilson v. Blue Cross of California*, 1990) have reaffirmed that "when a treating physician makes a decision to discharge a patient because an insurance company refuses to pay benefits, either or both may be liable if their conduct was 'a substantial factor in bringing about the harm'" (Stromberg & Dellinger, 1993, p. 13). Stromberg and Dellinger (1993) concluded that the practitioner should at least provide services on an emergency basis regardless of payment and "energetically seek approval for additional services the patient genuinely needs" (p. 13). Appelbaum (1993) provided further guidelines to limit legal liability within a managed-care system. These include a duty to appeal adverse decisions by the insurance company, a duty to disclose to the patients the economic implications of their managed-care plan and its possible impact on treatment, and a duty to continue treatment under certain circumstances even if benefits have been exhausted. Of course, all actions related to dealing with the managed-care system should be documented in writing.

Haas and Cummings (1991) presented considerations to take into account before becoming involved in a particular managed-care system. These include consideration of the following questions:

1. How much does the plan intrude into the patient–provider relationship?
2. What provisions exist for exceptions to the rule?
3. Are there referral resources if patient needs should exceed plan benefits?
4. Does the plan provide assistance or training in helping the provider to achieve treatment goals?

5. Are there ways in which the plan is open to provider input?
6. Do plans clearly inform their policyholders of the limits of benefits?

Undoubtedly, malpractice issues related to managed care will continue to arise as these systems become more complex and patients and clinicians are increasingly influenced by these pressures.

MINIMIZING MALPRACTICE RISKS

Several authors have formulated guidelines for minimizing the malpractice risks (Soisson, VandeCreek, & Knapp, 1987; Stromberg & Dellinger, 1993; VandeCreek & Stout, 1993). These can be summarized as follows:

- Maintain accurate records of patient care
- Obtain informed consent in writing of billing procedures and treatment plans
- Ensure that all practitioners remain current in knowledge and skills in their areas of practice
- Honor patient rights to confidentiality and privilege
- Be thorough in assessment of patients, especially where suicide and homicide may be potential factors
- Avoid dual relationships with patients and ex-patients
- Accept only as many patients as can be carefully treated
- Terminate treatment carefully and for the proper reasons
- Exercise caution with new modalities of treatment and systems of managed care

Taking these suggestions seriously and implementing them in everyday practice will not only help avoid any malpractice action but also improve the quality of care.

SUMMARY AND CONCLUSIONS

In this chapter, we outlined general concepts of malpractice law and delineated several areas of increased malpractice risk particularly relevant to the practice of clinical health psychology. We attempted to provide concrete examples of the more common dilemmas that occur in clinical health psychology practice. Even so, the clinical health psychology practitioner may be faced with unique ethical and legal problems on a frequent basis. Because clinical health psychology is a relatively young area, consultation with one's colleagues, ethical panels, and legal counsel is advisable when faced with professional practice issues.

SUGGESTED READINGS

Deardorff, W. W., Cross, H. J., & Hupprich, W. R. (1984). Malpractice liability in psychotherapy: Client and practitioner perspectives. *Professional Psychology: Research and Practice, 15,* 590–600.

Knapp, S., & VandeCreek, L. (1981). Behavioral medicine: Its malpractice risks for psychologists. *Professional Psychology, 13,* 677–683.

Knapp, S., & VandeCreek, L. (1993). Legal and ethical issues in billing patients and collecting fees. *Psychotherapy, 30,* 25–31.

Schutz, B. M. (1982). *Legal liability in psychotherapy: A practitioner's guide to risk management.* San Francisco: Jossey-Bass.

Stromberg, C., & Dellinger, A. (1993, December). Malpractice and other professional liability. In *The Psychologist's Legal Update, 3,* 1–15. (Available from National Register of Health Service Providers in Psychology, 1120 G Street, NW, Suite 330, Washington, DC 20005)

VandeCreek, L., & Knapp, S. (1993). *Tarasoff and beyond: Legal and clinical considerations in the treatment of life-endangering patients.* Sarasota, FL: Practitioner's Resource Series.

8

Future Issues for Clinical Health Psychology

The future of clinical health psychology depends on the course of events within the field itself as well as those external to the discipline of psychology. In this chapter, we elucidate some of the trends and changes we anticipate and provide our perceptions of their potential impact. Our purpose is to stimulate thinking, discussion, and research related to these issues rather than to detail particular positions.

TECHNOLOGICAL ADVANCES

Clinical health psychology will become increasingly technology oriented. More and more assessment tools will be computerized and easily available to nonpsychologist users, sometimes bypassing local psychologists within the health care system. With this change will come the potential for increased abuse of such services, especially given the absence of psychometrically and clinically trained professionals in the interpretation process at the clinical case level. To the extent that diagnostic labels are rendered or treatment decisions are made from such data, there will be increased risks of malpractice suits involving these techniques. Given this, and the fact that many measures have inadequate norms for medical–surgical patients, we could witness in health care the kind of backlash about testing that occurred within the school system surrounding the use of intelligence tests and within industry with respect to employee selection, honesty, and evaluations for promotion. Psychologists might need to take an increased role in both professional and patient advocacy with respect to this issue.

Another area of technological advance has to do with increased sophistication in psychophysiological measurement. Developments in ambulatory monitoring will permit more accurate psychophysiological profiling and assessment. In vivo treatment programming will be possible. The potential exists for developing a considerable data base for the biopsychosocial model in the real world and for facilitating generalization of treatment efforts.

Advances in technology also permit the creation of psychoeducational materials for patients, and we expect that psychologists will be active participants in these endeavors. Video technology might also provide access to specialized patient services in rural areas as well as distance education and supervision of psychologists or providers in the field.

As clinical health psychologists contribute their expertise in behavior change to the health care system, there are also more opportunities for coercive control of patients (e.g., to promote compliance with health care providers who reflect the values of the dominant culture). Research on issues of diversity in health psychology is necessary to provide increased knowledge of cultural differences relevant to health care and to increase our awareness and sensitivity to related issues.

Although Weiss (1982), in his 1980 presidential address to the Division of Health Psychology, warned about "technology run amok" p. 89; (given technology's inherent amorality), there still remains little focus in the literature on ethical issues in clinical health psychology. We encourage more attention to this area and hope that our chapter on ethical issues will stimulate increased discussion.

DEVELOPMENT OF THE PROFESSION

Subspecialization

As clinical health psychology develops, there will be increased need for subspecialization. This is already apparent with respect to pediatric psychology, rehabilitation psychology, and pain management and will also become evident within other areas. In fact, the American Board of Health Psychology is currently developing certification guidelines for a subspecialty in pain. One of the areas that we predict will have the greatest support is that of primary-care health psychology. These practitioners will need a broad base in mental health and clinical health psychology and will serve in front-line positions in the health care system of tomorrow. However, their roles will be predominantly consultation to primary-care physicians, triage, and program development. Direct-intervention services will be provided by less expensive health personnel.

With respect to education and training, we have repeatedly indicated that it is impossible for the clinical health psychologist to have in-depth knowledge and clinical expertise in the biopsychosocial aspects of such diverse areas as biofeedback for cardiac arrhythmias, treatment of chronic pain, genetic counseling, organ-donor evaluations, and death and dying. However, we believe that predoctoral training should continue to be generic in both clinical and health psychology, with more focus on problems seen in primary health care settings. Subspecialization should occur at the postdoctoral level. This will avoid the production of "blacksmiths" who might be quickly outdated without a firm grounding in the discipline of psychology.

With increased specialization does come the risk that patients will be chunked into health behavior patterns or problems. Clinicians might take a myopic view in the same manner that physicians have been accused of doing, given that profession's specialization around organ systems. Thus we could have weight-management psychologists, type A psychologists, stress-management psychologists, and so forth. We might attempt to simplistically treat "smoking behavior" without a full appreciation of the context of this behavior within the individual and his or her environment. This results in a split similar to the mind–body dualism for which we have criticized medicine. This new dualism might be called *behavior–person* dualism. If it occurs, health care will be increasingly fragmented. At best our treatments will be ineffective; at worst we will cause damage to our patients. We fully agree that the major *focus* in clinical health psychology is not on psychopathology, but we are dismayed by comments of health psychologists suggesting that expertise in this area is not important. The clinical health psychologist must understand behavior and behavior change within both "normal" and "abnormal" domains.

Professional Practice

There will continue to be increased attention in issues of credentialing and accreditation in health psychology. Although the certification of advanced competency in practice is now well established through the board-certification process, accreditation is in its infancy. However, the Council of Directors of Health Psychology Training Programs has recommended criteria for postdoctoral training in clinical health psychology, and the Interorganizational Council for the Accreditation of Postdoctoral Programs[1] is field testing accreditation procedures in 1994.

There will also be increased attention to accountability and effectiveness of the provider at the individual-practitioner level. These data are already being compiled on physicians, and soon consumer hotlines will be available as health care becomes more consumer oriented in nature. Measures of patient satisfaction with the psychologist will be gathered routinely by third-party payers, and the profession will be increasingly torn between models of excellence and consumerism as core values. There seems little doubt that the individual practitioner will experience a significant loss of autonomy and that this will be a jarring experience.

In practice, we also anticipate an increase in cross-referrals among psy-

---

[1]The Interorganization Council includes the major credentialing groups in professional psychology: American Board of Professional Psychology, American Psychological Association, Association of State and Provincial Psychology Boards, Canadian Psychological Association, and National Register.

chologists and a more prominent focus on training other disciplines in the delivery of specialized services as new information becomes available. Psychology will always give its knowledge away. We believe that psychology has the potential to survive current health care industry crises primarily because of our expertise in research, program development and evaluation, and measurement of behavior. Other disciplines will assume roles as therapists and do so less expensively. Unfortunately, our recent experiences with hiring suggest that many psychologists entering practice see themselves primarily as psychotherapists, with few other skills and training. Because policymakers in large organizations cannot appreciate important distinctions *within* psychology, our discipline might fail to live up to its potential in the health care system because of our own complacency about the reliability of the product of graduate training.

Growth of Knowledge

Health care reform is demanding empirically based health care services. There is an increased need for well-controlled clinical trials to assess costs, benefits, and side effects of various psychological interventions. Although we have often complained that our discipline has been held to a higher scientific standard than medical practice itself, the playing field is now more even. We anticipate more interdisciplinary clinical research and more rigorous searches for *interactions* among biological, psychological, and social interventions.

Related to this, we are concerned about the number of psychologists entering practice from graduate programs without training in the conduct of clinical research and minimal exposure to research methodology. Not only will these psychologists be unable to contribute to the body of knowledge but they might also lack the expertise to critically review current findings and make informed decisions about applications. They could therefore unwittingly contribute to a backlash in many areas of clinical health psychology, such as we have experienced to some extent in biofeedback and wellness programs. The focus on self-control and the popularization of related techniques have already produced a new clinical problem: the patient who feels guilty and incompetent that he or she cannot "will" or "visualize" the cancer away or bring all psychophysiological symptoms under control. We must not promise more than we can deliver, in terms of either quantity of service or power of our techniques.

CHANGES IN PSYCHIATRY

We view psychiatry's "remedicalization" as due perhaps as much to economics and the need to realign with medicine as to scientific developments in biological psychiatry. However, the trend toward a reaffirmation of the biological factors in mental illness and a focus on psychopharmacology actually increases opportunities for nonmedical providers of psychological treatment services. In addition, to the extent that psychologists continue to be trained in areas relevant to health care systems in which their psychiatric colleagues are not (e.g., research, program evaluation, and measurement of behavior), they will be assured roles on the health care team.

Psychiatry continues, as does traditional clinical psychology, to be viewed as being preoccupied with mental illness. Thus, the field of clinical health psychology is ripe for continued development. However, our previous prediction that increased competition in the health care industry could result in increased interprofessional conflict appears to have been accurate, a situation we find most unfortunate for psychology, psychiatry, and the general public.

CHANGES IN THE HEALTH CARE SYSTEM

For over a decade, a major revolution in the health care system has been predicted for the United States; it is now under way. The precursors were federal programs such as prospective payment systems and fixed-rate reimbursement for DRGs, which have already had significant effects on hospital practices. Currently under deliberation in Congress are a number of health reform acts, which could involve a major overhaul of the entire financing and service-delivery system. Major themes include universal access, comprehensive mandated health benefits, cost containment, quality, and accountability. Although the legislative outcome is not yet determined, that change will occur is accepted as fact. Unfortunately the response by psychology's major professional organization has sometimes been more reactionary than progressive. For example, the American Psychological Association primary advocacy objective has been the "protection of traditional areas of practice," with the major focus on mental health benefits. We predict (and hope) that this will change in the near future so as to take into account, and to promulgate, the scientific and practice contributions of clinical health psychology to the entire health care system. Our discipline provides health services and research—not just mental health services, although these too are very important.

In the private sector, it is clear that service provision as a cottage industry is waning as health care comes increasingly under corporate control. To survive as a practicing clinical health psychologist, sophistication in health maintenance organizations (HMOs), preferred provider organizations (PPOs), and physician–hospital organizations (PHOs) will be required, because it is estimated that the majority of Americans will be obtaining their health care through such organizations in the future. (The newest form of consolidation in the health care industry is the PHO, a legal entity that is jointly owned by a hospital and a group of physicians to further mutual interests. Its ability to contract with HMOs represents the most fully integrated form of managed health care.) Although these issues have not been extensively addressed in graduate education to date, psychologists will need to develop skills in dealing with corporate administrative structures, in providing evidence of accountability, and in using management information systems for cost–benefit analyses. Belar (1989) detailed the opportunities for psychologists in HMOs, with a focus on implications for graduate education and training.

How will clinical health psychology fare in this new world of health care? As discussed previously, mind–body dualism pervades the insurance industry; different benefit packages are developed for mental health and for physical health. And despite renewed attention to the importance of behavior throughout health care, there is a risk that psychological services will only be covered under mental health benefits. Belar (1991) noted how this already occurs (e.g., when the expense of penile prosthesis surgery is fully covered under a health plan but the cost of a presurgical psychological consultation regarding the appropriateness of surgery has significant copayment requirements under the mental health benefit portion of the health plan). Services such as those in clinical health psychology that bridge between mental health and physical health could find themselves without support, especially in the early years, until large systems experience first-hand the need for integration of medical and behavioral services.

Nearly a decade ago, Cummings (1986) voiced concern that psychologists were "ill prepared for the competitive market for their services that lies ahead" (p. 426). In his treatise, "The Dismantling of Our Health System," he pointed out how psychologists have historically eschewed marketing of their products and have been overly committed to notions of "cure" rather than "brief intermittent psychotherapy throughout the life cycle" (p. 429). In addition, the legislation affecting health care evolves through the political process, about which many psychologists tend to be either naive or uninterested. In our opinion, clinical health psychologists need to become politically involved in health policy at both institutional and legislative levels to ensure our survival. We have many opportunities, but only ourselves to meet the challenges.

SUGGESTED READINGS

Belar, C. D. (1989). Opportunities for psychologists in health maintenance organizations: Implications for graduate education and training. *Professional Psychology: Research and Practice, 29,* 390–394.

Lowman, R. L., & Resnik, R. (Eds.). (1994). *Mental health practitioners' guide to managed care.* Washington, DC: American Psychological Association.

Journals Relevant to Clinical Health Psychology

Given the wide range of special interests among health psychologists, specialty journals (e.g., *Pain*, *Headache*, and *Omega*) will not be listed. Rather, the following journals reflect general interests in the field.

American Journal of Preventive Medicine Journal of the American College of Preventive Medicine, Oxford University Press, 200 Madison Ave., New York, NY 10016. Information and research related to public health and preventive medicine.

American Journal of Public Health Public Health Association, 1015 15th Street, NW, Washington, DC 20005. Focus on risk factors, behavioral health, and risk-factor reduction.

Annals of Behavioral Medicine Publication of the Society of Behavioral Medicine, 103 South Adams Street, Rockville, MD 20850. Review articles, original research, and comprehensive abstracts of interest to biobehavioral researchers and clinicians.

Anxiety, Stress, and Coping Harwood Academic Publishers, PO Box 786, Cooper Station, New York, NY 10276. Research and theoretical articles related to anxiety dimensions, stress, and coping processes.

Archives of Physical Medicine and Rehabilitation Official journal of the American Academy of Physical Medicine and Rehabilitation. W. B. Saunders Company, The Curtis Center, Independence Square West, Philadelphia, PA 19106-3399. Original research and clinical experience in physical medicine and the diagnosis, therapy, and delivery of rehabilitation care.

Behavioral Medicine: An Interdisciplinary Journal of Research and Practice Heldref Publications, 1319 Eighteenth Street, NW, Washington, DC 20036-1802. An interdisciplinary journal focusing on behavioral and social influences on mental and physical health.

Biofeedback and Self-Regulation Journal of the Association for Applied Psychophysiology and Biofeedback. Plenum Publishing Corporation, 233 Spring Street, New York, NY 10013. Focus on scientific advances in methods and theory of self-regulation.

Biological Psychology Elsevier Science Publishers B.V., Journal Division, PO Box 211, 1000 AE Amsterdam, The Netherlands. Psychophysiology, biological correlates of psychological states.

"The Blue Sheet": Health Policy and Biomedical Research News of the Week F-D-C Reports, Inc., 5550 Friendship Blvd., Suite One, Chevy Chase, MD 20815-7278. A weekly newsletter that summarizes current legislation and research funding related to health issues.

Brain, Behavior and Immunity Academic Press, 525 B Street, Suite 1900, San Diego, CA 92101-4495. Research in psychoneuroimmunology.

British Journal of Medical Psychology British Psychological Society, St. Andrews House, 48 Princess Road, East, Leicester LEI 7 DR, United Kingdom. Psychology as applicable to medicine and psychotherapy.

General Hospital Psychiatry: Psychiatry, Medicine, and Primary Care Elsevier Science Publishing Company, Inc., 655 Avenue of the Americas, New York, NY 10010. A journal emphasizing a biopsychosocial approach to illness and health.

Harvard Health Letter Harvard Medical School Health Publications Group, 164 Longwood Avenue, Boston, MA 02115. Interprets current medical information for the general reader.

Health Affairs: The Policy Journal of the Health Sphere Project Hope, Suite 600, 7500 Old Georgetown Road, Bethesda, MD 20814. Exploration of domestic and international health policy issues.

Health Psychology Journal of the Division of Health Psychology, American Psychological Association, 750 First Street, NE, Washington, DC 20002. Broad spectrum of health psychology research.

International Journal of Behavioral Medicine The journal of the International Society for Behavioral Medicine, Lawrence Erlbaum Associates, 365 Broadway, Hillsdale, NJ 07642.

International Journal of Psychiatry in Medicine Baywood Publishing Company, 26 Austin Avenue, PO Box 337, Amityville, NY 11701. Psychological issues and health and illness.

International Journal of Psychosomatics International Psychosomatics Institute, PO Box 1296, Philadelphia, PA 19105. All aspects of psychosomatics.

Journal of Behavioral Medicine Plenum Publishing, 233 Spring Street, New York, NY 10013. Interdisciplinary journal emphasizing applications of research to prevention, treatment, and rehabilitation.

Journal of Clinical Psychology in Medical Settings Plenum Publishing, 233 Spring Street, New York, NY 10013. Articles on the science and practice of clinical psychology in the medical environment.

Journal of Clinical Psychopharmacology Williams & Wilkins, 428 East Preston Street, Baltimore, MD 21202. Intended for practicing clinicians and trainees to maintain current knowledge of clinical psychopharmacology.

Journal of Health Politics, Policy and Law Duke University Press, 905 W. Main Street, 18-B, Durham, NC 27701.

Journal of Health and Social Behavior Journal of the American Sociological Association, 1722 N Street, NW, Washington, DC 20036. Focus on the health care system, organizations and occupations; sociological perspectives of health and disease.

Journal of Human Stress Opinion Publications, Inc., RR1, Box 396, Shelburne Falls, MA 01370. Focuses on the relationship between stress and disease.

Journal of Pediatric Psychology Plenum Publishing Corporation, 233 Spring Street, New York, NY 10013. Focus on health and illness in children.

Journal of Psychosomatic Research Pergamon Press, 660 White Plains Road, Tarrytown, NY 10591-5153. Wide variety of health psychology research.

Journal of Rehabilitation and Health Plenum Publishing, 233 Spring Street, New York, NY 10013. Original and review articles on physical, emotional, cognitive, and sociological aspects of rehabilitation.

Mental Medicine Update: Mind–Body Newsletter Institute for the Study of

Human Knowledge, PO Box 176, Los Altos, CA 94032. Various articles on mind–body interaction issues.

New England Journal of Medicine Journal of the Massachusetts Medical Society, 1440 Main Street, PO Box 803, Waltham, MA 02254-0803. Some articles relevant to risk factors and the relationships between behavior and disease. Review articles and commentaries reflect prevailing attitudes in medicine.

Preventive Medicine Academic Press, 6277 Sea Harbor Drive, Orlando, FL 32887-4900. Focus on health promotion and disease prevention.

Professional Psychology: Research and Practice American Psychological Association, 750 First Street, NE, Washington, DC 20002-4242. Application of psychology, including scientific underpinnings of the profession of psychology.

Psychological Assessment American Psychological Association, 750 First Street, NE, Washington, DC 20002-4242. Empirical articles concerning clinical assessment and evaluation.

Psychological Bulletin American Psychological Association, 750 First Street NE, Washington, DC 20002. Occasional critical review articles relevant to health psychology.

Psychology and Health: An International Journal Harwood Academic Publishers, PO Box 786, Cooper Station, New York, NY 10276. Study and application of psychological approaches to health and illness.

Psychoneuroendocrinology Pergamon, Elsevier Science, Inc., 660 White Plains Road, Tarrytown, NY 10591-5153. Focus on relationships between behavior and endocrinology.

Psychophysiology Journal of the Society for Psychophysiological Research, Cambridge University Press, 40 West 20th Street, New York, NY 10011-4211. Basic and applied research in psychophysiology.

Psychosomatic Medicine Journal of the American Psychosomatic Society. Williams & Wilkins, PO Box 23291, Baltimore, MD 21298-9325. Wide variety of health psychology research, with a focus on psychosomatic disorders.

Psychosomatics Journal of the Academy of Psychosomatic Medicine, American Psychiatric Press, Inc., 1400 K Street, NW, Washington, DC 20005. General focus, with numerous case reports.

Psychotherapy and Psychosomatics S. Karger Publishers, 26 West Avon Road, PO Box 529, Farmington, CT 06085. Articles concerning psychotherapy research related to medical problems, strong clinical orientation.

Quality of Life Research Rapid Communications of Oxford, Ltd., The Old Malthouse, Paradise Street, Oxford, OX1 1LD, UK. Aspects of quality-of-life research in every aspect of health care.

Social Science and Medicine Pergamon, Elsevier Science Inc., 660 White Plains Road, Tarrytown, NY 10591-5153. All areas of sociobehavioral sciences and medicine, including the interrelationships between various disciplines.

Medical Abbreviations

This is a list of commonly used medical abbreviations. Although abbreviations tend to be standard across settings, when comparing approved lists from different hospitals, we have sometimes noted significant differences. It is imperative that the practitioner obtain the approved list of abbreviations before writing in any hospital's medical records. It is also important to know the conditions under which these abbreviations are used (e.g., usually never in discharge summaries).

A	assessment	bid	twice a day
$\bar{a}$	before	BF	Black female
AB	abortion	BK	below knee
A.D.	right ear	BM	bowel movement
ADL	activities of daily living	BMR	basal metabolic rate
ad lib	at pleasure	BO	bowel obstruction
AF	atrial fibrillation	BOM	bilateral otitis media
AK	above knee	BP	blood pressure
A.L.	left ear	BPH	benign prostatic hypertrophy
AMA	against medical advice	BRP	bathroom privileges
ANA	antinuclear factor	BS	breath sounds
ANS	autonomic nervous system	bs	bowel sounds
A&P	ascultation and percussion	BSO	bilateral salpingo-oophorectomy
ASA	aspirin	BUN	blood urea nitrogen
ASCVD	arteriosclerotic heart disease	Bx	biopsy
AU	both ears	$\bar{c}$	with
A&W	alive and well	CA	carcinoma
BAE, BE	barium enema	CA	calcium
B/C	birth control	CAT	computerized axial tomogram
BCP	birth control pills	CBC	complete blood count

CC   chief complaint
CCU   coronary care unit
CHD   coronary heart disease
CHF   congestive heart failure
CNS   central nervous system
C/O   complains of
COPD   chronic obstructive pul-
   monary disease
CP   cerebral palsy
CPR   cardiopulmonary resuscitation
Cr N   cranial nerve
CS, C/S   cesarean section
CSF   cerebrospinal fluid
CVA   cerebrovascular accident
CVD   cardiovascular disease
Cx   cervix
CXR   chest X ray
d   diastolic
D   dorsal spine
D&C   dilation and curettage
D/C'D   discontinued
DIFF   differential blood count
DM   diabetes mellitus
DOA   dead on arrival
DOB   date of birth
DOE   dyspnea on exertion
DTRs   deep tendon reflexes
Dx   diagnosis
EA   emergency area
ECG   electrocardiogram
EEG   electroencephalogram
EENT   eyes, ears, nose, throat
EMG   electromyogram
ENT   ears, nose, throat
EOM   extraocular movements
ESR   erythrocyte sedimentation rate

EUA   examination under anesthesia
FB   foreign body
FBS   fasting blood sugar
FH   family history
F/U   follow-up
FUO   fever of unknown origin
FVC   forced vital capacity
Fx   fracture
G, Gr   gravida
GB   gallbladder
GC   gonococcus
GE   gastroenterology
GG   gamma globulin
GI   gastrointestinal
gr   grain
GSW   gunshot wound
gt   drop
gtt   drops
GU   genitourinary
HA   headache
HBP   high blood pressure
HEENT   head, ears, eyes, nose, throat
H&L   heart and lungs
HNP   herniated nucleus pulposus
H&P   history and physical
HPI   history of present illness
htn   hypertension
hs   at bedtime
Hx   history
ICU   intensive care unit
ID   intradermal
I&D   incision and drainage
IH   infectious hepatitis
IM   intramuscular
IMP   impression
imp   improved

in situ   in normal position

IOP   intraocular pressure

IPPD   intermittent positive pressure breathing

IUP   intrauterine pregnancy

IV   intravenous

IVP   intravenous pyelogram

JRA   juvenile rheumatoid arthritis

KJ   knee jerk

KUB   kidney, ureter, bladder

L&A   light and accommodation

LAB   laboratory results

LAP   laparotomy

LLE   left lower extremity

LLL   left lower lobe

LLQ   left lower quadrant

LMD   local medical doctor

LMP   last menstrual period

LOC   level of consciousness

LP   lumbar puncture

LS   lumbosacral

LSK   liver, spleen, kidney

MH   marital history

MI   myocardial infarction

MM   malignant melanoma

MMR   measles, mumps, and rubella immunization

MOD   medical officer of the day

NA   not applicable

NAA   no apparent abnormalities

NB   newborn

NC   no change

N/C   no complaints

NK   not known

NL   normal

NPO   nothing by mouth

NR   nonreactive

NSD   no significant difference

NSR   normal sinus rhythm

NSSP   normal size, shape, position

N&V   nausea and vomiting

O   objective

OB   obstetrics

OBS   organic brain syndrome

Od   overdose

od   right eye

OM   otitis media

OPC   outpatient clinic

OS   mouth

os   left eye

ou   both eyes

$\bar{p}$ after

p   pulse

P   plan

PARA   number of pregnancies

PE   physical examination

PERLA   pupils equal, react to light and accommodation

PERRLA   pupils equal, round, regular, react to light and accommodation

PH   past history

PI   present illness

PID   pelvic inflammatory disease

PM   postmortem

PMH   past medical history

PMT   premenstrual tension

PNS   peripheral nervous system

po   by mouth

prn   as needed

PS   prescription

PTA   prior to admission

PVC   premature ventricular contraction
Px   physical examination
Q   every
qd   every day
qh   every hour
qid   four times a day
qm   every morning
qn   every night
QNS   quantity not sufficient
qod   every other day
qs   enough
R   respiration
RBC   red blood count
REM   rapid eye movement
R/O   rule out
ROM   range of motion
ROS   review of systems
RR   recovery room
RTC   return to clinic
RTW   return to work
Rx   prescription, treatment
s̄   without
S   subjective
SB   stillbirth
SCC   squamous cell carcinoma
S&O   salpingo-oophorectomy
SOB   shortness of breath
SPP   suprapubic prostatectomy
SP   spinal
S/P   status post
SUBQ   subcutaneous
SRG   surgery
SX   symptoms
Sx   signs

T   temperature
T&A   tonsillectomy and adenoidectomy
TAB   therapeutic abortion
TAH   total abdominal hysterectomy
TBLC   term birth, living child
TC   throat culture
TIA   transient ischemic attack
tid   three times a day
TL   tubal ligation
TPR   temperature, pulse, respiration
TURP   transurethral resection of prostate
TVH   total vaginal hysterectomy
UA   urinalysis
U&C   usual and customary
UCHD   usual childhood diseases
UK   unknown
URI   upper respiratory infection
UTI   urinary tract infection
V   vein
VDRL   Veneral Disease Research Laboratory (syphilis)
VS   vital signs
VSS   vital signs stable
W   widowed
WBC   white blood cells
WDWN   well developed, well nourished
WF   White female
WM   White male
WNL   within normal limits
XM   cross-match
YO   year old
?   question of

Professional and Disease-Specific Organizations

PROFESSIONAL ORGANIZATIONS

Academy of Behavioral Medicine
  Research
Department of Medical Psychology
4301 Jones Bridge Road
Bethesda, MD 20814-4799

Academy of Psychosomatic Medicine
5824 N. Magnolia
Chicago, IL 60660

American Board of Health Psychology
2100 E. Broadway
Suite 313
Columbia, MO 65201

American Geriatrics Society
770 Lexington Ave., Suite 300
New York, NY 10021

American Health Care Advisory
  Association
223 E. College Street
Grapevine, TX 76051

American Psychological Association
750 First Street, NE
Washington, DC 20002-4242

American Psychosomatic Society
6728 Old McLean Village Drive
McLean, VA 22101

American Public Health Association
1015 15th Street, NW
Washington, DC 20005

American Society of Clinical Hypnosis
2200 E. Devon Ave., Suite 291
Des Plaines, IL 60018-4534

Association for Applied Psychophysiology and Biofeedback
10200 W. 44th Ave.
Wheat Ridge, CO 80033

Association for the Care of Children's
  Health
7910 Woodmont Ave., Suite 300
Bethesda, MD 20814

Association of Medical School
  Professors of Psychology
PO Box 9137
Morgantown, WV 26506-9137

Gerontolological Society of America
1275 K Street, NW, Suite 350
Washington, DC 20005

Group Health Association of America
1129 20th Street, NW, Suite 600
Washington, DC 20036

International Academy of Behavioral
   Medicine, Counseling and
   Psychotherapy
6750 Hillcrest Plaza, Suite 304
Dallas, TX 75230

National Hospice Organization
1901 N. Moore Street, Suite 901
Arlington, VA 22209

National Minority Health Association
PO Box 11876
Harrisburg, PA 17108

National Rehabilitation Association
633 South Washington Street
Alexandria, VA 22314

National Women's Health Network
1325 G Street, NW
Washington, DC 20005

Society for Adolescent Medicine
19401 E. 40 Highway, Suite 120
Independence, MO 64055

Society for Psychophysiological
   Research
c/o Robert J. Gatchel
University of Texas Southwestern
   Medical Center
Psychology Department
5323 Harry Hines Blvd.
Dallas, TX 75235-9044

Society of Behavioral Medicine
103 South Adams Street
Rockville, MD 20850-2315

DISEASE-SPECIFIC ORGANIZATIONS

Alzheimer's Association
919 N. Michigan Ave.
   Suite 1000
Chicago, IL 60611

American Anorexia/Bulimia
   Association
418 E. 76 Street
New York, NY 10021

American Association for the Study
   of Headache
875 Kings Highway, Suite 200
Woodbury, NJ 08096-3172

American Association of Spinal Cord
   Injury Psychologist and Social
   Workers
75–20 Astoria Blvd.
Jackson Heights, NY 11370-1177

American Brain Tumor Association
3725 N. Talman Ave.
Chicago, IL 60618

American Burn Association
c/o Andrew M. Munster, MD
Baltimore Regional Burn Center
Francis Scott Key Hospital
4940 Eastern Ave.
Baltimore, MD 21224

American Cancer Society
1599 Clifton Road, NE
Atlanta, GA 30329

American Chronic Pain Association
PO Box 850
Rocklin, CA 95677

American Council for Headache
    Education
875 Kings Highway, Suite 200
Woodbury, NJ 08096

American Council of the Blind
1155 15th Street, NW, Suite 720
Washington, DC 20005

American Diabetes Association
National Center
PO Box 25757
1660 Duke Street
Alexandria, VA 22314

American Epilepsy Foundation
638 Prospect Ave.
Hartford, CT 06105-4298

American Fertility Association
2140 11th Ave, South, Suite 200
Birmingham, AL 35205-2800

American Foundation for AIDS
    Research (AMFAR)
5900 Wilshire Blvd., 2nd Floor
Los Angeles, CA 90036

American Heart Association
7272 Greenville Ave.
Dallas, TX 75231-4596

American Liver Foundation
1425 Pompton Ave.
Cedar Grove, NJ 07009

American Lung Association
1740 Broadway
New York, NY 10019

American Pain Society
5700 Old Orchard Road, First Floor
Skokie, IL 60077-1024

American Paralysis Association
500 Morris Ave.
Springfield, NJ 07081

American Sleep Disorders Association
1610 14th Street, NW, Suite 300
Rochester, NY 55901

American Society of Clinical Oncology
435 N. Michigan Ave., Suite 1717
Chicago, IL 60611-4067

American Society of Rheumatology
   Health Professionals
Suite 150, 60 Executive Park South
Atlanta, GA 30329

American Tinnitus Association
PO Box 5
Portland, OR 97207

Arthritis Foundation
1314 Spring Street, NW
Atlanta, GA 30309

Association of Rheumatology Health
   Professionals
Suite 150
60 Executive Park South
Atlanta, GA 30329

Crohn's and Colitis Foundation of
   America
444 Park Ave., South, 11th Floor
New York, NY 10016-7374

Cystic Fibrosis Foundation
6931 Arlington Road, No. 200
Bethesda, MD 20814

Huntington's Disease Society of
   America
140 W. 22nd Street, 6th Floor
New York, NY 10011-2420

International Association for the
   Study of Pain
909 N.E. 43rd Street
Suite 306
Seattle, WA 98105-6020

Lupus Foundation of America
4 Research Place, Suite 180
Rockville, MD 20850–3226

Muscular Dystrophy Association
3300 E. Sunrise Drive
Tucson, AZ 85718

National AIDS Information Clearing-
   house
PO Box 6003
Rockville, MD 20850

National Association for Hearing and
   Speech Action
10801 Rockville Pike
Rockville, MD 20852

National Association of the Deaf
814 Thayer Ave.
Silver Spring, MD 20910

National Brain Injury Research
   Foundation
1612 K Street, NW, Suite 204
Washington, DC 20006

National Chronic Pain Outreach
   Association
7979 Old Georgetown Road, Suite 100
Bethesda, MD 20814-2429

National Digestive Diseases Information Clearinghouse
Box NDDIC
9000 Rockville Pike
Bethesda, MD 20892

National Headache Foundation
5252 N. Western Ave.
Chicago, IL 60625

National Head Injury Foundation
1776 Massachusetts Ave, NW, Suite 100
Washington, DC 20036

National Kidney Foundation
30 E. 33rd Street, Suite 1100
New York, NY 10016

National Multiple Sclerosis Society
733 3rd Ave.
New York, NY 10017

National Osteoporosis Foundation
1150 17th Street, NW, Suite 500
Washington, DC 20037

National Stroke Association
300 E. Hampden Ave., Suite 240
Englewood, CO 80110-2654

National Sudden Infant Death Syndrome Clearinghouse
8201 Greenboro Drive, Suite 600
McLean, VA 22102

Paget Foundation for Paget's Disease of Bone and Related Disorders
200 Varick Street, Suite 1004
New York, NY 10014-4810

Parkinson's Educational Program
3900 Birch Street, No. 105
Newport Beach, CA 92660

People with AIDS Coalition
31 W. 26th Street
New York, NY 10010

Reflex Sympathetic Dystrophy Association
PO Box 821
Haddenfield, NJ 08033

Spina Bifida Association of America
4590 MacArthur Blvd., NW, Suite 250
Washington, DC 20007

NOTE. For further information on other organizations, see the following two references:

Backus, K. (Ed.).(1993). *Medical and health information directory: Vol. 1. Organizations, agencies, and institutions* (6th ed.). Detroit, MI: Gale Research.
Daniels, P. K., & Schwartz, C. A. (Eds.). (1994). Health and medical organizations. In *Encyclopedia of associations: Vol. 1. Part 2: National organizations of the U.S.* (28th ed., pp. 1415–1700). Detroit, MI: Gale Research.

Medical Problems That Present With Psychological Symptoms

ADDISON'S DISEASE (ADRENAL CORTICAL INSUFFICIENCY) Depression, negativism, apathy, suspiciousness, thought disorder, confusion, weight loss

CUSHING'S DISEASE (HYPERADRENALISM) Varied presentation, depression, anxiety, thought disorder, bizarre somatic delusions, weight gain, fatigue

HYPERTHYROIDISM Anxiety, depression, hyperactivity, grandiosity, heat intolerance, tremor

HYPOTHYROIDISM Lethargy, anxiety, irritability, thought disorder, somatic delusions, hallucinations, paranoia

HYPOGLYCEMIA (ISLET CELL ADENOMA) Anxiety, fear, depression, fatigue, agitation, confusion

INTRACRANIAL TUMORS Varied presentation, depression, anxiety, personality changes, headache, loss of memory and judgment

PANCREATIC CARCINOMA Depression, sense of imminent doom, loss of motivation, weight loss

PERNICIOUS ANEMIA Depression, guilt feelings, confusion, weight loss

PHEOCHROMOCYTOMA Anxiety, panic, fear, apprehension, trembling, sweating, headache

MULTIPLE SCLEROSIS Varied presentation, depression, mood swings, sometimes bland euphoria, speech difficulties

SYSTEMIC LUPUS ERYTHEMATOSUS Varied presentation, thought disorder, depression, confusion

PORPHYRIA (ACUTE INTERMITTENT) Anxiety, mood swings, extremes of excitement or withdrawal, emotional outbursts

HYPERCALCEMIA   Lack of energy, fatigue, irritability, memory deficit, anorexia, nausea, vomiting

HYPOCALCEMIA   Perioral numbness, increased nervousness, irritability, anxiety, increased emotional lability

NORMAL PRESSURE HYDROCEPHALUS   Apathy, psychomotor retardation, forgetfulness, unsteadiness of gait, incontinence

VITAMIN B DEFICIENCIES   Clinical evidence of vitamin deficiency occurs only when tissue stores are sharply depleted and these include: sore tongue, weakness, parathesias, lemon-yellow complexion, visual disturbances

WILSON'S DISEASE (HEPATOLENTICULAR DEGENERATION)   Can mimic almost any psychiatric disorder; family history may reveal a relative has died at an early age of liver disease, neurological disease or in a psychiatric hospital

NOTE.   See also R. C. Hall (Ed.). (1980). *Psychiatric presentations of medical illness: Somatopsychic disorders.* New York: SP Medical and Scientific Books.

References

Ader, R., & Cohen, N. (1993). Psychoneuroimmunology: Conditioning and stress. *Annual Review of Psychology, 44,* 53–85.

Ader, R., Weiner, H., & Baum, A. (1988). *Experimental foundations of behavioral medicine: Conditioning approaches.* Hillsdale, NJ: Erlbaum.

Agras, W. S. (1984). The behavioral treatment of somatic disorders. In W. D. Gentry (Ed.), *Handbook of behavioral medicine* (pp. 479–525). New York: Guilford Press.

Alexander, F. (1950). *Psychosomatic medicine.* New York: Norton.

American Psychiatric Association. (1994). *Diagnostic and statistical manual of mental disorders* (4th ed.). Washington, DC: Author.

American Psychological Association. (1953). *Ethical standards of psychologists.* Washington, DC: Author.

American Psychological Association. (1981). Ethical principles of psychologists. *American Psychologist, 36,* 633–638.

American Psychological Association. (1985a). *A hospital practice primer for psychologists.* Washington, DC: Author.

American Psychological Association. (1985b). *Standards for educational and psychological testing.* Washington, DC: Author.

American Psychological Association. (1986). *Guidelines for computer-based tests and interpretations.* Washington, DC: Author.

American Psychological Association. (1987). *General guidelines for providers of psychological services.* Washington, DC: Author.

American Psychological Association. (1992). Ethical principles of psychologists and code of conduct. *American Psychologist, 47,* 1597–1611.

American Psychological Association Ethics Committee. (1993). Report of the ethics committee: 1991–1992. *American Psychologist, 48,* 811–820.

Andersen, B. L. (1992). Psychological interventions for cancer patients to enhance the quality of life. *Journal of Consulting and Clinical Psychology, 60,* 552–568.

Appelbaum, P. S. (1993). Legal liability and managed care. *American Psychologist, 48,* 251–257.

Asken, M. J. (1979). Medical psychology: Toward definition, clarification, and organization. *Professional Psychology, 10,* 66–73.

Austad, C. S., & Berman, W. H. (Eds.). (1991). *Psychotherapy in managed health care: The optimal use of time and resources.* Washington, DC: American Psychological Association.

Bagheri, A. S., Lane, L. S., Kline, F. M., & Araujo, D. M. (1981). Why physicians fail to tell patients a psychiatrist is coming. *Psychosomatics, 22,* 407–419.

Baker v. United States, 226 F. Supp. 129 (S.D. Iowa 1964).

Bandura, A. (1969). *Principles of behavior modification.* New York: Holt, Rinehart & Winston.

Barton, W. E., & Sanborn, C. J. (1978). *Law and the mental health professional.* New York: International Universities Press.

Bazelon, D. L. (1974). Psychiatrists and the adversary process. *Scientific American, 290,* 18–23.

Beck, A. T. (1972). *Depression: Causes and treatment.* Philadelphia: University of Pennsylvania Press.

Beck, A. T., Rush, A. J., Shaw, B. F., & Emery, G. (1979). *Cognitive therapy of depression.* New York: Guilford Press.

Beck, A. T., Steer, R. A., & Garbin, M. G. (1988). Psychometric properties of the Beck Depression Inventory: Twenty-five years of evaluation. *Clinical Psychology Review, 8,* 77–100.

Becker, D. M., Hill, D. R., Jackson, J. S., Levine, D. M., Stillman, F. A., & Weiss, S. M. (Eds.). (1992). *Health behavioral research in minority populations: Access, design, and implementation* (NIH Publication No. 92–2965). Washington, DC: U.S. Department of Health and Human Services.

Beecher, H. K. (1956). Relationship of the significance of wound to the pain experienced. *Journal of the American Medical Association, 161,* 1609–1613.

Beigler, J. S. (1984). Tarasoff v. confidentiality. *Behavioral Sciences and the Law, 2,* 273–289.

Belar, C. D. (1980). Training the clinical psychology student in behavioral medicine. *Professional Psychology, 11,* 620–627.

Belar, C. D. (1989). Opportunities for psychologists in health maintenance organizations: Implications for graduate education and training. *Professional Psychology: Research and Practice, 20,* 390–394.

Belar, C. D. (1991). Behavioral medicine. In C. S. Austad & W. H. Berman (Eds.), *Psychotherapy in managed health care* (65–79). Washington, DC: American Psychological Association.

Belar, C. D., Deardorff, W. W., & Kelly, K. E. (1987). *The practice of clinical health psychology.* New York: Pergamon Press.

Belar, C. D., & Kibrick, S. (1986). Biofeedback in the treatment of chronic back pain. In A. Holzman & D. Turk (Eds.), *Pain management: A handbook of psychological treatment approaches* (pp. 131–150). New York: Pergamon Press.

Belar, C. D., & Perry, N. W. (1992). National conference on scientist–practitioner education and training for the professional practice of psychology. *American Psychologist, 47,* 71–75

Belar, C. D., & Siegel, L. J. (1983). A survey of postdoctoral training programs in health psychology. *Health Psychology, 2,* 413–425.

Belar, C. D., Wilson, E., & Hughes, H. (1982). Health psychology training in doctoral psychology programs. *Health Psychology, 1,* 289–299.

Bergner, M., Bobbitt, R. A., Carter, W. B., & Gilson, B. S. (1981). The Sickness Impact Profile: Development and final revision of a health status measure. *Medical Care, 19,* 787–806.

Bernard, L. C., & Krupat, E. (1994). *Health psychology: Biopsychosocial factors in health and illness.* Orlando, FL: Holt, Rinehart & Winston.

Bernstein, D. A., & Borkovec, T. D. (1973). *Progressive relaxation training: A manual for the helping professions.* Champaign, IL: Research Press.

Berry v. Moench, 8 Utah 2d 191, 331 P.2d 814 (1958).

Billowitz, A., & Friedson, W. (1978–1979). Are psychiatric consultants' recommendations followed? *International Journal of Psychiatry in Medicine, 9,* 179–189.

Blanchard, E. G. (1993). Irritable bowel syndrome. In R. J. Gatchel & E. B. Blanchard. (Eds.), *Psychophysiological disorders: Research and clinical applications* (pp. 23–62). Washington, DC: American Psychological Association.

Blechman, E. A., & Brownell, K. D. (Eds.). (1988). *Handbook of behavioral medicine for women.* New York: Pergamon.

Bleiberg, J., Ciulla, R., & Katz, B. L. (1991). Psychological components of rehabilitation programs for brain-injured and spinal-cord-injured patients. In J. J. Sweet, R. H. Rozensky, & S. M. Tovian (Eds.), *Handbook of clinical psychology in medical settings* (pp 375–400). New York: Plenum.

Bongar, B., Maris, R. W., Berman, A. L., & Litman, R. E. (1992). Outpatient standards of care and the suicidal patient. *Suicide and Life-Threatening Behavior,* *22,* 453–478.

Bradley, L. A., McDonald-Haile, J., & Jaworski, T. M. (1992). Assessment of psychological status using interviews and self-report instruments. In D. C. Turk & R. Melzack (Eds.), *Handbook of pain assessment* (pp. 193–213). New York: Guilford Press.

Brantley, P. J., & Bruce, B. K. (1986). Assessment in behavioral medicine. In A. R. Ciminero, K. S. Calhoun, & H. E. Adams (Eds.), *Handbook of behavioral assessment* (2nd ed., pp. 673–710). New York: Wiley

Brodman, K., Erdman, A. J., & Wolff, H. G. (1949). *Cornell Medical Index Health Questionnaire.* New York: Cornell University Medical College.

Brownell, K. D., & Wadden, T. A. (1992). Etiology and treatment of obesity: Understanding a serious, prevalent, and refractory disorder. *Journal of Consulting and Clinical Psychology, 60,* 505–517.

Budman, S. H., & Gurman, A. S. (1988). *Theory and practice of brief therapy.* New York: Guilford Press.

Budman, S. H., Hoyt, M. F., & Friedman, S. (1992). *The first session in brief therapy.* New York: Guilford Press.

Burish, T. G., & Bradley, L. A. (Eds.). (1983). *Coping with chronic disease.* New York: Academic Press.

Bursztajn, H., Gutheil, T. G., Hamm, R. M., & Brodsky, A. (1983). Subjective data and suicide assessment in the light of recent legal developments: Part II. Clinical uses of legal standards in the interpretation of subjective data. *International Journal of Law and Psychiatry, 6,* 331–350.

Butcher, J. N., Dahlstrom, W. G., Graham, J. R., Tellegen, A. M. & Kaemmer, B. (1989). *MMPI–2: Manual for administration and scoring.* Minneapolis: University of Minnesota Press.

Cacioppo, J. T., Petty, R. E., & Marshall-Goodell, B. (1985). Physical, social, and inferential elements of psychophysiological measurement. In P. Karoly (Ed.), *Measurement strategies in health psychology* (pp. 263–300). New York: Wiley.

Caplan, B. (Ed.). (1987). *Rehabilitation psychology desk reference.* Rockville, MD: Aspen.

Cassileth, B. R., Zupkis, R. V., Sutton-Smith, K., & March, V. (1980). Informed consent: Why are its goals imperfectly realized? *The New England Journal of Medicine, 302,* 896–900.

Cattell, R. B., Eber, H. W., & Tatsouka, M. M. (1970). *Handbook for the Sixteen Per-*

sonality Factor Questionnaire (16PF). Champaign, IL: Institute for Personality and Ability Testing.

Cautela, J. R. (1967). Covert sensitization. *Psychological Reports, 20,* 459–468.

Chambers v. Ingram, 858 F.2d 351, 356 (7th Cir. 1988).

Charles, S. C. (1993). The doctor–patient relationship and medical malpractice litigation. *Bulletin of the Menninger Clinic, 57,* 195–207.

Cohen, R. J. (1979). *Malpractice: A guide for mental health professionals.* New York: Free Press.

Cohen, R. J., & Mariano, W. E. (1982). *Legal guidebook in mental health.* New York: Free Press.

Corah, N. L. (1969). Development of a Dental Anxiety Scale. *Journal of Dental Research, 48,* 396.

Costa, P. T., & VandenBos, G. R. (1990). *Psychological aspects of chronic conditions, fatal diseases, and clinical care.* Washington, DC: American Psychological Association.

Cox, D. J., Gonder-Frederick, L, & Saunders, J. R. (1991). Diabetes: Clinical issues and management. In J. J. Sweet, R. H. Rozensky, & S. M. Tovian (Eds.), *Handbook of clinical psychology in medical settings* (pp. 473–495). New York: Plenum.

Creer, T. L., & Bender, B. G. (1993). Asthma. In R. K. Gatchel & E. B. Blanchard. (Eds.), *Psychophysiological disorders: Research and clinical applications* (pp. 151–203). Washington, DC: American Psychological Association.

Creer, T. L., Reynolds, R. V., & Kotses, H. (1991). Psychological theory, assessment, and interventions for adult and childhood asthma. In J. J. Sweet, R. H. Rozensky, & S. M. Tovian (Eds.), *Handbook of clinical psychology in medical settings* (pp. 497–515). New York: Plenum.

Cross, H. K., & Deardorff, W. W. (1987). Malpractice in psychotherapy and psychological evaluation. In J. R. McNamara & M. A. Appel (Eds.), *Critical issues, developments, and trends in professional psychology* (Vol. 3, pp. 55–79). New York: Praeger.

Cummings, N. A. (1985). Assessing the computer's impact: Professional concerns. *Computers in human behavior, 1,* 293–300.

Cummings, N. A. (1986). The dismantling of our health care system. *American Psychologist, 41,* 426–431.

Dana, R. H. (1984). Assessment for health psychology. *Clinical Psychology Review, 4,* 459–476.

Dana, R. H., & Hoffman, T. A. (1987). Health assessment domains: Credibility and legitimization. *Clinical Psychology Review, 7,* 539–555.

Davis, M., Eshelman, E. R., & McKay, M. (1988). *The relaxation and stress reduction workbook* (3rd ed.). Oakland, CA: New Harbinger Publications.

Dawidoff, D. (1966). The malpractice of psychiatrists. *Duke Law Journal*, 696–716.

Deardorff, W. W., Cross, H. J., & Hupprich, W. (1984). Malpractice liability in psychotherapy: Client and practitioner perspectives. *Professional Psychology: Research and Practice, 15*, 590–600.

DeGood, D.E. (1983). Reducing medical patients' reluctance to participate in psychotherapies: The initial session. *Professional Psychology: Research & Practice, 14*, 570–579.

Derogatis, L. R. (1983). *SCL–90–R: Administration, scoring and procedures manual— II for the revised version.* Towson, MD: Clinical Psychometric Research.

Derogatis, L. R. (1986). The Psychosocial Adjustment to Illness Scale (PAIS). *Journal of Psychosomatic Research, 30*(1), 77–91.

Derogatis, L. R., & Lopez, M. C. (1983). *The Psychosocial Adjustment to Illness Scale (PAIS & PAIS–SR): Administration, scoring and procedures manual: I.* Baltimore: Johns Hopkins University School of Medicine.

Dershimer, R. A. (1990). *Counseling the bereaved.* Des Moines, IA: Allyn & Bacon.

Division of Health Psychology. (1991). *Doctoral and postdoctoral training programs in health psychology.* Washington, DC: Author.

Doleys, D. M., Meredith, R. L., & Ciminero, A. R. (1982). *Behavioral medicine: Assessment and treatment strategies.* New York: Plenum.

Dorken, H. (1990). Malpractice claims experience of psychologists: Policy issues, cost comparisons with psychiatrists, and prescription privilege implications. *Professional Psychology: Research and Practice, 21*, 150–152.

Dubin, S. S. (1972). Obsolescence or lifelong education: A choice for the professional. *American Psychologist, 27*, 486–496.

Elfant, A. B. (1985). Psychotherapy and assessment in hospital settings: Ideological and professional conflicts. *Professional Psychology: Research and Practice, 16*(1), 55–63.

Ellis, A. (1962). *Reason and emotion in psychotherapy.* New York: Lyle Stuart.

Engel, G. L. (1977, April). The need for a new medical model: A challenge for biomedicine. *Science, 196*, 129–136.

Fabrega, H. (1974). *Disease and social behavior.* Cambridge, MA: MIT Press.

Feldman, S. R., & Ward, T. M. (1979). Psychotherapeutic injury: Reshaping the implied contract as an alternative to malpractice. *North Carolina Law Review, 58*, 63–96.

Fisher, K. (1985). Malpractice: Charges catch clinicians in cycle of shame, slip-ups. *American Psychological Association Monitor, 16*, 6–7.

Flor, H., & Turk, D. C. (1989). Psychophysiology of chronic pain: Do chronic pain patients exhibit symptom-specific psychophysiological responses? *Psychological Bulletin, 105,* 215–259.

Folstein, M. F., Folstein, S. E., & McHugh, P. R. (1975). "Mini-mental state": A practical method for grading the cognitive state of patients for the clinician. *Journal of Psychiatric Research, 12,* 189–198.

Fordyce, W. E. (1976). *Behavioral methods for chronic pain and illness.* St. Louis: Mosby.

Fowler, R. D., & Butcher, J. N. (1986). Critique of Matarazzo's views on computerized testing: All sigma and no meaning. *American Psychologist, 41,* 64–96.

Frank, R. G., Gluck, J. P., & Buckelew, S. P. (1990). Rehabilitation: Psychology's greatest opportunity? *American Psychologist, 45,* 757–761.

Freedman, R. R. (1993). Raynaud's disease and phenomenon. In R. K. Gatchel & E. B. Blanchard. (Eds.), *Psychophysiological disorders: Research and clinical applications* (pp. 245–267). Washington, DC: American Psychological Association.

Fried, R. (1993). *The psychology and physiology of breathing.* New York: Plenum.

Furniss v. Fitchett, N.Z.L.R. 396 S. Ct. (1958).

Furrow, B. (1980). *Malpractice in psychotherapy.* Lexington, MA: Heath.

Garfield, S. L. (1989). *The practice of brief psychotherapy.* New York: Pergamon.

Garner, D. M., & Olmsted, M. P. (1984). *The Eating Disorder Inventory Manual.* Odessa, FL: Psychological Assessment Resources.

Gatchel, R. J., & Blanchard, E. B. (Eds.). (1993). *Psychophysiological disorders: Research and clinical applications.* Washington, DC: American Psychological Association.

Gentry, W. D. (Ed.). (1984). *Handbook of behavioral medicine.* New York: Guilford Press.

Gentry, W. D., & Matarazzo, J. D. (1981). Medical psychology: Three decades of growth and development. In C. K. Prokop & L. A. Bradley (Eds.), *Medical psychology: Contributions to behavioral medicine* (pp. 5–15). New York: Academic Press.

Gentry, W. D., & Owens, D. (1986). Pain groups. In A. D. Holzman & D. C. Turk (Eds.), *Pain management: A handbook of psychological treatment approaches* (pp. 100–112). New York: Pergamon Press.

Gentry, W. D., Street, W. J., Masur, F. T., & Asken, M. J. (1981). Training in medical psychology: A survey of graduate and internship training programs. *Professional Psychology, 13,* 397–403.

Golden, W. L., Dowd, E. T., & Friedberg, F. (1987). *Hypnotherapy: A modern approach.* New York: Pergamon Press.

Goldfried, M. R., & Davison, G. (1976). *Clinical behavioral therapy*. New York: Holt, Rinehart & Winston.

Goodstein, L. D. (1985). *White paper on duty to protect*. Washington, DC: American Psychological Association Committee on Legal Issues.

Graham, J. R. (1977). *The MMPI: A practical guide*. New York: Oxford University Press.

Greene, R. L. (1980). *The MMPI: An interpretive manual*. New York: Grune & Stratton.

Greene, R. L. (1991). *The MMPI-2/MMPI: An interpretive manual*. Boston: Allyn & Bacon.

Grimaldi, K. E., & Lichtenstein, E. (1969). Hot, smoky air as an aversive stimulus in the treatment of smoking. *Behaviour Research and Therapy, 7*, 275–282.

Gruen, W. (1975). Effects of brief psychotherapy during the hospitalization period on the recovery process in heart attacks. *Journal of Consulting and Clinical Psychology, 43*, 223–232.

Grunder, T. M. (1980). On the readability of surgical consent forms. *The New England Journal of Medicine, 302*, 900–902.

Guggenheim, F. G. (1978). Suicide. In T. P. Hackett & N. H. Cassen (Eds.), *Massachusetts General Hospital: Handbook of general hospital psychiatry* (pp. 250–263). St. Louis, MO: Mosby.

Gutheil, T. G., Bursztajn, H., Hamm, R. M., & Brodsky, A. (1983). Subjective data and suicide assessment in the light of recent legal developments: Part I. Malpractice prevention and the use of subjective data. *International Journal of Law and Psychiatry, 6*, 317–329.

Gylys, B. A., & Wedding, M. E. (1988). *Medical terminology: A systems approach* (2nd ed.). Philadelphia: Dans.

Haas, L. J., & Cummings, N. A. (1991). Managed outpatient mental health plans: Clinical, ethical, and practical guidelines for participation. *Professional Psychology: Research and Practice, 22*, 45–51.

Hall, H., Minnes, L., & Olness, K. (1993). The psychophysiology of voluntary immunomodulation. *International Journal of Neuroscience, 69*, 221–234.

Halperin, D. A. (1980). "Misinformed consent." *Bulletin of the American Academy of Psychiatry and Law, 8*, 175–178.

Hamilton, M. (1959). The assessment of anxiety status by rating. *British Journal of Medical Psychology, 32*, 50–55.

Hammer v. Rosen, 7 N.Y.2d 376, 165 N.E.2d 756, 198 N.Y.S.2d (1960).

Harrar, W. R., VandeCreek, L, & Knapp, S. (1990). Ethical and legal aspects of clinical supervision. *Professional Psychology: Research and Practice, 21*, 37–41.

Harris, M. (1973). Tort liability of the psychotherapist. *University of San Francisco Law Review, 8*, 405–436.

Hathaway, S. R., & McKinley, J. C. (1967). *The Minnesota Multiphasic Personality Inventory manual.* New York: Psychological Corporation.

Heide, F. J., & Borkovec, T. D. (1984). Relaxation-induced anxiety: Mechanisms and theoretical implications. *Behavior Research and Therapy, 22*(1), 1–12.

Hilgard, E. R., & Hilgard J. R. (1994). *Hypnosis in the relief of pain.* New York: Brunner/Mazel.

Hofer, P. J., & Bersoff, D. N. (1983). *Standards for the administration and interpretation of computerized psychological testing.* (Available from D. N. Bersoff, Suite 511, 1200 Seventeenth Street, NW, Washington, DC 20036)

Hogan, D. (1979). *The regulation of psychotherapists: Vol. 3. A review of malpractice suits in the United States.* Cambridge, MA: Ballinger.

Holmes, T. H., & Rahe, R. H. (1967). A Social Readjustment Rating Scale. *Journal of Psychosomatic Research, 11*, 213–218.

Holzman, A. D., & Turk, D. C. (1986). *Pain management: A handbook of psychological treatment approaches.* Elmsford, NY: Pergamon Press.

House, J. S., Landis, K. R., & Umberson, D. (1988, July). Social relationships and health. *Science, 241*, 540–545.

Houston, B. K. (1988). Division 38 survey: Synopsis of results. *The Health Psychologist, 10*, 2–3.

Isselbacher, K. J., Braunwald, E., Wilson, J. D., Martin, J. B., Fauci, A. S., & Kasper, D. L. (Eds.). (1994). *Harrison's principles of internal medicine* (13th ed.) New York: McGraw-Hill.

Jablonski by Pahls v. United States, 712F.2d 391 (1983).

Jacob, R. G., & Moore, D. J. (1984). Paradoxical interventions in behavioral medicine. *Journal of Behavior Therapy and Experimental Psychiatry, 15*, 205–213.

Jacobs, D. F. (1983). The development and application of standards of practice for professional psychologists. In B. D. Sales (Ed.), *The professional psychologists' handbook.* New York: Plenum.

Jacobs, J., Bernhard, R., Delgado, A., & Strain, J. J. (1977). Screening for organic mental syndromes in the medically ill. *Annals of Internal Medicine, 86*, 40.

Jacobson, E. (1939). *Progressive relaxation.* Chicago: University of Chicago Press.

Janis, I. L. (1958). *Psychological stress: Psychoanalytic and behavioral studies of surgical patients.* New York: Wiley.

Jenkins, C. D., Zyzanski, S. J., & Rosenman, R. H. (1979). *Jenkins Activity Survey manual.* New York: The Psychological Corporation.

Johnston, M., & Vogele, C. (1993). Benefits of psychological preparation for surgery: A meta-analysis. *Annals of Behavioral Medicine, 15,* 245–256.

Jones, E., & Nisbett, R. (1971). The actor and observer. Divergent perceptions of the causes of behavior. In E. E. Jones, D. E. Kanouse, H. H. Kelly, R. E. Nisbett, S. Valins, & B. Weiner (Eds.), *Attribution: Perceiving the causes of behavior.* Morristown, NJ: General Learning Press.

Kamenar, P. D. (1984). Psychiatrists' duty to warn of a dangerous patient: A survey of the law. *Behavioral Sciences and the Law, 2,* 259–272.

Kanner, A. D., Coyne, J. C., Schaefer, C., & Lazarus, R. S. (1981). Comparison of two modes of stress measurement: Daily hassles and uplifts versus major life events. *Journal of Behavioral Medicine, 4,* 1–39.

Kaplan, R. M., Sallis, J. F., & Patterson, T. L. (1993). *Health and human behavior.* New York: McGraw-Hill.

Karoly, P. (1985). *Measurement strategies in health psychology.* New York: Wiley.

Karoly, P. (Ed.). (1988). *Handbook of child health assessment: Biopsychosocial perspectives.* New York: Wiley.

Katz, S. T., Downs, H., Cash, H., & Grotz, R. (1970). Progress in the development of the index of ADL. *The Gerontologist, 10,* 20–30.

Keefe, F. J., & Blumenthal, J. A. (Eds.). (1982). *Assessment strategies in behavioral medicine.* New York: Grune & Stratton.

Keith-Spiegel, P., & Koocher, G. P. (1985). *Ethics in psychology.* New York: Random House.

Kelly, J. A., & Murphy, D. A. (1992). Psychological interventions with AIDS and HIV: Prevention and treatment. *Journal of Consulting and Clinical Psychology, 60,* 576–585.

Kerns, R. D., Turk, D. C., & Rudy, T. E. (1985). The West Haven–Yale Multidimensional Pain Inventory. *Pain, 23,* 345–356.

Klein, J. I., & Glover, S. I. (1983). Psychiatric malpractice. *International Journal of Law and Psychiatry, 6,* 131–157.

Kleinman, A., Eisenberg, L., & Good, B. (1977). *Culture, illness, and care: Clinical lessons from anthropological and cross-cultural research.* Unpublished report.

Knapp, S. (1980). A primer on malpractice for psychologists. *Professional Psychology, 11,* 606–612.

Knapp, S., & VandeCreek, L. (1981). Behavioral medicine: Its malpractice risks for psychologists. *Professional Psychology, 12,* 677–683.

Knapp, S., & VandeCreek, L. (1990). Application of the duty to protect to HIV-positive patients. *Professional Psychology: Research and Practice, 21,* 161–166.

Knapp, S., & VandeCreek, L. (1993). Legal and ethical issues in billing patients and collecting fees. *Psychotherapy, 30,* 25–31.

Koocher, G. P. (1983). Ethical and professional standards in psychology. In B. D. Sales (Ed.), *The professional psychologist's handbook* (pp. 77–109). New York: Plenum.

Koocher, G. P. (1994). APA and the FTC: New adventures in consumer protection. *American Psychologist, 49,* 322–328.

Korchin, S. J. (1976). *Modern clinical psychology.* New York: Basic Books.

Landau-Stanton, J., & Clements, C. D. (1993). *AIDS, health and mental health: A primary sourcebook.* New York: Brunner/Mazel.

Landrine, H., & Klonoff, E. (1992). Culture and health-related schemas: A review and proposal for interdisciplinary integration. *Health Psychology, 11,* 267–276.

Lang, P. J., & Melamed, B. G. (1969). Avoidance conditioning therapy of an infant with chronic ruminative vomiting. *Journal of Abnormal Psychology, 74,* 139–142.

LeCron, L. (1970). *Self hypnosis.* New York: New American Library.

Leigh, H., & Reiser, M. F. (1980). *Biological, psychological, and social dimensions of medical practice.* New York: Plenum.

Leo, J. (1984, October). Polling for mental health. *Time,* 80.

Ley, P. (1982). Studies of recall in medical settings. *Human Learning, 1,* 223–233.

Lichtenstein, E., & Glasgow, R. E. (1992). Smoking cessation: What have we learned over the past decade? *Journal of Consulting and Clinical Psychology, 60,* 518–527.

Linden, W. (1991). *Autogenic training: A clinical guide.* New York: Guilford Press.

Lipowski, Z. J. (1967). Review of consultation psychiatry and psychosomatic medicine: I. General principles. *Psychosomatic Medicine, 29,* 153–171.

Lipowski, Z. J. (1977). Psychosomatic medicine in the seventies: An overview. *American Journal of Psychiatry, 134*(3), 233–243.

Loeser, J. (1986). Herpes Zoster and postherpetic neuralgia. *Pain, 25,* 149–164.

Lowman, R. L, & Resnick, R. J. (Eds.). (1994). *The mental health professional's guide to managed health care.* Washington, DC: American Psychological Association.

Lucente, F. E., & Fleck, S. (1972). A study of hospitalization anxiety in 408 medical and surgical patients. *Psychosomatic Medicine, 34,* 304–312.

Magrab, P. R., & Papadopoulou, Z. L. (1977). The effect of a token economy on dietary compliance for children on hemodialysis. *Journal of Applied Behavior Analysis, 10,* 573–578.

Malament, I. B., Dunn, M. E., & Davis, R. (1975). Pressure sores: An operant conditioning approach to prevention. *Archives of Physical Medicine and Rehabilitation, 56,* 161–165.

Markus, R. M. (1965). Conspiracy of silence. *Cleveland Law Review, 14,* 520–533.

Martin, P. R. (1993). *Psychological management of chronic headaches.* New York: Guilford Press.

Maslach, C. (1982). *Burnout: The cost of caring.* Englewood Cliffs, NJ: Prentice Hall.

Matarazzo, J. D. (1980). Behavioral health and behavioral medicine. *American Psychologist, 35,* 807–817.

Matarazzo, J. D. (1983). Computerized psychological testing. *Science, 221,* p. 323.

Matarazzo, J. D. (1986). Computerized clinical psychological test interpretation: Unvalidated plus all mean and no sigma. *American Psychologist, 41,* 14–21.

Matarazzo, J. D., Weiss, S. M., Herd, J. A., Miller, N. E., & Weiss, S. M. (Eds.). (1984). *Behavioral health: A handbook of health enhancement and disease prevention.* New York: Wiley.

Maxmen, J. S. (1991). *Psychotropic drugs: Fast facts.* New York: Norton.

McKay, M., Davis, M., & Fanning, P. (1981). *Thoughts and feelings: The art of cognitive stress intervention.* Richmond, CA: New Harbinger.

Mechanic, D. (1972). Social psychological factors affecting the presentation of bodily complaints. *New England Journal of Medicine, 286,* 1132–1139.

Meenan, R. R., Gertman, P. M., & Mason, J. H. (1982). The Arthritis Impact Measurement Scales: Further investigation of a health status measure. *Arthritis and Rheumatology, 25,* 1048–1053.

Meichenbaum, D. (1977). *Cognitive behavior modification: An integrative approach.* New York: Plenum.

Meichenbaum, D., & Turk, D. C. (1987). *Facilitating treatment adherence: A practitioner's guidebook.* New York: Plenum.

Melamed, B. G., & Siegel, L. J. (1980). *Behavioral medicine: Practical applications in health care.* New York: Springer.

Melamed, B. G., & Williamson, D. J. (1991). Programs for the treatment of dental disorders: Dental anxiety and tempomandibular disorders. In J. J. Sweet, R. H. Rozensky, & S. M. Tovian (Eds.), *Handbook of clinical psychology in medical settings* (pp. 539–565). New York: Plenum.

Melzack, R. (1975). The McGill Pain Questionnaire: Major properties and scoring methods. *Pain, 1,* 277–299.

Melzack, R., & Wall, P. D. (1983). *The challenge of pain.* New York: Basic Books.

Miller, T. W. (1981). Professional services evaluation in a medical setting. In C. K. Prokop & L. A. Bradley (Eds.), *Medical psychology: Contributions to behavioral medicine* (pp. 471–483). New York: Academic Press.

Millon, T. (1982a). *Millon Clinical Multiaxial Inventory manual* (3rd ed.). Minneapolis, MN: National Computer Systems.

Millon, T. (1982b). On the nature of clinical health psychology. In T. Millon, C. J. Green, & R. B. Meagher (Eds.), *Handbook of clinical health psychology* (pp. 1–27). New York: Plenum.

Millon, T., Green, C. J., & Meagher, R. B. (1982b). *Millon Behavioral Health Inventory manual.* Minneapolis: National Computer Systems.

Monahan, J. (1993). Limiting therapist exposure to Tarasoff liability: Guidelines for risk containment. *American Psychologist, 48,* 242–250.

Moos, R. H. (1974). *Evaluating treatment environments: A social ecological approach.* New York: Wiley.

Moos, R. H. (Ed.) (1977). *Coping with physical illness.* New York: Plenum.

Moos, R. H. (1981). *Work Environment Scale manual.* Palo Alto, CA: Consulting Psychologists Press.

Moos, R., & Moos, B. (1981). *Family Environment Scale manual.* Palo Alto, CA: Consulting Psychologists Press.

Moos, R. H., & Schaefer, J. A. (1987). Evaluating health care work settings: A holistic conceptual framework. *Psychology and Health, 1,* 97–122.

Morin, C. M. (1993). *Insomnia: Psychological assessment and management.* New York: Guilford Press.

Morrow, G., & Clayman, D. (1982). *A membership survey of the division of health psychology, American Psychological Association.* Unpublished manuscript.

Mumford, E., Schlesinger, H. J., & Glass, G. V. (1982). The effects of psychological intervention on recovery from surgery and heart attacks: An analysis of the literature. *American Journal of Public Health, 72,* 141–151.

Nader, R., Petkas, P., & Blackwell, K. (Eds.). (1972). *Whistle blowing.* New York: Bantam Books.

Newman, A. S. (1981). Ethical issues in the supervision of psychotherapy. *Professional Psychology, 12,* 690–695.

Noll, J. D. (1976). The psychotherapist and informed consent. *American Journal of Psychiatry, 133,* 1451–1453.

Olson, R. A., Mullins, L. L., Gillman, J. B., & Chaney, J. M. (Eds.). (1994). *The sourcebook of pediatric psychology.* Des Moines, IA: Allyn & Bacon.

Olton, D. S., & Noonberg, A. R. (1980). *Biofeedback: Clinical applications in behavioral medicine.* Englewood Cliffs, NJ: Prentice Hall.

Osler, W. (1971). In W. P. D. Wrightsman (Ed.), *The emergence of scientific medicine.* Edinburgh, Scotland: Oliver & Boyd.

Petrucci, R. J., & Harwick, R. D. (1984). Role of the psychologist on a radical head and neck surgical service team. *Professional Psychology, 15,* 538–543.

Philips, C. (1978). Tension headache: Theoretical problems. *Behavior Research and Therapy, 16,* 249–261.

Pilisuk, M., Boylan, R., & Acredolo, C. (1987). Social support, life stress, and subsequent medical care utilization. *Health Psychology, 6,* 273–288.

Piotrowski, C., & Lubin, B. (1990). Assessment practices of health psychologists: Survey of APA Division 38 clinicians. *Professional Psychology, Research and Practice, 21,* 99–106.

Polonsky, W. H. (1993). Psychosocial issues in diabetes mellitus. In R. K. Gatchel & E. B. Blanchard. (Eds.), *Psychophysiological disorders: Research and clinical applications* (pp. 357–381). Washington, DC: American Psychological Association.

Pope, K. S. (1990). Ethical and malpractice issues in hospital practice. *American Psychologist, 45,* 1066–1070.

Pope, K. S. (1992). Responsibilities in providing psychological test feedback to clients. *Psychological Assessment, 4,* 268–271.

Pope, K. S., Keith-Spiegel, P., & Tabachnick, B. G. (1986). Sexual attraction to clients: The human therapist and the (sometimes) inhuman training system. *American Psychologist, 41,* 147–158.

Pope, K. S., Simpson, H. J., & Myron, M. F. (1978). Malpractice in outpatient psychotherapy. *American Journal of Psychotherapy, 32,* 593–600.

Pope, K. S., Tabachnick, B. G., & Keith-Spiegel, P. (1987). Ethics of practice: The beliefs and behaviors of psychologists and therapists. *American Psychologist, 42,* 993–1006.

Pope, K. S., & Vetter, V. A. (1992). Ethical dilemmas encountered by members of the American Psychological Association. *American Psychologist, 47,* 397–411.

Poppen, R. (1988). *Behavioral relaxation training and assessment.* New York: Pergamon Press.

Professional negligence. (1973). *University of Pennsylvania Law Review, 121,* 627.

Prokop, C. K., & Bradley, L. A. (Eds.). (1981). *Medical psychology: Contributions to behavioral medicine.* New York: Academic Press.

Quinn, K. M. (1984). The impact of Tarasoff on clinical practice. *Behavioral Sciences and the Law, 2,* 319–329.

Rachlin, S. (1984). Double jeopardy: Suicide and malpractice. *General Hospital Psychiatry, 6,* 302–307.

Radloff, L. S. (1977). The CES–D scale: A self-report depression scale for research in the general population. *Journal of Applied Psychological Measurement, 1,* 385–401.

Rando, T. A. (1984). *Grief, dying and death: Clinical interventions for caregivers.* Champaign, IL: Research Press.

Ray, W. J., Raczynski, J. M., Rogers, T., & Kimball, W. H. (1979). *Evaluation of clinical biofeedback.* New York: Plenum.

Resolutions approved by the National Conference on Graduate Education in Psychology. (1987). *American Psychologist, 42,* 1070–1084.

Rodin, J., & Collins, A. (Eds.). (1991). *Women and new reproductive technologies: Medical, psychosocial, legal, and ethical dilemmas.* Hillsdale, NJ: Erlbaum.

Rodrigue, J. R., Greene, A. G., & Boggs, S. R. (1994) Current status of psychological research in organ transplantation. *Journal of Clinical Psychology in Medical Settings, 1,* 41–70.

Rosen, R. C., Brondolo, E., & Kostis, J. B. (1993). Nonpharmacological treatment of essential hypertension: Research and clinical applications. In R. J. Gatchel & E. B. Blanchard (Eds.), *Psychophysiological disorders: Research and clinical applications* (pp. 63–110). Washington, DC: American Psychological Association.

Rosenbaum, L. (1983). Biofeedback-assisted stress management for insulin-treated diabetes mellitus. *Biofeedback and Self Regulation, 8*(1), 519–532.

Rosenman, R. (1978). The interview method of assessment of the coronary-prone behavior pattern. In T. M. Dembroski, S. M. Weiss, J. L. Shields, S. G. Haynes, & M. Feinleib (Eds.), *Coronary-prone behavior.* New York: Springer-Verlag.

Routh, D. K. (Ed.). (1988). *Handbook of pediatric psychology.* New York: Guilford Press.

Roy v. Hartogs, 85 Misc.2d 891, 381 N.Y.S.2d 587 (1975).

Russo v. Ascher, 545 A.2d 714 (Md. App. 1988).

Russo, D.C., Bird, P. O., & Masek, B.J. (1980). Assessment issues in behavioral medicine. *Behavioral Assessment, 2*(1), 1–18.

Sadoff, R. L. (1979). Changes in mental health law: Progress for patients—Problems for psychiatrists. In S. Halleck (Ed.), *New directions for mental health services: Coping with the legal onslaught,* No. 4. San Francisco: Jossey-Bass.

Sajwaj, T., Libet, J., & Agras, W. S. (1974). Lemon-juice therapy: The control of life-threatening rumination in a six-month-old infant. *Journal of Applied Behavior Analysis, 7,* 557–566.

Salmon, P. (1992). Psychological factors in surgical stress: Implications for management. *Clinical Psychology Review, 12,* 681–704.

Sarason, I. G., Johnson, J. H., & Siegel, J. M. (1978). Assessing the impact of life changes: Development of the Life Experiences Survey. *Journal of Consulting and Clinical Psychology, 46,* 932–946.

Sayette, M. A., & Mayne, T. J. (1990). Survey of current clinical research trends in clinical psychology. *American Psychologist, 45,* 1263–1266.

Schag, C. A., Heinrich, R. L., Aadland, R. L., & Ganz, P. A. (1990). Assessing problems of cancer patients: Psychometric properties of the Cancer Inventory of Problem Situations. *Health Psychology, 9,* 83–102.

Schenkenberg, T., Peterson, L., Wood, D., & DaBell, R. (1981). Psychological consultation/liaison in a medical and neurological setting: Physicians' appraisal. *Professional Psychology, 12,* 309–317.

Schindler, R. J. (1976). Malpractice—Another new dimension of liability: A critical analysis. *Trial Lawyer's Guide,* 129–151.

Schofield, W. (1969). The role of psychology in the delivery of health services. *American Psychologist, 24,* 565–584.

Schultz, J. H., & Luthe, W. (1969). *Autogenic therapy.* New York: Grune & Stratton.

Schuster v. Altenberg, 424 N.W.2d 159 (Wis. 1988).

Schutz, B. M. (1982). *Legal liability in psychotherapy: A practitioner's guide to risk management.* San Francisco: Jossey-Bass.

Schwartz, G. E., & Weiss, S. M. (1978). Behavioral medicine revisited: An amended definition. *Journal of Behavioral Medicine, 1,* 249–251.

Schwartz, M. S. (1987). *Biofeedback: A practitioner's guide.* New York: Guilford Press.

Schwitzgebel, R. L., & Schwitzgebel, R. K. (1980). *Law and psychological practice.* New York: Wiley.

Seeburg, K. N., & DeBoer, K. F. (1980). Effects of EMG biofeedback on diabetes. *Biofeedback and Self Regulation, 5,* 289–293.

Shabsin, H. S., & Whitehead, W. E. (1991). Psychological characteristics and treatment of patients with gastrointestinal disorders. In J. J. Sweet, R. H. Rozensky, & S. M. Tovian (Eds.), *Handbook of clinical psychology in medical settings* (pp. 517–537). New York: Plenum.

Shanteau, J., & Harris, R. J. (Eds.). (1990). *Organ donation and transplantation: Psychological and behavioral factors.* Washington, DC: American Psychological Association.

Shapiro, A., & Baum, A. (Eds.). (1991). *Behavioral aspects of cardiovascular disease.* Hillsdale, NJ: Erlbaum.

Sheridan, E. P., Matarazzo, J. D., Boll, T. J., Perry, N. W., Weiss, S. M., & Belar, C. D. (1988). Post doctoral education training for clinical service providers in health psychology. *Health Psychology, 7,* 1–17.

Shevitz, S. A., Silberfarb, P. M., & Lipowski, Z. J. (1976). Psychiatric consultations in a general hospital: A report on 1,000 referrals. *Diseases of the Nervous System, 37,* 295–300.

Shorter, E. (1992). *From paralysis to fatigue: A history of psychosomatic illness in the modern era.* New York: Free Press.

Shows, W. D. (1976). Problem of training psychology interns in medical schools: A case of trying to change the leopard's spots. *Professional Psychology, 7,* 393–395.

Simmons v. United States, 805 F2d 1363 at 1366 (9th Cir. 1986).

Skorupa, J., & Agresti, A. A. (1993). Ethical beliefs about burnout and continued professional practice. *Professional Psychology: Research and Practice, 24,* 281–285.

Slovenko, R. (1978). Psychotherapy and informed consent: A search in judicial regulation. In W. E. Barton & C. J. Sanborn (Eds.), *Law and the mental health professions: Friction at the interface* (pp. 51–70). New York: International Universities Press.

Smith, T. S., McGuire, J. M., Abbott, D. W., & Blau, B. I. (1991). Clinical ethical decision making: An investigation of the rationales used to justify doing less than one believes one should. *Professional Psychology: Research and Practice, 22,* 235–239.

Sobel, D. S. (1991). The placebo effect: Using the body's own healing mechanisms. In R. Ornstein & C. Swencionis (Eds.), *The healing brain: A scientific reader* (pp. 63–74). New York: Guilford Press.

Soisson, E. L., VandeCreek, L., & Knapp, S. (1987). Thorough record keeping: A good defense in a litigious era. *Professional Psychology: Research and Practice, 18,* 498–502.

Southard, M. J., & Gross, B. H. (1982). Making clinical decisions after Tarasoff. In B. Gross & L. E. Weinberger (Eds.), *New directions for mental health services: Vol. 16: The mental health professional and the legal system* (pp. 93–101). San Francisco: Jossey-Bass.

Spence, A. P. (1982). *Basic human anatomy.* Menlo Park, CA: Benjamin/Cummings.

Spielberger, C. D. (1988). *State–Trait Anger Expression Inventory.* Odessa, FL: Psychological Assessment Resources.

Spielberger, C. D., Gorsuch, R. L., & Lushene, R. (1970). *The State–Trait Anxiety Inventory manual.* Palo Alto, CA: Consulting Psychologists Press.

Stabler, B., & Mesibov, G. B. (1984). Role functions of pediatric and health psychologists in health-care settings. *Professional Psychology: Research and Practice, 15*(2), 142–151.

Stone, A. A. (1979). Informed consent: Special problems for psychiatry. *Hospital and Community Psychiatry, 30,* 321–327.

Stone, G. C. (1979). Psychology and the health system. In G. C. Stone, F. Cohen, & N. Adler (Eds.), *Health psychology: A handbook* (pp. 47–75). San Francisco: Jossey-Bass.

Stone, G. C. (Ed.). (1983). National Working Conference on Education and Training in Health Psychology. *Health Psychology, 2*(Suppl. 5), 1–153.

Stone, G. C., Weiss, S. M., Matarazzo, J. D., Miller, N. E., Rodin, J., Belar, C. D., Follick, M. J., & Singer, J. E. (Eds.). (1987). *Health psychology: A discipline and a profession.* Chicago: University of Chicago Press.

Stricker, G. (1983). Peer review systems in psychology. In B. D. Sales (Ed.), *The professional psychologists' handbook.* New York: Plenum.

Stricker, G., & Cohen, L. H. (1984). APA/CHAMPUS peer review project: Implications for research and practice. *Professional Psychology: Research and Practice, 15,* 96–108.

Stromberg, C. D., & Dellinger, A. (1993, December). Malpractice and other professional liability. In *The Psychologist's legal update* (pp. 1–15). Washington, DC: National Register of Health Service Providers in Psychology.

Sturgis, E. T., & Gramling, S. (1988). Psychophysiological assessment. In A. S. Bellack & M. Hersen (Eds.), *Behavioral assessment* (3rd ed., pp. 213–251). Needham Heights, MA: Allyn & Bacon.

Sutton, E., & Belar, C. D. (1982). Tension headache patients versus controls: A study of EMG parameters. *Headache,* 133–136.

Sweet, J. J., Rozensky, R. H., & Tovian, S. M. (Eds). (1991). *Handbook of clinical psychology in medical settings.* New York: Plenum.

Tarasoff v. Regents of University of California, 131 Cal. Rptr. 14, 551 P2d 334 (1976).

Tarshis, C. B. (1972). Liability for psychotherapy. *University of Toronto Faculty Law Review, 30,* 75–96.

Temoshok, L., & Baum, A. (Eds.). (1990). *Psychosocial perspectives on AIDS.* Hillsdale, NJ: Erlbaum.

Theaman, M. (1984). The impact of peer review on professional practice. *American Psychologist, 39,* 406–414.

Thoreson, C. E., & Powell, L. H. (1992). Type A behavior pattern: New perspectives on theory, assessment and intervention. *Journal of Consulting and Clinical Psychology. 60,* 595–604.

Tiep, B. L., Burns, M., Kao, D., Madison, R., & Herrera, J. (1986). *Biofeedback augmented pursed lips breathing training in patients with chronic obstructive lung disease.* Paper presented at the 17th annual meeting of the Biofeedback Society of America, San Francisco.

Totten, G., Lamb, D. H., & Reeder, G. D. (1990). Tarasoff and confidentiality in AIDS-related psychotherapy. *Professional Psychology: Research and Practice, 21,* 155–160.

Tovian, S. M. (1991). Integration of clinical psychology into adult and pediatric oncology programs. In J. J. Sweet, R. H. Rozensky, & S. M. Tovian (Eds.), *Handbook of clinical psychology in medical settings* (pp. 331–352). New York: Plenum.

Travis, C. B. (1988a). *Women and health psychology: Biomedical issues.* Hillsdale, NJ: Erlbaum.

Travis, C. B. (1988b). *Women and health psychology: Mental health issues.* Hillsdale, NJ: Erlbaum.

Trzepacz, P. T., & Baker, R. W. (1993). *The Psychiatric Mental Status Examination.* New York: Oxford University Press.

Turk, D. C., & Meichenbaum, D. (1991). Adherence to self-care regimens. In J. J. Sweet, R. H. Rozensky, & S. M. Tovian (Eds.), *Handbook of clinical psychology in medical settings* (pp. 249–266). New York: Plenum.

Turk, D. C., Meichenbaum, D., & Genest, M. (1983). *Pain and behavioral medicine: A cognitive–behavioral perspective.* New York: Guilford Press.

Turk, D. C., & Melzack, R. (Eds.). (1992). *Handbook of pain assessment.* New York: Guilford Press.

Turkington, C. (1986). Response to crisis: Pay up or go naked. *American Psychological Association Monitor, 17*, 6–7.

Ulrich, R. S. (1984). View through a window may influence recovery from surgery. *Science, 224*, 420–421.

VandeCreek, L., & Knapp, S. (1993). *Tarasoff and beyond: Legal and clinical considerations in the treatment of life-endangering patients.* Sarasota, FL: Practitioner's Resource Series.

VandeCreek, L., & Stout, C. E. (1993). Risk management in inpatient psychiatric care. In D. Ruben, C. Stout, & M. Squire (Eds), *Current advances in inpatient psychiatric care: A handbook* (pp. 53–67). New York: Greenwood.

VandenBos, G., & DeLeon P. H. (1988). The use of psychotherapy to improve physical health. *Psychotherapy, 25*, 335–343.

Wall, P. D., & Melzack, R. (1994). *Textbook of pain* (3rd ed.). New York: Churchill Livingstone.

Wallston, K. A., Wallston, B. S., & DeVellis, R. (1978). Development of the Multidimensional Health Locus of Control (MHLC) scales. *Health Education Monographs, 6*, 160–170.

Weeks, G. R. (Ed.). (1991). *Promoting change through paradoxical therapy.* New York: Brunner/Mazel.

Weisman, A. D. (1978). Coping with illness. In T. P. Hackett & N. H. Cassem (Eds.), *Massachusetts general hospital handbook of general hospital psychiatry.* St. Louis: Mosby.

Weiss, S. M. (1982). Health psychology: The time is now. *Health Psychology, 1*, 81–91.

Weiss, S. M., Anderson, R. T., & Weiss, S. M. (1991). Cardiovascular disorders: Hypertension and coronary heart disease. In J. J. Sweet, R. H. Rozensky, & S. M. Tovian (Eds.), *Handbook of clinical psychology in medical settings* (pp. 353–373). New York: Plenum.

Weiss, S., Fielding, J. E., & Baum, A. (Eds.). (1990). *Health at work.* Hillsdale, NJ: Erlbaum.

Wesley, A. L., Gatchel, R. J., Polatin, P. B., Kinney, R. K., & Mayer, T. G. (1991). Differentiation between somatic and cognitive/affective components in commonly used measurements of depression in patients with chronic low-back pain—Let's not mix apples and oranges. *Spine, 16*, No. 6 Supplement, S213–S215.

Wettstein, R. M. (1984). The prediction of violent behavior and the duty to protect third parties. *Behavioral Sciences and the Law, 2*, 291–317.

White, L., Tursky, B., & Schwartz, G. E. (Eds.). (1985). *Placebo.* New York: Guilford Press.

Whitehead, W. E. (1992). Behavioral medicine approaches to gastrointestinal disorders. *Journal of Consulting and Clinical Psychology, 60,* 605–612.

Wickline v. California, 228 Cal. Rptr. 661, 670 (Cal. App. 2d Dist. 1986).

Widiger, T. A., & Frances, A. (1987). Interviews and inventories for the measurement of personality disorders. *Clinical Psychology Review, 7,* 49–75.

Widiger, T. A., & Rorer, L. G. (1984). The responsible psychotherapist. *American Psychologist, 39,* 503–515.

Wilkins, M. A., McGuire, J. M., Abbott, D. W., & Blau, B. I. (1990). Willingness to apply understood ethical principles. *Journal of Clinical Psychology, 46,* 539–547.

Wilson v. Blue Cross of California, 271 Cal. Rptr. 276 (Cal. App. 2d Dist. 1990).

Winiarski, J. G. (1992). *AIDS-related psychotherapy.* Des Moines, IA: Allyn & Bacon.

Wolff, H. G. (1953). *Stress and disease.* Springfield, IL: Charles C. Thomas.

Wolff, H. G., & Wolf, S. (1951). The management of hypertensive patients. In E. T. Bell (Ed.), *Hypertension.* Minneapolis: University of Minnesota Press.

Wolpe, J. (1958). *Psychotherapy by reciprocal inhibition.* Stanford, CA: Stanford University Press.

Wright, R. H. (1981). Psychologists and professional liability (malpractice) insurance. *American Psychologist, 36,* 1484–1493.

Young, L. D. (1993). Rheumatoid arthritis. In R. K. Gatchel & E. B. Blanchard (Eds.), *Psychophysiological disorders: Research and clinical applications* (pp. 269–298). Washington, DC: American Psychological Association.

Zerubavel, E. (1980). The bureaucratization of responsibility: The case of informed consent. *Bulletin of the American Academy of Psychiatry and Law, 8,* 161–167.

Author Index ·

Numbers in italics refer to listings in the reference sections.

Subject Index

About the Authors

Cynthia D. Belar received her PhD in clinical psychology from Ohio University in 1974 after an internship at Duke University Medical Center. From 1974 to 1984, she was on the faculty of the Department of Clinical and Health Psychology at the University of Florida Health Science Center, where she developed the Pain and Stress Management Laboratory as well as the medical psychology service and training components of the doctoral and internship programs. From 1983 to 1990, she served as chief psychologist and clinical director of behavioral medicine for the Kaiser Permanente Medical Care Program in Los Angeles.

She is currently director of the doctoral program in clinical psychology at the University of Florida, president-elect of the Division of Health Psychology of the American Psychological Association, and chairman of the Council of University Directors of Clinical Psychology. Her research has been in the areas of pain, stress management, and biofeedback.

William W. Deardorff received his doctorate in clinical psychology from Washington State University in 1985, after an internship at the University of Washington Medical School. He then completed a postdoctoral fellowship in clinical health psychology at the Kaiser Permanente Medical Care Program, Los Angeles.

He is board certified in health psychology by the American Board of Professional Psychology. He is a Fellow of the American Academy of Health Psychology and is currently serving as the organization's president. He is in private practice with a multidisciplinary group specializing in disorders of the spine. His research and clinical interests include pain, psychological factors in medical disorders, psychological preparation for surgery, and legal and ethical issues in clinical health psychology practice.